OFFICIAL

Netscape
Java 1.1
PROGRAMMING BOOK

ALL PLATFORMS

An imprint of
Ventana Communications Group

Java Language and the JFC,
plus Techniques for the Internet
and the Enterprise

DANIEL I. JOSHI
PAVEL A. VOROBIEV, PH.D.

VENTANA

Official Netscape Java 1.1 Programming Book

Copyright © 1998 by Daniel I. Joshi and Pavel A. Vorobiev, PhD

Library of Congress Cataloging-in-Publication Data

Joshi, Daniel I. and Pavel A. Vorobiev
Official Netscape Java 1.1 Programming Book / Daniel I. Joshi.
p.   cm.
Includes index.
ISBN 1-56604-766-8
1. Java (Computer program language) 2. Netscape. I. Title.
QA76.73.J38J675 1997
005.2'762—dc21   97-30076
  CIP
First Edition 9 8 7 6 5 4 3 2 1

Printed in the United States of America

Published and distributed to the trade by Ventana Communications Group
P.O. Box 13964, Research Triangle Park, NC 27709-3964
919.544.9404
FAX 919.544.9472
http://www.vmedia.com

Ventana Communications Group is a division of International Thomson Publishing.

Netscape Publishing Relations
Suzanne C. Anthony
Netscape Communications Corporation
501 E. Middlefield Rd.
Mountain View, CA 94043
http://home.netscape.com

President
Michael E. Moran

Associate Publisher
Robert Kern

Editorial Operations Manager
Kerry L. B. Foster

Production Manager
Jaimie Livingston

Brand Manager
Jamie Jaeger Fiocco

Art Director
Marcia Webb

Creative Services Manager
Diane Lennox

Acquisitions Editor
Neweleen A. Trebnik

Project Editor
Adam F. Newton

Development Editor
Michelle Corbin Nichols

Copy Editor
Norma Emory

CD-ROM Specialist
Shadrack Frazier

Technical Reviewer
Richard Jessup

Desktop Publisher
Caroline Heine McKenzie

Proofreader
Beth Snowberger

Indexer
Sherry Massey

Interior Designer
Patrick Berry

Cover Illustrator
Lisa Gill

About the Authors

Daniel I. Joshi is a veteran writer and senior R & D specialist for Joshi Publishing & Marketing LLC (www.joshipublishing.com). Among his most recent titles are Ventana's *The Java 1.1 Programmer's Reference, Migrating from Java 1.0 to Java 1.1, The Comprehensive Guide to the JDBC SQL API*, and *The Comprehensive Guide to Visual J++*.

Pavel A. Vorobiev, PhD is a doctoral graduate in both Physics and Mathematics, and currently works as a senior C++ and Java developer for RCC Consultants, Inc. He is coauthor of Ventana's *The Java 1.1 Programmer's Reference* and *Migrating from Java 1.0 to Java 1.1*. He is also a technical editor for *The Comprehensive Guide to Visual J++* and *The Comprehensive Guide to the JDBC SQL API*.

Acknowledgments

I would like to acknowledge Neweleen Trebnik for fighting the fires so I could get this book out. To Michelle Nichols for helping me facilitate better information design, and to Adam Newton, whose efficiency is nothing less than impressive. I would also like to acknowledge Richard Jessup for his meticulous review of the material and Norma Emory for all her added efforts. And, last but not least, I would like to thank Pavel Vorobiev for helping to make this book a reality.

—D. I. J.

I thank my wife Marina for all of the encouragement, love, and support that she gave me throughout the process of writing this book. I would also like to thank my partner, Dan Joshi, for providing such an excellent work environment.

—P. A. V.

Contents

PART III

Introducing the JFC

P A R T   I V

Appendix

Introduction

The *Official Netscape Java 1.1 Programming Book* is designed with two specific goals: (1) To provide a vigorous overview of Java; and (2) to introduce the Java Foundation Classes (JFC). In giving an overview of Java, we assume that you have not necessarily had prior knowledge of or working experience with the language itself. We do not assume, though, that you have never programmed before. So, we hope we have provided a balanced presentation, making the book's Java coverage vigorous and comprehensive, but not overbearing.

Java is fast becoming the foundation upon which many Netscape (and Internet) technologies are built. Netscape technologies such as NetscapeONE, Netscape's Internet Foundation Classes (IFC), JavaScript, and Netscape's version of Dynamic HTML incorporate, build upon, assume, or resemble Java. Soon, being versed in Java technology and the Java language itself will no longer be an option for Internet developers. This book is designed to give you detailed and technical coverage of Java from the source (i.e., the Java 1.1 platform as defined by Sun Microsystems). Also included in this book is special coverage of Netscape's and JavaSoft's latest Java technology—the Java Foundation Classes (JFC). You will learn what the JFC is and how Netscape's IFC is being integrated into the JFC.

If you haven't already done so, take a look at the Table of Contents. You will see that the JFC is specifically mentioned in the title of Chapter 11 alone. So, if you are measuring the amount of JFC material by the number of times the abbreviation appears, you will be misled into thinking that it is truly covered only in part of Part III. This is not so: A number of existing Java technologies, generic concepts, and accepted standards were used to create the JFC. Furthermore, if you do not have a very solid understanding of how to program in Java to begin with, many parts of the JFC will appear not to make sense or may simply seem abstruse.

In summary, you will find very little useless information in this book. You also will find that there is little information that does not relate (either directly or indirectly) to the JFC, which is why this book is a useful tool to fully understand the JFC.

Stay Up-to-Date With Netscapepress.com

Netscapepress.com is the place to go for the latest information about Netscape Press. Connect via http://www.netscapepress.com to access a complete catalog of Netscape Press titles, technical support, and updated information related to the *Official Netscape Java 1.1 Programming Book.*

Netscapepress.com is also the home of *Navigate!*—the official electronic publication of Netscape Press and your best source for articles and reviews aimed at Netscape users. *Navigate!* features interviews with industry icons and experts as well as articles excerpted from upcoming Netscape Press titles.

Netscape Press is a joint effort between Ventana and Netscape Communications Corporation and serves as the publishing arm of Netscape.

Chapter 12 Last-Minute Update

Due to modifications in the Swing set, the following examples in Chapter 12 were updated just before this book went to the printers (but just after the CD was burned):

```
SwingBorderTest.java
SwingButtonTest.java
SwingCheckboxTest.java
SwingInternalFrameTest.java
SwingTabbedPaneTest.java
```

Visit Netscapepress.com to get these up-to-date examples.

What's Inside?

The *Official Netscape Java 1.1 Programming Book* has three major parts. The first is a rigorous introduction to the Java programming language and basic programming techniques. The second part delves into how Java is being used on the Internet through the use of Java applets. Part II also discusses key technologies that (as you will see later on in Part III) are used by the JFC. Finally, the last part gives you a first look at the JFC.

Part I: The Java Fundamentals

Chapter 1, "Introducing Java." In this chapter, you will learn a little bit about where Java came from and where it is going. You will also be introduced to Java, including a definition of what it is, types of programs you can create, and the key features that make it so useful.

Chapter 2, "The Java Language Syntax." This chapter gives you a detailed overview of the Java language specification. We'll look at topics that relate to Java syntax as well as other fundamental parts of the language that are essential to program in Java and to understand the key Java technologies that follow in later chapters.

Chapter 3, "Java's Object-Orientation." Object-oriented programming (OOP) organizes your programs in a more efficient and easier-to-understand format. This chapter covers Java's implementation of OOP, assuming that you have never created/used objects before. Related OOP topics, such as an introduction to object-oriented design (OOD) and advanced OOP Java concepts, are also discussed in this chapter.

Chapter 4, "Exceptions & Multithreading in Java." This chapter starts with an introduction to exceptions—what they are, how to use them, and what to do to handle them. The chapter then moves on to introduce multithreading and to provide information on how to implement multithreading at the linguistic level in Java.

Chapter 5, "The AWT." The Abstract Window Toolkit (AWT) is one of the most significant parts of Java and one of the biggest building blocks behind the JFC. The AWT represents the complete Graphical User Interface (GUI) toolkit that facilitates services, tools, and components necessary to create front ends in Java. This chapter gives you a reference-based profile of all the AWT components, saving the services and tools of the AWT for the next chapter.

Chapter 6, "Using the AWT." This chapter picks up where the last chapter left off. Starting with a huge section on event handling (with many examples), you will learn how the delegation event-handling model works in Java. You will also learn about other AWT features and services, such as customizing mouseless operation, setting the colors of your Java GUI to the user's system colors, and printing in Java.

Part II: Java on the Internet

Chapter 7, " Introduction to Java Applets." In this chapter, you will learn about Java applets, what they are, how they work, and how they are different from applications. You will also learn how to embed an applet in a HyperText Markup Language (HTML) page. Finally, you will have a chance to create a sample applet that will be expanded on in the next chapter to show how applets communicate via the Net.

Chapter 8, "Creating Interactive Web Sites With Applets." This chapter will introduce you to a very high-level understanding of how communication takes place in Java and on the Net. You will learn what you need to know to effectively design a Java program to connect to the Internet, a server on a network, or even another applet. A complete discussion of networking and Java could easily be the topic for an entire book. So, this chapter gives only a whistle-stop tour, touching on a few of the key concepts and programming techniques, with several examples to complement the discussions.

Chapter 9, "Java Archives & Trusted Applets." This chapter is going to give you a hands-on look at Java ARchives (JAR) files and how they are used in conjunction with digital signatures to give applets trusted status.

Chapter 10, "Java Beans." Components are to object-oriented programming what objects were to procedural programming. They represent the next giant step forward in software reusablilty. In Java, components are "beans." This chapter introduces you to the Java Beans architecture and Application Programming Interface (API). The chapter ends with an example that takes you through the steps to create a real Beans component.

Part III: Introducing the JFC

Chapter 11, "Introduction to the JFC." This chapter gives you a high-level overview of the JFC, where it came from and where it is going. It discusses the reasoning behind the needs for the JFC and explains how these needs are being met.

Chapter 12, "The Swing Set." This chapter introduces you to the Swing set, which is JFC's suite of GUI components. Included in this chapter are numerous examples with corresponding figures and numerous notes discussing features that were works-in-progress at the time of this writing. By the end of this chapter, you should have had a fairly good dose of JFC/Swing.

Conventions Used in This Book

As with any book that deals with a programming language, a set of conventions, formatting, and wording had to be chosen. Obviously, most of the conventions used in this book are generic to the Java community. Nonetheless, there are still several conventions that may be ambiguous or simply nonstandard in the Java community.

Vocabulary

Several words used in this book may need to be clarified:

- **appletcation**. This is a nonstandard term used for a Java program that can be executed as either a Java applet or an application (depending on from where it is executed).

- **parameter**. Arguments for a given method or constructor are referred to as parameters.

- **pseudoexample**. Any time you see this statement, it means that the code to which it refers is syntactically correct but would not compile (or would compile but, when executed, would not produce the desired result). Pseudoexamples are code snippets used for illustration purposes only.

- **runnable example**. The term *runnable* is meant to let you know that the code it references is meant to be compiled and executed in Java.

- **user**. A *user* is anyone who is executing a given Java program. Obviously, this can be a programmer who's testing code or simply a person "using" a Java program.

Formatting

We've tried to reconcile potentially ambiguous situations when talking about Java by using the following conventions:

- Java keywords, code references (such as object and class names), and names of Java Development Kit (JDK) tools are presented in a computer code font. This helps to avoid ambiguous statements such as: "This for loop executes for the duration of the loop." To the uninitiated, this sounds odd because of the Java keyword for. This book presents the sentence as follows: "This `for` loop executes for the duration of the loop."

- In the snippets of code, you may notice that some comments are italicized. These comments either let you know that the piece of code is an instruction, or that you should replace the italicized code with your own code. For example:

```
for (x = 0; x < 5; x++) {
    //Body of the loop
}
```

The comment *Body of the loop* tells you that, if this were real, the body of the loop would be contained there.

- Italics may also be used at the first mention of a buzzword, technical term, or obscure vocabulary word.

- All method names in this book end with open-and-close parentheses, as in, setState( ).

- When referring to a generic set of methods, three crosses (XXX) are used. For example, isXXX() (in which XXX represents a primitive data type) would be used to allude to this given collection of "is" methods as a whole.

Feedback

If you have a tip, trick, example, or anything else that you think would be a help to other readers; or, if you wish to send us feedback about what you liked/disliked about this book, please e-mail the following address:

feedback@joshipublishing.com

Note: We may not be able to reply individually to every message.

Moving On

Despite all of the published books, online documentation, and other resources available for Java, there still appear to be several fundamental holes. This is probably because Java is growing exponentially, and with this growth comes much hype—sometimes making it hard to distinguish between fact and fiction. We hope that this book will help you, the task-oriented Java programmer, both to get up-to-speed on Java and to get a solid introduction to the JFC.

Daniel I. Joshi

Pavel A. Vorobiev, Ph.D.

## PART I

The Java Fundamentals

Introducing Java

I n this short chapter you will learn a little bit about where Java came from and where it is going. You also will have an introduction to Java, including a definition of what it is, the types of programs you can create with it, and the key features that make it so useful.

In 1991, Sun Microsystems started a project to create software for portable electronic devices such as Personal Digital Assistants (PDAs) and television sets. The idea behind the project was to make such electronic devices more intelligent. James Gosling (the curator of Java) was assigned to the project, and he began implementing solutions using C++. However, it soon became apparent to Gosling and others that C++ was not the right programming language for the project. Because of its use of direct references (i.e., pointers), and its reliance on the programmer for memory management, C++ was not stable enough for the job. So Gosling began to develop a new language that would compensate for these risks/inadequacies yet retain the robustness of C++. That language—known then as Oak (named after a tree outside Gosling's window)—was designed to be portable, safe, and robust. Although the Oak language was revolutionary at the time, it never gained widespread acceptance in the consumer electronics industry. And it wasn't until 1994—after the Internet's commercialization and subsequent, explosive growth—that Sun began to look at using Oak's capabilities to create distributed applications on the Net.

In spring 1995, Java experienced a new beginning. At that time, HotJava—the first Java-compliant browser written in the Java language—became available to the public. HotJava, designed to port the use of Java to the Internet by using a special type of Java application known as an *applet,* made a big hit on the Net. Applets, it turned out, were a perfect fit to take advantage of Java's powerful and portable capabilities.

With the release of HotJava, Java broke into the Internet, gained public acceptance, and was endorsed by the top software and hardware companies in the computer industry. This changed the Net considerably as Java allowed a new level of interactivity in worldwide information sharing.

Around the time that HotJava was making such a splash, Netscape Communications released its first (Sun's HotJava excluded) browser to support Java (as of Navigator 2.0). Since then, Netscape has gone from simply supporting Java to completely embracing it. Netscape continues to work with JavaSoft (Sun's company for Java technologies) to enhance and improve the technology. Netscape also pioneers new Java-related technologies (e.g., JavaScript), which have helped developers facilitate better Java/Internet solutions.

TIP

Today, HotJava and Navigator are not the only Internet browsers to support Java applets. Just about every Internet browser in the industry allows the use of Java applets and other Java-related technologies.

Defining Java

Java is modeled after the very robust programming language, C++. C++ is used widely as the primary programming language for application development. Applications developed for environments ranging from UNIX to Macintosh to Windows use one form of C/C++. The problem is that, at the linguistic and binary level, C/C++ is not easily portable across each of these platforms. The operating systems mentioned above (as well as many others) all use C++, but each system uses the language in a way that is optimized to the specific environment's needs. Although this is beneficial for performance, it means that when you move between platforms, you usually have to rewrite and recompile the program with a compiler that is specific to the environment on which you wish to run. Sound complex? It can be. Java, however, does not have these limitations because it is both modeled on the robustness of C++ and inherently designed to be portable over many different platforms. In this way, Java has taken distributed computing to the next level.

Aside from being platform independent, Java also is easier to use than C++. In fact, you could say that Java is "easy to learn." This is an opinion and myth in the industry, but compared to other languages (like C++, Smalltalk, and even Visual Basic), Java is easy to learn. Java incorporates and enhances the strengths of C++ while removing the overly complex/dangerous parts. Java also borrows several concepts from Smalltalk.

For people coming from older structured programming languages (like Pascal and BASIC), the most intimidating aspect of Java is the fact that it is object-oriented. Unlike its predecessors, and unlike C, Visual Basic, and a host of scripting languages for the Net, including JavaScript and VBScript, an object-oriented programming (OOP) language like Java can pose a threateningly complex way to create programs. (Visual Basic only partially implements true OOP design, thus it is considered object-*based*.) Despite the complexities inherent in OOP, though, objects are the future of programming. Once you learn to use one object-oriented language, you will find it easier to learn others.

Differentiating Java From JavaScript

Netscape has developed a Java-based scripting language known as JavaScript. It is very important to differentiate between the two: JavaScript is an object-*based* language acting as an extension to HyperText Markup Language (HTML). It allows you to perform client-side error checking of HTML forms, for instance. On the other hand, Java is a fully capable OOP language that allows for the design of real programs that can be used on the Net or executed as applications on the user's desktop.

Java Applets & Applications

Java has defined two different types of program formats: the *applet* and the application. In Java, applets are special types of Java programs. Applets are unique because Web pages can call them, and they have a different structure of invoking actions in the program (based on a life-cycle model). Applets are designed to be much more secure than traditional applications in order to protect themselves (and others) from the inherent security risks that a powerful language like Java brings to the Internet.

Java applications are more traditional in the sense that they are similar to the typical programs that you would create using other programming languages. Java applications have fewer security restrictions than their applet counterparts, but applications are not directly accessible from the Internet.

TIP

Appletcations *are a unique blend, sort of a half-breed between Java applets and Java applications. An appletcation can be either an applet or an application, depending on where it is invoked. Note, however, that appletcations are merely a programming* technique; *they do not change any of the definitions for applets and applications that you have just read about.*

The applet is unique to Java and is tailored for use on the Internet. One of the biggest spurs to creating the Java applet model was Java's power. If such a powerful language were used with malicious intent, it could be potentially dangerous to its user's environment (the Web browser's hosting environment). In order to protect the user's system, the applet's design is inherently self-limiting. An applet runs in an area commonly referred to as the *sandbox*, an area that is secure and separate from your system's files and other resources (see the "Java Is Secure" section below). Furthermore, most of the Internet browsers also exercise increased security on Java applets to ensure that no harm, intentional or otherwise, can result from a Java applet. You will have a chance to get a detailed look at applets in Chapter 7.

TIP

Java has defined a set of security application programming interfaces (APIs) that lets Java applets be signed digitally. In this way, the integrity and origin of a given applet can be verified, and then it can be given freedom to do things that used to be reserved only for applications. For more information, please see Chapter 9.

Understanding Java

Knowing what Java is and why it is hot, and understanding the key points that make Java so useful are two different topics. While the first part of this chapter introduced you to the former, the following sections give you an understanding of some key points that make Java so powerful.

Java Is Based on C/C++

Java is based on C++ but is designed to be easier to use. In this section, we will take a closer look at some of the similarities and differences between the two languages:

- In Java, as in C/C++, a line of code is terminated by a semicolon (;). Technically speaking, white spaces and carriage returns are ignored.

- Java does not use pointers. Instead, Java uses a sort of indirect pointer called a *reference*.

Defining Pointers

A pointer is a variable that contains the address (i.e., memory location) of another variable or type. Pointers can "point" to variables that contain data or they can even "point" to another pointer.

Pointers are a very powerful and useful tool; however, they also are difficult to understand. Furthermore, pointers are one of the major contributors to software bugs. Hence, Java does not support the use of pointers.

- Unlike C/C++, Java requires that every function, which in Java is called a *method*, be attached to a class.

- Unlike C++, which supports multiple inheritance, Java only supports single inheritance (see Chapter 3 for more information on inheritance in Java).

- Java does not support the use of templates.

Defining Templates in C++

A template in C++ is a generic function that houses the overall framework for a set of similar functions, leaving it to the compiler to decide exactly which implementation of this generic function to use. Java uses *method overloading*, which is very similar to templates (see Chapter 3 for more information).

- Java does not support the preprocessor model used in C and C++.

- Java does not use **const, struct,** and **union.**

For more information about the basic structure of Java and the similarities/ differences it shares with C/C++, see Chapter 2.

Java Is Multithreaded

Multithreading at the linguistic level is one of Java's strongest legs. Explicitly, using threads can benefit almost any program, because it gives that program the ability to execute in a concurrent fashion. In the same way that two instances of Netscape Navigator can be loading different sites at the same time, one Java program can be designed to have a number of different tasks working at once.

Chapter 4 gives a complete introduction to and discussion of threads and how to program them in Java.

Java Is Object Oriented

At its core, Java is an object-oriented programming (OOP) language. OOP means that Java organizes its programs into a hierarchy of classes that define its behavior. This is certainly not unique to Java. In fact, Java's OOP design has been borrowed from other programming languages, including C++ and Smalltalk. As you will see later on, Java does have the advantage of being easier to understand (particularly when compared to C++). Chapter 3 details OOP in Java.

Java Is Platform Independent

One of the really powerful features of the Java language is that it is platform independent. This means that Java programs port across different operating systems. You do not need to reconfigure your Java applets to have them move from one environment to the next. Java takes care of everything.

Java Is Architecture Neutral

This is a more technical term for platform independence, meaning that Java is 100 percent portable between platforms. It doesn't matter if you use a Mac, Windows, or UNIX system; Java runs on them all.

TIP

Some critics contend that Java's platform independence is useless because the majority of computer users employ Windows. However, even if one were to follow this ill-founded logic, the truth of the matter is that Java's platform independence inherently improves its versatility. In the case of the Internet, for instance, different types of systems and platforms are utilized. Thus, Java's platform independence is a perfect fit.

Java Is Secure

Java is a compiled and interpreted language. When a Java program is compiled, the source code for the program is converted into bytecodes. Then, when the Java program is executed, these bytecodes are translated to machine language instructions specific to the hosting environment. Bytecodes can be verified. So, when the program loads, it is verified, making sure that it has not been changed, distorted, or tampered with. Also, as you learned earlier, certain Java applets are subject to sandbox restrictions.

TIP

> *The word* sandbox *is used to denote the local "firewall" behind which Java applets are resigned to execute. This ensures that applets that are either intentionally or incidentally malicious will not be able to directly lock, access, or mutilate resources on the user's system.*

Java Is Dynamic

Java manages memory allocation through a dynamic process called *garbage collection*. In C/C++, programmers were responsible for memory management, but Java does memory management automatically; it alleviates the opportunity for incorrect memory deallocation.

Memory leaks occur when a program takes free memory from the environment to construct its objects as it starts. Throughout the life of the program, it is creating and destroying many objects, thereby taking and freeing memory. In theory, when the program finally quits, it releases all the memory it used to the user's environment. But this happens only to a perfect program that is able to keep track of every ounce of used memory. All of the objects constructed need to be destroyed, thus all of the memory taken for the program would be released into the environment.

However, in the real world, perfect memory management is not always going to happen. In most cases, the program does not completely clean up after itself upon leaving the user's environment, and this results in poor memory management. The key difference between Java and C/C++ is that in C/C++ it is up to the programmer to make sure the program releases memory that is no longer used. The larger and more complex the program, the more room for errors in memory management. Memory leaks are a very real and expected part of a program.

In C++, you have to keep track of all the objects you create to make sure that they are all properly destroyed; however, this is not so in Java. Java will take care of all the memory operations. It is really that simple.

Where Is Java Going?

The first half of 1996 marked Java's official release (i.e., version 1.0). However, the momentum behind Java was so strong that solutions to problems in version 1.0 were being implemented even before its release. While 1.0 made big strides in portability, it lacked many of the basic characteristics contained in other environments, so Java was considered an "infant" in the computer programming language arena. But in the months following 1.0's release, extension APIs were continually being developed and released by Sun, adding specific functionality to Java.

Then, early in 1997, the next version of Java (1.1) neared completion. Containing the extension APIs created in the last year as well as numerous other enhancements, version 1.1 was a big step in the growth of Java as a technology.

As for the version following 1.1, it may be available in the beta version for public review by the time you read this. Probably the single biggest enhancement will be its inclusion of the Java Foundation Classes (JFCs), a joint development between JavaSoft, Netscape, and IBM that will create a high-powered graphical user interface (GUI) development environment. There is no doubt that JFCs will be the single largest step to solidify Java's place in professional application development. Chapters 11 and 12 give you a first look at the JFC and its key services and components.

Moving On

In this chapter you broke ground, learning about the various aspects of Java, including its origins, program types, and basic attributes. The next chapter both gears you toward learning the Java language syntax and builds a foundation for you to understand Java's structure. If you are already familiar with the Java structure, you may want to move forward to the OOP coverage in Chapter 3.

The Java Language Syntax

This chapter is an overview of the syntax for the Java language. The syntax of Java is a very fundamental part of Java. It is essential to programming in Java and understanding key Java technologies. Topics covered include: *literals*, *data types*, *operators*, and *control-flow statements*, among others.

If you have had any exposure to programming in other languages (especially C/C++), this should be review. On the other hand, if you are not comfortable with your programming skills, use this section to build your foundation.

Keywords

Java, being similar to the C/C++ programming language, has a predefined number of *keywords*. Keywords represent reserved words designated for a specific purpose. In many cases, you will mix and match various keywords in your code to perform certain actions. Table 2-1 shows a list of keywords that comprise the core building blocks that define the Java language.

abstract	double	int	super
boolean	else	interface	switch
break	extends	long	synchronized
byte	final	native	this
case	finally	new	throw
catch	float	package	throws
char	for	private	transient
class	goto	protected	try
const	if	public	void
continue	implements	return	volatile
default	import	short	while
do	instanceof	static	

Table 2-1: Keywords in the Java language.

Note: The keywords goto and const are part of the Java language, but they do not have any specific functionality with the current release of the Java language specification. Though carried over from C/C++, they no longer are useful in the Java language.

Literals

A literal is any lexical value expressed as itself. There are several types of literals, including: integers, floating-point values, and booleans (collectively referred to as numerical literals); as well as characters and string literals (collectively referred to as nonnumerical literals).

On the other hand, *data types* (which will be discussed in detail later on) are lexical values that represent other values (i. e. variables). This is very similar to algebra, in which X can mean more than just X. X could be 2, the square root of -5, or the gross national product. As you will learn later on, Java has a specific set of data types for holding certain values.

Note: Technically speaking, Java interprets a literal to a corresponding data type. In a way, a literal is a data type without a variable name specifying a value that represents itself. For more information on data types, please see the later section, "Primitive Data Types."

Numerical Literals

In Java, numerical literals represent quantitative values. Java supports several different numerical systems, including *decimal* (a numbering system of base 10), *binary* (a numbering system of base 2), *octal* (a numbering system of base 8), and *hexadecimal* (using a base of 16). However, most of what you see here will be in either decimal (base 10) or binary (base 2). An int is the default data type used for integer literals. If needed, you can specify the literal to be of type long by appending the letter *l* or *L*:

24050000L

TIP

Use appended letters to specify a particular data type with any kind of literal (case is not sensitive). For example, both 10000l and 10000L specify this literal to be a numerical type long. *Extremely large values utilize the integer type* long.

Floating-point values (numbers that have fractional parts, such as 3.14159) are automatically assumed to be a type double. However, if you wish to use the smaller floating-point type float, then you will need to append a letter *f* to represent that data type:

2.313f

Note: Floating-point types also let you specify scientific notation by using *e* (or *E*) to represent the exponential power. For example, the value 2.54 X 10^5 represented in Java is 2.54e5 or 2.54e5f housed in the float type.

Unlike C and C++, Java represents *boolean* values as either true or false (rather than as a numerical value as with C/C++).

Nonnumerical Literals

There are two types of nonnumerical literals in Java. The first, character literals, represent a single Unicode character surrounded by single quotation marks. The second, string literals, represent a sequence of Unicode characters, all of which are surrounded by double quotation marks. Let's take a closer look at each.

Unicode

Unicode is a new coding format based on 16-bit characters. Unlike the older ANSI/ASCII standards used in C and C++ that are only half that length (8 bits) and thereby capable of having 255 characters, the Unicode standard can contain 65,536 characters.

Unicode contains symbols for almost every major dialect in the world. You can directly reference a given Unicode character in Java by using \u*XXXX*, with the *X*s representing a hexadecimal value.

Character Literals

Character literals represent a single Unicode or ASCII (which is a subset of Unicode) character and are housed in the char type. Character literals are always encased in single quotation marks. The following shows several examples:

`'A' 'z' '>'`

However, some characters are not so obvious or simply cannot be encased in quotation marks. That is where *character escapes* come in. Table 2-2 shows commonly used escape characters to print the not-so-obvious values.

Character Escape	Meaning
\b	Backspace
\f	Form feed
\n	New line
\t	Tab
\r	Carriage return
\\	Backslash
\'	Single quote
\"	Double quote
XXX	ASCII character (as denoted by its *XXX* value, where *X* is an octal value)
\u*XXXX*	Unicode character (as denoted by its *XXXX* value, where *X* is a hexadecimal value)

Table 2-2: Character escapes in Java.

String Literals

String literals are merely collections of character literals. Java stores these literals in String objects (you will learn more about objects and String objects in the next chapter). This is very different from C or C++. In C, a string literal represents an array of characters (using the `char` primitive data type). The following code provides some examples of the use of a string literal:

```
"This is a test";
"This is a \t test";
```

The first line simply prints out the following statement:

```
This is a test
```

The second line prints out the same thing but places a tab where the \t is so that, when printed, it will look something like the following:

```
This is a    test
```

TIP

You can use character escapes in both string and character literals.

Primitive Data Types

Literals are a fairly simple concept because they do nothing more than represent themselves. Nevertheless, in many instances, you may want to have a value represent something else, or you may need a variable in which you can place values temporarily. In Java, you have two forms of variables (usually known as data types). The ones discussed here are primitive data types. The other data types are object oriented in nature and have been saved for the next chapter.

Primitive data types represent fundamental elements (denoted by the keywords `byte`, `int`, `short`, `long`, `boolean`, and `char`) that hold a certain type of data in a specific range. You use a data type to hold information depending on its type and the amount of data.

Java Is Strongly Typed

You may have heard the statement, "Java is strongly typed." This means that you must declare all variables before you can use them in your Java programs. However, you can declare a variable anywhere in your Java program. Also, note that a variable that is declared but is not assigned a specific value reverts to a default one.

In Java and other programs, you need to have a place to store data. However, the type and size of the data directly affect what data type you can (or should) use. You need to be careful of this, because storing data in the wrong data type can cause the values to become distorted and/or reported incorrectly. Furthermore, all data types have finite boundaries, and it is important that the data you are storing do not go beyond these ceilings. You will learn about all of these attributes for each primitive data type in the following sections.

Integers

In mathematics, an integer is a whole number that can have either a positive or a negative value. The values -10, 0, 5, and 2,040,506 are all examples of integers. Moreover, in mathematics, an integer can be any fixed value from negative to positive infinity, with no theoretical limitation—except maybe the size of your chalkboard. This is somewhat similar in data types. You can have a wide range of values for integer data types, but memory allocation (i.e., your computer's chalkboard) inherently limits an integer's overall size.

Computers store their information based on the binary (a number of base 2) number system in the form of bits. A *bit* is the smallest piece of information stored in a computer.

Note: *Bit* is the shortened name for the term *binary digit*.

A *byte* is a series of eight bits and comprises the arrangement for how bits are stored in a computer. So, it is no surprise that byte is the smallest integer data type in Java. Since byte is the smallest size of the integers in Java, it is the most efficient to use. However, as a result, byte also has the smallest range. You can assign a byte to have a value of -128 to +127. Following is an example of declaring a byte variable:

```
byte myVal;
```

Understanding Identifiers

In the sample code, myVal is an identifier. Identifiers are lexical tokens that are used as the name for a variable, with the preceding data type (byte in this case) specifying what type of data myVal can store.

Note that the identifier must start from a Unicode language letter, the underscore (_), or the dollar sign ($) followed by letters, digits, or both. Also, note that identifiers are case sensitive. So, for instance, myval and myVal will be regarded as two different variables by the compiler.

The next level up is the short data type, which is also an integer, but it is 16 bits in length. Since short's bit width is twice as long as byte's, its range is increased by a power of 2. Thus, the integer data type short has a range of -32,768 to +32,767.

Note: All integral data types in Java are signed, wherein the leftmost bit is reserved for the sign (0 being positive and 1 being negative). Unlike C/C++, there is no unsigned keyword in Java.

Because of its name, int is probably the easiest to remember. This data type is a 32-bit value, twice the size of short, which makes its range increase from short by a power of 2. Notice how Java organizes its integer data types so that each one will increase in range by a power of 2. The range of int is -2,147,483,648 to +2,147,483,647. And the last and largest integer value that you can have in Java is the data type long. As you probably guessed, long is 64 bits in length, with a range of -9,223,372,036,854,775,808 to +9,223,372,036,854,775,807. The long is the single largest data type for integers in the Java language.

Note: Unlike C/C++, you cannot append multiple numerical data types in a given declaration. So for instance, short int declarations would be illegal.

Booleans

Booleans are very simple in that they can contain only two values: either true or false.

Note: As you will learn a little later, data types can convert from one form to another, through casting. However, unlike the BOOL keyword in C++ or the boolean keyword in Visual Basic, Java booleans cannot convert to other data types.

Unless assigned, booleans default to a value of false. The following shows several examples of initializing a boolean value:

```
boolean x = true;
boolean y; //defaults to false
boolean z = false;
```

TIP

In Java, you can declare a variable and assign it a value in the same line.

Characters

The keyword char denotes the character data type. The char type is like char in C/C++, with only one major difference: The char type in Java stores its values using the 16-bit Unicode format.

The following is an example of a char. Notice that there are single quotation marks around the actual character. That denotes that X is a character literal:

```
char myChar = 'X';
```

TIP

The sample code line shows an example of a declared and initialized variable in the same line. However, you can alternatively declare a variable and initialize it later:

```
char myChar; //Declared
//Later on in the program: myChar = 'X';
```

Also, if you wish to declare more than one variable of the same data type, you can accomplish this in a single line of code by separating each declaration with a comma. For example:

```
int a, b, c;
char d = 'Z', e = 'Y', f = 'X';
```

The first line of code declares all three variables (a, b, and c) of the int type. The second line declares and initializes values to the variables d, e, and f.

Some characters cannot be printed on the screen directly without some sort of assistance. In other cases, you need to use a special font to display Unicode characters above the 256 value. For example, what if you wanted to have a single quotation mark as a value in the previous snippet of code? In that case, you need to use one of the character escapes that you learned about earlier in the discussion of character literals.

Floating Points

Noninteger decimal numbers use Java's floating-point types. There are two floating-point types in the Java language: float and double. Both of these floating-point data types conform to the IEEE 754 specifications. (IEEE stands for the Institute of Electrical and Electronic Engineers, an organization noted for setting standards in the computer industry.) There are several formats for specifying a floating-point value, including using exponential notation:

```
2.232    4.234e5    1.2E-56
```

Starting with the smaller of the two, the float is a 32-bit (4-byte) data type that contains 7 significant digits (any significant digits after 7 are truncated). It is known as a single-precision data type and is suitable for most calculations.

Significant Digits

You can determine the number of significant digits in a value by finding the length of values that begin and end with nonzero values. For example, 4,500 has 2 significant digits, 1,001,000 has 4 significant digits, and 0.000123 has 3 significant digits.

However, in certain situations you may need to have a more precise way of keeping track of your values. In that case, you would use the double value. This double-precision floating-point value is 64 bits (8 bytes in length) and holds 15 significant digits. Table 2-3 shows a summary of the two floating-point types.

Keyword	Size in Bits	Size in Bytes	Range
float	32	4	+/-3.40282347E+38 to +/-1.40239846E-45
double	64	8	+/-1.79769313486231570E+308 to +/-4.94065645841246544E-324

Table 2-3: Floating-point types.

Casting

One way to manipulate data is to change the variable from one type to another. This form of conversion is known as *casting*. The actual syntax for casting between values is fairly simple. Put the data type to which you want to cast in parentheses in front of the variable, as follows:

```
int A;
char B;
A = (int) B;
```

However, there is a tricky part: You need to make sure that you understand all of the ins and outs of casting, because if you are not careful, you could lose data during the cast. This is possible if the data type to which you are casting is smaller than the original type.

TIP

Probably the most common use for casting is to convert from an int *data type to a* char *data type or vice versa.*

You can safely cast to a smaller data type but only if the actual value does not exceed the smaller data type's range. Of course, if you are casting to a larger data type, then you can be sure that there will be no loss of data. Table 2-4 lists all casts considered safe for any value of the original data type.

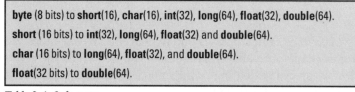

byte (8 bits) to **short**(16), **char**(16), **int**(32), **long**(64), **float**(32), **double**(64).

short (16 bits) to **int**(32), **long**(64), **float**(32) and **double**(64).

char (16 bits) to **long**(64), **float**(32), and **double**(64).

float(32 bits) to **double**(64).

Table 2-4: Safe casts.

Note that casting from a type of equal or larger bit width can be done implicitly (i.e., you can directly assign the two types to each other without having to explicitly put the parenthetical type reference).

Operators

Operators are symbols that the compiler uses to perform specific tasks in a given *statement* or *expression*. Whenever you work with variables, literals, or combinations of the two, you need to understand all of the operators available to you. Most of the operators in Java relate to the operators found in C/C++, with only very minor discrepancies.

Note: A statement represents a line of code (as denoted by an appended semicolon). An expression is similar to a statement except that it yields a value.

In this chapter you have already been exposed to the "=" operator that you used to initialize a variable. For instance, the following shows how you would declare and initialize a variable:

```
float a = 1.41459;
```

You can see that it is the job of = to assign the value (1.41459) to the identifier (a). You will have a chance to learn more about the assignment operators later on in this chapter. Let's take a closer look at the various operators available in Java.

Arithmetic Operators

Arithmetic operators are probably one of the easiest operators to understand because they deal directly with basic mathematical topics such as adding, subtracting, multiplying, and dividing. Table 2-5 gives an outline and an overview of each arithmetic operator in which $a = 4$ and $b = 2$:

Operator	Definition	Java Representation	Algebra Representation	Solution
+	Addition	a + b	a + b	6
−	Subtraction	a − b	a − b	2
++	Increment	a++ (or ++a)	a + 1 (or 1 + b)	5 (or 3)
−−	Decrement	a −− (or −− a)	a −− 1 (or 1 −− b)	3 (or 1)
*	Multiplication	a * b	(a)(b)	8
/	Division	a / b	a ÷ b	2
%	Modulus	a % b	a mod b	0

Table 2-5: Arithmetic operators.

A few things to mention about the arithmetic operators before moving forward: First, it is important to understand the difference between prefixing or suffixing the increment/decrement operators. When an increment/decrement operator is executed as part of a larger expression, prefixing it will cause the operator to execute first; suffixing it will cause it to execute second. For example, consider the following:

```
int a = 5;
int b = ++a * 2;
```

This will result in b equal to 12 since the increment is prefixed. The following will result in b equal to 10:

```
int a = 5;
int b = a++ * 2;
```

Also, the minus sign (-) can be used as a unary negation operator using only one operand. The following shows an example of using the negation operator on the integer variable X:

```
-X;
```

Now, the value X has been negated (e.g., if X were 5, it would now be -5).

Modulus

The modulus operator (%) returns the remainder for the result of the division of the two operands. The following shows a few examples:

```
7 % 2; // results in 1
4 % 9; // results in 4
-20 % 5; // results in 0
```

When performing calculations, you may not always have starting values or results that all belong to the same type. Java handles this in one of several ways. If the two operands are int types, then the resulting value will be an integer. If one or both of the two operands are floating-point values, the arithmetic expression returns a floating-point value after the nonfloating operand has been *promoted* to a floating point. *Promoted* means it is automatically cast to a data type containing a larger bit width. The order in which types are checked is double, float, long and int. So if in some calculation one of the operands is a double value, the other will be promoted to double as well. Or if a given calculation had a double and float, the float type would be promoted to double.

Note: While numerical promotion is often apparent in the arithmetic operations, it also is used by a number of other operators that perform calculations between two operands.

Relational Operators

Sometimes you want to compare the relationship between two values. In Java, just as in C and C++, this can be done using a set of *relational operators*. However, unlike in C and C++, the result of the comparison is not a numerical expression (0 for false and nonzero for true). In Java, it returns a boolean type that will have a value of either true or false. Table 2-6 shows the relational operators and an example of using them; $a = 7$ and $b = 3$.

Operator	Definition	Example	Result
==	equal to	a == 7	true
		b == 7	false
!=	not equal to	a != 7	false
		b != 7	true
<	less than	a < 7	false
		b < 7	true
>	greater than	a > 7	false
		b > 7	false
<=	less than or equal to	a <= 7	true
		b <= 7	true
>=	greater than or equal to	a >= 7	true
		b >= 7	false

Table 2-6: Relational operators.

Boolean Operators

Another set of operators that also returns a boolean type are the boolean operators. These let you evaluate two expressions using various logic to return a collective true or false. Table 2-7 shows an overview of the boolean operators (* the right side of this expression is not evaluated).

Operator	Definition	Expression	Result
&&	AND	a && b	false
		b && a	false*
		a && a	true
		b && b	false*
&	AND	a && b	false
		b && a	false
		a && a	true
		b && b	false

Operator	Definition	Expression	Result
||	OR	a || b	true*
		b || a	true
		a || a	true*
		b || b	false
|	OR	a || b	true
		b || a	true
		a || a	true
		b || b	false
!	NOT	!a	false
		!b	true

Table 2-7: Logical operators.

Note: In the preceding table, *a* = true and *b* = false.

The && is the AND operator, and just as in C/C++, it evaluates two operands and returns true only if both sides are true; otherwise, it returns false. In && operations, if the left side is evaluated to false, then the whole expression returns false and the right side is never evaluated. Alternatively, if you want to always perform evaluations of both sides, you can use the bitwise & operator.

The | | is the OR operator and behaves in a somewhat inverse fashion: It returns true if either side is true or if both sides are true. The only time it will return false is if both sides are false. If the left side of an | | operation returns true, then the whole expression returns true and the right side is not evaluated. Alternatively, you can use the bitwise | operator to enforce evaluations of both sides regardless.

TIP

Using && and | | as opposed to & and | can be particularly useful when you put the less complex evaluation on the left, leaving the more complex one for the right. In this way, you minimize the opportunity for the more complex to be executed, thereby saving execution time. Also, this is useful if you have two evaluations where one is not valid unless the first evaluation is true.

The ! is the NOT operator and is used as a negation tool that inverses the value for a particular expression. For instance, consider the following expression where X is an integer:

```
X > 2;
```

If for some value of X this is true, then the following would be false:

`!(X > 2);`

Note: The logical NOT can be used to do *not equal to* evaluations (!=). For more information, see the preceding section on relational operators.

Bitwise Operators

Bitwise operators are similar to the boolean operators you dealt with in the last section, except with bitwise operators you are dealing at the binary level. Bitwise operators work with primitive integral data types and give you the ability to access these types at a very low level. This is useful for networking, operating systems, and performing other lower-level solutions in Java.

Bitwise operators, because they work at such a low level (i.e., the individual bits), are able to perform certain tasks very efficiently. In fact, many compilers will take a higher-level operation and convert it to a more efficient bitwise operation during compilation. Table 2-8 shows the AND, OR, XOR, and NOT bitwise operators in which *a* is a bit with a value of 1, and *b* is a bit with a value of 0.

Operator	Definition	Expression	Result
&	AND	a & b	0
		b & a	0
		a & a	1
		b & b	0
|	OR	a | b	1
		b | a	1
		a | a	1
		b | b	0
^	XOR	a ^ b	1
		b ^ a	1
		a ^ a	0
		b ^ b	0
~	NOT	~a	0
		~b	1

Table 2-8: Bitwise AND, OR, XOR, and NOT operators.

Bitwise operations perform their evaluations with each binary value in the integral data type. To illustrate, let's take a look at a binary value of 40 (that is, 0000 0000 0010 1000) and the value 24 (0000 0000 0001 1000). Table 2-9 shows the result of the & operation on the two values.

Bit number	1	2	3	4	5	6	7	8	9	10	11	12	13	14	15	16
Value of 40	0	0	0	0	0	0	0	0	0	0	1	0	1	0	0	0
Value of 24	0	0	0	0	0	0	0	0	0	0	0	1	1	0	0	0
Result 8	0	0	0	0	0	0	0	0	0	0	0	0	1	0	0	0

Table 2-9: Result of the & operation on the values 40 & 24.

The result for this operation in Table 2-9 is 8 (0000 0000 0000 1000).

The left and right *shift operators* move bits in one direction or another, depending on which shift operator you choose and how many times you wish to shift it. << shifts to the left, and >> shifts to the right, adding zeros when needed to either the right or the left side. Remembering that Java types are signed values when performing a shifting operation, the leftmost bit is not moved, thereby retaining the sign of the value. In the event that you wish to shift all bits, Java facilitates an unsigned right shift operator (>>>).

Because shifting is done at the binary level, it is extremely fast and is sometimes preferred over more traditional operations. Operating systems, networking software, and other low-level software take advantage of various shifting techniques. Table 2-10 summarizes the shifting operators available for Java in which a = 5 and b = -10.

Operator	Definition	Example	Solution
<<	left shift	a << 5	160
		b << 5	-320
>>	right shift	a >> 2	1
		b >> 2	-3
>>>	unsigned right shift	a >>> 1	2
		b >>> 1	2147483643

Table 2-10: Bitwise shifting operators.

In Table 2-10, the bits in a would be shifted left by one, adding a 0 to the right-hand side. Table 2-11 shows the binary interpretation for 75 before and after a << shift operation.

Bit number	1	2	3	4	5	6	7	8	9	10	11	12	13	14	15	16
Value of 75	0	0	0	0	0	0	0	0	0	1	0	0	1	0	1	1
Result 150	0	0	0	0	0	0	0	0	1	0	0	1	0	1	1	0

Table 2-11: Binary interpretation of 75 << 1.

Notice that the bits were merely bumped to the left, a 0 was added, and the decimal value for the result of the shift is 150 (0000 0000 1001 0110). If you had specified 2 for the number of shifts, it would result in the bits shifting two places to the left and two zeros being added to the right.

One of the important uses for shifting is to multiply by powers of 2 with left shifts and divide by powers of 2 with right shifts. The following shows the mathematical equations for both of these shifts:

```
X << A  = X*2^A
X >> A  = X/2^A
```

Notice, however, that in shifting, 1's can get cut off from the right-hand side. This also can happen to shifts that move the bits too far to the left. It is important to be aware of these losses in shifts.

Assignment Operators

You've been working with assignment since the beginning of this chapter. So at this point it should be obvious that Java assigns in a right-to-left fashion. Nonetheless, consider the following more complicated example:

```
x = y = 10;
```

Here, y will be assigned 10 and the "subexpression" y = 10, which evaluates to 10, will be assigned to x. Therefore, x equals 10. However, the assignment operator can work with a number of other operators to create compound assignment operators. So, for example:

```
a += 5;
```

is the same as:

```
a = a + 5;
```

Table 2-12 gives a complete overview of assignment operators where x = 5.

Operator	Java Representation	Algebra	Example	Solution
=	a = b	a = b	x = 6	6
+=	a += b	a = a + b	x += 5	10
-=	a -= b	a = a - b	x -= 5	0
*=	a *= b	a = a * b	x *= 5	25
/=	a /= b	a = a / b	x /= 5	1
%=	a %= b	a = a % b	x %= 5	0
&=	a &= b	a = a & b	x &= 2	0
|=	a |= b	a = a	b	x |= 2	7
^=	a ^= b	a = a ^ b	x ^= 2	7
<<=	a <<= b	a = a << b	x <<= 2	20
>>=	a >>= b	a = a >> b	x >>= 2	1
>>>=	a >>>= b	a = a >>> b	x >>>= 2	1

Table 2-12: Compound assignment operators.

Operator Precedence

At this point, all of the primitive data types in the Java language and the operators for Java have been introduced. But before moving on, it is important to know a little more about *operator precedence*.

Operator precedence is a very easy to understand process of organizing operators to execute over other operators in the same expression. The idea behind operator precedence is very similar to that concept in algebra.

Operator Precedence in Algebra

You'll recall that, in algebra, there are rules of operation that cause one operator to execute prior to others. To illustrate, let's evaluate the following expression:

```
1 + 2 * 3 - 4 = y
```

Now, if you were not following the rules of operation as defined in algebra, you might be tempted to solve for y using the following methodology:

```
1.  1 + 2 * 3 - 4 = y
2.  3 * 3 - 4 = y
3.  9 - 4 = y
4.  5 = y
```

This is incorrect. The correct answer is 3. You arrive at the correct answer if you remember that multiplication and division operations in algebra take priority over addition and subtraction operations. So the correct procedure to solve this equation is:

1. 1 + 2 * 3 - 4 = y
2. 1 + 6 - 4 = y
3. 7 - 4 = y
4. 3 = y

Understanding why 3 is the correct answer and 5 is incorrect is easy. Still, in algebra and in Java, you have the ability to bend these rules and specify when certain operations should take priority over others. And that is done using parentheses. By surrounding a particular operation with parentheses, you give it precedence to execute first, regardless of what other operators are present.

Let's go ahead and make some changes to our algebraic equation so that 5 is the correct answer for y by adding parenthetical citations:

(1 + 2) * 3 - 2 = y

If you now go through the logic of solving this equation, you will receive 5 as your correct answer:

1. (1 + 2) * 3 - 4 = y
2. 3 * 3 - 4 = y
3. 9 - 4 = y
4. 5 = y

Operator Precedence in Java

Operator precedence in the Java language mirrors the methodology previously explained from algebra, except in Java there are other types of operators. Table 2-13 lists all the operators. Some of them have not been discussed thus far, but by the end of this book, you will have been introduced to all of the very useful ones. The first (or top) line has the highest priority; in each line, the item to the far left has the highest priority for that line.

Note: The top left has highest priority.

.	[]	()				
++	--	!	-	~	**new** (*cast*)	
*	/	%				
+	-					
<<	>>	>>>				
<	<=	.	>=	>**instanceof**		
==	!=					
&						
^						
|						
&&						
||						
=	*=	/=	%=	+=	-=	<< = >>= &= |= ^= >>>=

Table 2-13: Operator precedence.

Note: Even though new and instanceof are words (and not symbols), they are operators in the Java language.

Control Flow

In the last section, you dealt with the details of operations in the Java language. However, another fundamental part of programming is the use of control-flow structures to determine if a particular line (or block) of code should be executed. Control-flow structures give you the ability to create all sorts of decision trees in your application.

Diagramming Control Flow

Control-flow diagrams (also referred to as pseudocode diagrams) are formats for visually interpreting the programs you write without getting caught up in the actual details of how to write them in some programming language. Diagrams give you the ability to design your programs so that anyone (not just Java-literate programmers) can view them. This provides a unique way for you to perform an analysis of your program and determine what it should (and should not) be doing. Figure 2-1 diagrams what to do when driving a vehicle approaching an intersection with a light.

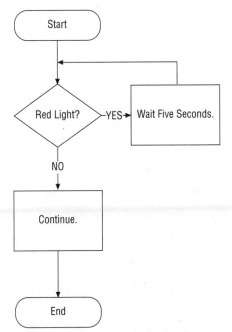

Figure 2-1: Diagram of what to do when approaching an intersection.

In Figure 2-1, you come into an intersection and perform an evaluation to determine if the light is red. If this is true, then you wait five seconds and perform the evaluation again. However, if this is false, you continue through the intersection.

Notice that it does not matter what vehicle you are using nor at what exact intersection you are. In Figure 2-1, you have a relevant drawing showing a diagram for what to do at just about any intersection.

The if Statement

The if statement is a control statement that executes a line (or block) of code based on the result of an evaluation. The following shows the syntax for using a simple if statement:

```
if (condition)
```

```
statement;
```

Notice in the previous code that if the *condition* returns true, then it causes *statement* to execute. However, if the *condition* returns false, then it causes *statement* not to execute, and the program continues after the if statement.

To illustrate, let's imagine that you had an integer variable x and you wanted to determine if its value is greater than 200. The diagram in Figure 2-2 illustrates the design needed to implement this logic.

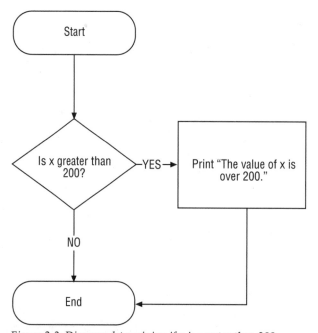

Figure 2-2: Diagram determining if x is greater than 200.

The following shows how to implement this logic using a simple if statement:

```
int x;
if (x > 200)
    System.out.println("The value of x is over 200.");
```

Note: This is a method used to display the specified text on the user's console. You will have a chance to learn more about it in the next chapter.

Using the if statement, you have the ability to execute several lines of code enclosed in brackets (referred to as a block of code). This is also true for just about all the other control-flow structures discussed here:

```
if (condition) {
    block of code;
}
```

In this syntax, you are able to execute a block of statements if the *condition* returns true. Returning to our variable x example, imagine you now want to determine if x is at least 200 and if so display a message to the user and then subtract 50 from x. Figure 2-3 shows an updated diagram.

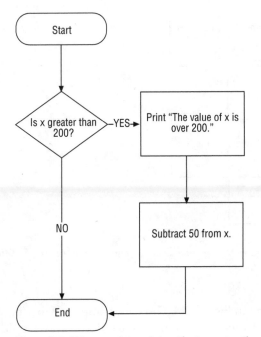

Figure 2-3: Diagram determining if x is greater than 200 and if so subtracting 50 from it.

Going to a code implementation, the if statement stays the same, but the code inside it needs to be changed:

```
int x;
if (x > 200) {
    System.out.println("The value of x is over 200.");
    x -= 50;
}
```

In the preceding code, if x is greater than 200, it displays a message to the user and then, using the -= assignment operator, the program also subtracts 50 from x. Let's add a little more functionality to this statement so that if x is less then 200, 50 gets added to it. Figure 2-4 shows an updated diagram.

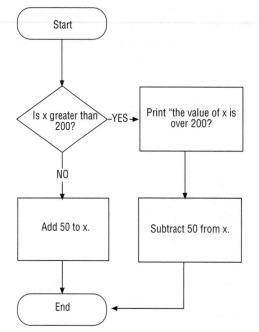

Figure 2-4: Diagram determining if x is greater than 200 and if so subtracting 50 from it, otherwise adding 50 to it.

Looking at the diagram in Figure 2-4, you could employ two separate if statements to do the job. However, another, more efficient way would be to add functionality to the original if statement by having it execute code if the evaluation returns a false using the else keyword in the if conditional. The following shows the syntax for an if-else statement:

```
if (condition) {
    //If condition is true this gets executed.
    block of code;
} else {
    //If condition is false this gets executed.
    block of code;
}
```

Applying else to our variable x example where you add 50 to x if it is less than 200, the if conditional now looks like the following:

```
int x;
if (x > 200) {
    System.out.println("The value for x is over 200.");
    x -= 50;
} else {
    x += 50;
}
```

The preceding example exemplifies most of the functionality behind the if statement. However, one more topic to touch upon before moving on is the ability to have several conditions being evaluated in a consecutive order in the same if statement using an else-if combination:

```
if (condition) {
    block of code;
} else if (condition) {
    block of code;
//Add more else-if conditionals here
} else {
    block of code;
}
```

Looking back to the variable x example, let's add the functionality that if x is equal to 200, you want to print out a statement on the screen and do nothing to x. Figure 2-5 shows a final diagram of this logic.

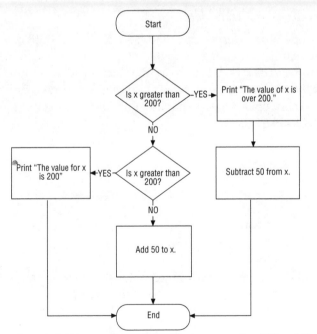

Figure 2-5: Diagram determining if x is greater than 200 and if so subtracting 50 from it; if x is equal to 200, doing nothing; otherwise, adding 50 to it.

The following shows the code implementation for the diagram in Figure 2-5.

```
int x;
if (x > 200) {
    System.out.println("The value for x is over 200.");
    x -= 50;
} else if (x == 200) {
    System.out.println("The value for x is 200.");
} else {
    x += 50;
}
```

The ? Operator

The ? (known as the ternary) operator is carried over from the C/C++ language. The *ternary operator* could be considered an if statement shorthand notation. The following is the syntax for the ternary operator:

```
condition ? statement1 : statement2;
```

The ternary operator is very simple and has been saved until now because it demonstrates similar functionality to that of an if statement. Ternary operators evaluate the *condition* and if it is true, then *statement1* is returned. On the other hand, if the *condition* is false, then *statement2* is returned. Converting the syntax of the ternary operator shown in the previous line code to an if statement syntax looks like this:

```
if (condition) {
    statement1;
} else {
    statement2;
}
```

The only difference between the ternary operator and this if conditional, besides syntax, is that the ternary operator returns a value so you can use it in expressions.

Note: The ternary operator is so named because *ternary* means the involvement of three, and the ternary operator has three terms.

The for Loop

The for loop behaves in a repetitious fashion, looping indefinitely until it meets certain conditions. In every for loop, there is an *initialization* section called once when the for loop starts. Then the for loop will continue to cycle between executing a statement (or block), each time calling an incrementing (or decrementing) *expression* and retesting the *conditional*. The following shows the general syntax of a for loop that executes only one statement:

```
for (initialization; condition; expression)
    statement;
```

Or, if you wish to have a block in your for loop, the following shows the syntax:

```
for (initialization; conditional; expression) {
    block of code;
}
```

Note: all of the parts of a for loop are optional. Depending on what you want to do, you can leave out any and/or all parts of the for loop. For example, leaving out the middle conditional would make the for loop cycle infinitely, which might be useful in responding to some sort of indefinite input.

Let's take a look at an example. In this case, you need to print out all the even numbers contained between the numbers 1 and 10. Now, with what you have learned thus far, you can do this by using the following code:

```
System.out.println("2");
System.out.println("4");
System.out.println("6");
System.out.println("8");
System.out.println("10");
```

This snippet of code does exactly what you need it to do. However, this brings up an important note about why there is control flow. Control flow helps the programmer write less code and perform more complex tasks in a more efficient manner. There is an easier and smarter way to do this same task. Let's implement a for loop performing the same operation but this time write less code:

```
for (int i = 1; i <= 5; i++)
    System.out.println(i * 2);
```

Note: In the previous code you can declare variables inside the for loop. Note that these variables only exist inside the loop and may not have the same identifier as a variable already present outside the loop.

In this case, the for loop will cycle through, incrementing at every step and printing out another even number. Using a for loop, you were able to condense five lines of code into two.

With `for` loops, you also can decrement, so that the code cycles in reverse. In the previous example, all of the even numbers between 1 and 10 are printed. The following sample snippet of code shows exactly the same task accomplished, except this time it prints the numbers in reverse order:

```
for (int i = 5; i >= 1; i--)
    System.out.println(i * 2);
```

Note: A `for` loop badly constructed may be infinite in nature and never quit looping. Or the `for` loop may never start looping to begin with.

The previous example prints all five even numbers on the screen in reverse order. Let's take a look at one more example: You have a loop that goes from 1 to 10, but this time you need to have the program test to see if the number is even or odd with each pass:

```
for (int i = 1; i <= 10; i++) {
    if ( i % 2 == 0)
        System.out.println("The number " + i + " is even");
else System.out.println("The number " + i + " is odd");
}
```

This shows an example of having one control-flow structure inside another. This is a very common and useful programming practice.

One final thing to touch upon is that you can declare more than one variable in the initialization and incrementing/decrementing parts as long as they are separated by commas. The following shows an example in which two variables (`i` and `j`) are used to display the values between 1 and 10 in an incrementing fashion for `i` and a decrementing fashion for `j`:

```
for (int i = 1, j = 10; i < 11; i++, j--) {
    System.out.println("i equals " + i);
    System.out.println("j equals " + j);
}
```

Figure 2-6 shows a diagram for the preceding logic.

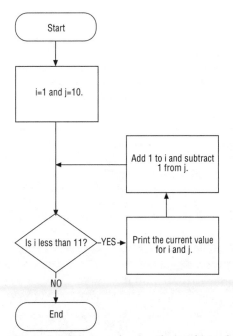

Figure 2-6: Diagram showing the i and j for *loop.*

The i and j for loop will produce the following output:

```
i equals 1
j equals 10
i equals 2
j equals 9
i equals 3
j equals 8
i equals 4
j equals 7
i equals 5
j equals 6
i equals 6
j equals 5
i equals 7
j equals 4
i equals 8
j equals 3
i equals 9
j equals 2
i equals 10
j equals 1
```

The while & do-while Loop

The while loop is similar to the for loop, except it does not have initialization or expression parts. Moreover, unless the body of the while loop eventually causes the *condition* to become false, it is assumed to continue looping forever. The following shows the syntax for a while loop with one statement and a while loop with a block of statements:

```
while (condition)
    statement;
```

or:

```
while (condition) {
    block of code;
}
```

while loops are very simple in that they test for a particular condition: If true, then they execute *statement* (or blocks of statements) and finally go back and retest *condition*. This will continue to loop until the *condition* becomes false.

The other loop related to the while loop is the do-while loop. Once you understand the while loop, the do-while loop is very easy to understand. Simply stated, the only difference between a while loop and a do-while loop is that with a do-while loop the *statement* (or block of statements) executes first, then the *condition* is evaluated. In other words, the logical pattern followed is to execute the statements and then evaluate the *condition*. The following shows the syntax for the do-while loop:

```
do
    statement;
while (condition);
```

or:

```
do {
    block of code;
} while (condition);
```

TIP

> *Note that it is possible that some given* while *loop may never be executed, but a do-while loop will always be executed at least once.*

The switch Statement

Sometimes, it is not convenient to have a conditional evaluate only a `boolean` result for determining which way your program should flow. In these cases, you can implement the `switch` statement. Carried over from C/C++, the `switch` statement is very useful for situations in which you have multiple selections going at one time for a given integral expression. The following is the syntax for a switch statement:

```
switch (expression) {

    case constant1:
        statement;
        break;
    case constant2:
        statement;
    case constant3:
        statement;
        break;

    .
    .
    .

    default:
        statement;
}
```

The `switch` statement is very easy to understand. Starting from the top, the *expression* returns an integral value. Then the value matches itself to one of the case constants (e.g., *constant1* or *constant2*). At this point, the *statement* contained inside that case executes and continues to execute down the switch statement until the keyword `break` is reached.

Note: In the previous syntax for the `switch` statement the `break` keyword is optional for each case. This means, however, that if a case does not contain a break, the program executes through the other cases following it until it reaches a break statement or comes to the end of the `switch` statement. Meaning that two cases in one `switch` statement cannot have exactly the same constant.

The last part of the previous syntax is the default part. In the event that the *expression* returns a value that does not match any of the cases in the `switch` statement, the *default* and its corresponding *statement* is executed. Note that the *default* is an optional part of the syntax for a `switch` statement.

TIP

It is a good practice to always put `default` *in a* `switch` *statement, since you might not always know for sure what data will be evaluated in the expression.*

Breaking Out of Loops

As mentioned in the keywords section, Java does not have any functional use for the goto keyword. As a result, Java has added extra functionality with labeled breaks in control-flow operations.

There are three types of jumping that help you circumvent the need to use goto: *breaking loops, breaking nested loops using labels,* and *continuing.*

Breaking

The first process to understand is the idea of breaking out of a loop. In these examples, you are in a loop (e.g., a for loop) and you are cycling through. However, every time you cycle, you are testing for something. If that evalua-tion returns true, then you call break to jump out of the loop.

For instance, imagine you have a variable x from which you wish to sub-tract 1,000 in 10 increments of 100. But if the account runs out of funds, you want the process to stop and print out what was not subtracted so no more subtractions take place thereby making x negative. Figure 2-7 shows the logic for this.

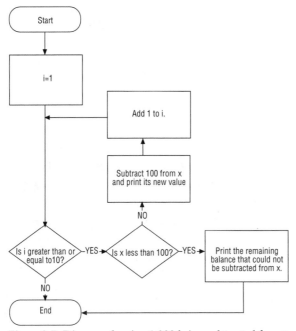

Figure 2-7: Diagram showing 1,000 being subtracted from x.

The following shows the code to implement the previous logic:

```java
int x;
for (int i = 1; i <= 10; i++) {
    if (x < 100) {
        System.out.println((1000 - 100 * (i-1)) + " could not be subtracted
from x.");
        break;
    }
    x -= 100;
    System.out.println("100 has been subtracted from x.");
    System.out.println("x now equals " + x);
}
```

None of the previous code should be new to you. However, the key area that you want to focus on now is the if statement. First, notice that it is inside a for loop (which is perfectly legal in Java) and is referred to as a *nested loop*. If x is less than 100, then the remaining balance is displayed and the break keyword is used to exit the for loop. So, to illustrate, if x were equal to 700, this is what the output would look like:

```
100 has been subtracted from x.
x now equals 600
100 has been subtracted from x.
x now equals 500
100 has been subtracted from x.
x now equals 400
100 has been subtracted from x.
x now equals 300
100 has been subtracted from x.
x now equals 200
100 has been subtracted from x.
x now equals 100
100 has been subtracted from x.
x now equals 0
300 could not be subtracted from x.
```

Note: Although it may seem wrong at a glance if when creating a nested control-flow solution (e.g., a nested loop for example) the only thing contained inside the outer control statement is the inner control statement, the brackets for the outer are optional. For example the following is legal:

```java
if (x == 1)
    while (true) {
        //Body of the while loop
    }
```

Breaking With Labels

Sometimes breaking out of a loop is just not that simple. Sometimes you want to not only break but also jump to a specific location in the program. In other languages, such as C and C++, goto functionality allows you to accomplish these tasks. In Java, goto is not an option; instead, you can use a labeled break.

Before continuing, you need to understand how to create labels in the Java language. Consider the following:

```
label1:
```

A label is nothing more than a name (similar to a name you might give a variable) immediately followed by a colon. When performing a labeled break, you type the keyword break (just as you did in the last section to remove yourself from a loop), followed by the label to which you want to jump:

```
HERE:

Body of Program

for (int I = 1; I < 100; I++) {
    //Body of outer for Loop
    if (condition)
        break THERE;
    for (int a = 1; a < 10; a ++) {
        //Body of inner for Loop
        if(condition)
            break HERE;
    }
}

THERE:
```

If you look closely at the preceding example, you will notice that if you were simply to specify break, you would break out of the inner for loop only, not the outer. Second, even if you were able to break out of both for loops by using two breaks, your program would continue execution at the end of the outer for loop and not at the specified label.

TIP

As with goto in C/C++ labeled breaks in Java are not the best solutions to a programming problem and should be implemented only as a last resort.

Continuing

The last technique to be discussed along the lines of breaking is how to prematurely advance in a for loop. This handy technique can prove quite useful. Simply stated, you have a loop that cycles through, and inside that loop, you may have a situation arise in which you want to advance to the next loop without executing all of the statements. Using the continue keyword and the following syntax provides your solution:

```
<Beginning of a Loop> {
    statement(s)1;
    <Conditional (if true execute the following block)> {
        statement(s);
        continue;
    }
    statement(s)2;
}
```

Notice in the previous example that every time this loop cycles, *statement(s)1* executes. However, *statement(s)2* executes only if the conditional returns a false. Otherwise, the block inside the conditional will execute the continue statement that will automatically advance the loop to the next cycle without executing *statement(s)2*. Continue can be a very handy technique in certain situations.

Moving On

In this chapter, you learned Java's basic language structure. However, there is more to Java since it is an object-oriented programming language. The next chapter will introduce you to object-oriented programming in Java and give you a chance to create your first Java program.

Java's Object-Orientation

Object-oriented programming (OOP) organizes your programs in a more efficient and, more important, easier-to-understand format. Java is by no means the first (or last) programming language to be object oriented. Nonetheless, Java is special as an OOP language: It is relatively easy to understand and even easier to implement compared to other OOP languages currently on the market.

OOP languages are designed around a modular theme. In object-oriented programming, one key point is the ability to have communication between the objects via function calls rather than by directly accessing the actual data in a given object. In this way, data are effectively encapsulated.

Also, you do not have any omnipresent global variables. You can grant certain classes (or parts thereof) to have varying levels of exposure to other classes. Figure 3-1 shows a diagram of a very simple distributed Java program.

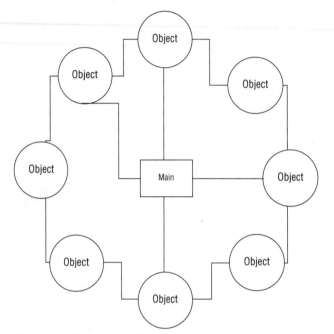

Figure 3-1: Diagram of a simple object-oriented program.

In OOP, objects replace less sophisticated functions (or procedures) and data structures. Furthermore, objects can have relationships with one another, giving you greater flexibility to enhance your program without changing any of the original source code. In summary, objects give you the ability to better organize distributed programs.

What are *objects*? Let's look at an analogy out of the real world—a car. A collection of properly integrated, interconnected components creates a car. Thanks to Henry Ford, all of these components are interchangeable and self-contained (i.e., understanding the inner workings of a given component is not critical to implementing it in the car). When you put all of these components together, you get a car. However, Ford does not create all the components for its vehicles; rather, it gets most of the components for a car from various third-party sources.

Note: If you disassemble one of these components, you will get smaller, more "basic" subcomponents and so on.

Objects in computer programming follow a very similar metaphor. All of your programs divide into reusable "components" (i.e., objects), which also are distributable to other programs. Each of these components has the ability both to interact with others and to store various real-time data. Some components you create; others you borrow from those already available; still others are a combination, when you specialize a component already available with your own customizations.

Note: Can you program Java without objects? No. You must program with objects when using Java.

This chapter details how objects and their behaviors are implemented in Java. For instance, how can you design the blueprints (so to speak) for an object and then actually create objects from that blueprint? You also will learn about the various properties and member types that an object can have and even how objects can effectively interact with one another.

Classes

Up to this point, everything discussed dealt strictly with the theoretical topic of objects in any given OOP language. However, in Java, a *class* represents the framework for an object. It is not until you have it constructed that it is a "living and breathing" object in Java. You will learn more about constructing a little later on. Right now, let's focus our attention on creating a Java class. The following shows the syntax for a very basic class in which you use the `class` keyword in the declaration line followed by brackets. Anything contained inside the brackets is code belonging to the class:

```
class ClassName {
Body of class
}
```

Let's look at a sample real-world class called `Computer`:

```
class Computer {
}
```

Notice in the previous code that `class` is part of the formal declaration for the class. Following that is the actual class name. This class is called `Computer`. Everything inside of the brackets is part of the class `Computer`. At a very basic level, that is really all there is to creating a class. However, as you can see, the class `Computer` does not have any functionality (i.e., it does not contain anything and is not doing anything) because there is no code inside its brackets to define any behavior for it.

Instance Fields

As mentioned in the last chapter, *variables* represent a holding tank for information that helps you save and access information within your Java programs. There are two important things to note about using variables in the Java language:

- Every variable must be a member of a class or defined locally in a block of code (which is in turn somehow tied to a class). In other words, you cannot have a stand-alone variable in Java.

- There are no global variables in Java (which is an indirect result of the first statement). In the following code, the integer variable, speed, is a member of class Computer:

```
class Computer {
int speed = 200;
  }
```

This is primarily all that you need to do in order to make a field available to the entire class Computer (i.e., the int variable could be used in any method belonging to this class). As you will learn later on, other objects can see this variable, but that directly depends on their relationship with class Computer.

Note: You see in the previous code that a value was explicitly specified. If you do not specify an initial value, Java uses a default one (either 0 or null, whichever is more appropriate). However, it is always a good idea to specify an initial value.

Instance Methods

Method is the object-oriented word for a function in structured-language talk. A method is exactly like a function, except that it is a member of a class. Hence, the method is a member of the class to which it belongs.

Note: Java does not support stand-alone functions. The only way to employ a method is to wrap it inside a class.

Methods, like functions, perform a set of actions when called. They are usually named after some sort of action, such as start( ), stop( ), kill( ), run( ), and so on. It also is not uncommon in Java for several classes to call the same method. The following code shows the syntax for declaring a simple method:

```
[modifier(s)] returnType methodName( ) {

    // Body of method

}
```

Modifiers will be discussed later. At this point, notice that just like a function, a method can have a return type. The *returnType* in front of the word *methodName()* represents the location where you designate a return type for this method. When you declare a method, you use the *returnType* to declare what type of data returns from this method. Unlike C, Java does not assume any default return type.

TIP

> *In some cases, you do not need to return a type. In those cases, replace the* returnType *with the keyword* void, *meaning nothing returns.*

Notice the parentheses after the name *methodName*. Within these, you can place variables to be passed to the method (hereafter known as *parameters*). When the parentheses are empty (as in the previous syntax), you have no parameters for this method. Notice that even though you do not have any parameters, you still need the parentheses after the method name.

Note: All parameters are passed by value, meaning that they are copied inside the method. So, changing a parameter value inside the method does not affect it outside the method. However, as you will learn later on, this is true for primitive types only. Java objects themselves are passed by reference, meaning any changes *do* affect the original object.

The following shows two methods added to the Computer class:

```
class Computer {

    int speed = 200;

    int getSpeed() {
        return speed;
    }
    void setSpeed(int newSpeed) {
        speed = newSpeed;
    }
```

The first method getSpeed() specifies int in front of its name. This means that the method will return an integer value. The code inside getSpeed() is an expression with the return keyword. This is the method's cue to return the value of the expression immediately following return. The second method setSpeed() has an int parameter declared. This means that any time this method is called, an integer needs to be specified to change the speed of the variable.

Looking at the previous example should help you better appreciate the essence of OOP and understand the selector and mutator methods. Notice that other objects calling this class do not access the speed field directly. Instead, they call an appropriate get*XXX*( ) method to retrieve the value or a set*XXX*( ) to change it. This represents the essence of the *encapsulation,* or *data hiding,* that is used in OOP. The actual data for the class (in this case speed) are encapsulated or "hidden" inside the object. If you are already familiar with Java you may have noticed that speed is not truly encapsulated because it should be modified with private. This has been removed for the sake of simplicity, but later on in the chapter you will have a chance to learn about modifiers.

Constructors

In order to instantiate a class, you must call one of the class's *constructors* (for more information on instantiating, please see "Instance-Initialization Blocks," two sections later). Constructors are just like the methods described earlier, except for a few syntactical points:

- Constructors must have the same name as the class they are constructing.

- Constructors do not specify a return type.

- Constructors must be called in conjunction with the new operator (you do not have the option to call them like a typical method you learned about earlier). The following shows the syntax for instantiating classes:

    `ClassName variableName = new ClassName( );`

> **TIP**
>
> *Unlike C++, the following code does not create any object; it just declares a reference of* Computer:
>
> `Computer myComputer;`
>
> *As you will learn more later on, to actually create an object in Java, you always need to use a* new *operator.*

In the preceding code, *ClassName* is the name of a class; *variableName* is the name of the *ClassName* object that will be created using the *ClassName* constructor *ClassName( ).* Note that just like methods you have the option of placing parameters inside the parentheses. Throughout the rest of this chapter, you will have a chance to construct instances of classes (i.e., objects).

Note: Must a class define a constructor? No. If you do not define any constructors in your class, Java will supply and use a default one (i.e., one with no parameters) that will be called when it is instantiated.

Inside the constructor, you include the initialization code you want to use for the creation of a class instance. The following shows the syntax of a constructor:

```
ClassName {
    ClassName() {

        //Constructor code here

    }
//Rest of the class
}
```

A class certainly can define more than one constructor as long as they do not specify the same parameters. For instance, looking at our Computer class, the following shows two constructors for it:

```
class Computer {

//Fields
    int speed = 200;
    String name  = "Unknown";

//Constructors
    Computer() {
        //Constructor code here
    }
    Computer(String newName) {
        //Constructor code here
    }

//Methods
    int getSpeed() {
        return speed;
    }
    setSpeed(int newSpeed) {
        speed = newSpeed;
    }
}
```

In the previous example, you can instantiate a Computer class using one of the two constructors. Consider the following:

```
//Default Constructor
Computer myComputer = new Computer();

//Constructor with a String specified
Computer myComputer2 = new Computer("DELL");
```

> **TIP**
>
> *If you don't need a variable identifier reference to some object, you do not have to declare one. You can simply leave the right side off and instantiate the object anonymously. However, it then turns into an expression* that *evaluates to the corresponding object type.*
>
> *For example, the following demonstrates* anonymous instantiating *by passing an anonymous instance of* Computer *as a parameter to the method* testMethod( ), *which has a* Computer *object parameter:*
>
> ```
> testMethod(new Computer("IBM"));
> ```

Destructors?

In this section you learned about constructors and how to create objects. However, you may be wondering what goes on when you are finished with an object. Unlike C++, Java handles the destruction of all objects automatically through what is known as a *garbage collector* (a technology borrowed from Smalltalk). This helps make Java programming easier and removes any chance of having memory-management-related errors. Technically speaking, the garbage collector keeps tabs on an object to see how many references it has; at the point when there are no more references to that object, it is destroyed.

Every object in Java does have a finalize( ) method that you can define to specify any cleanup code. However, it is *not* recommended that you use this method since you can never be sure when the garbage collector will clean up that object. The better solution is to define your own method (e.g., cleanUp( )) and call it manually when you are finished using some non-memory-related resource (e.g., a file).

Overloading

In the source code and examples in the previous sections, one of the OOP programming techniques employed was *overloading*. Specifically, you can create methods (or constructors) with similar functionality that have the same name. Java automatically chooses the correct method to execute based on what was given in the method call. Method overloading in Java is carried over from C++. However, C++ refers to it as function overloading.

Note: In C++, you can explicitly overload operators (+, -, *, etc.) so that they perform different functions in addition to their primary function in the language. However, because this functionality can overcomplicate programs, the ability for the programmer to overload an operator has been removed from the Java language. However, please do not be misled—several of Java's operators are overloaded.

Overloading can be very useful. It can be used to create several methods of the same name (with different input variables) to perform very similar tasks. Each overloaded method is designed to handle a different set of input variables but perform similar functions. Method overloading is a very important part of the modern programming paradigm in Java.

Instance-Initialization Blocks

Sometimes you may need to instantiate variable(s) in a more complex manner than in just one line; these cases usually involve a loop. At such times, you can use an instance-initialization block. The following code shows initialization of the factors array (you'll learn about arrays later in the chapter):

```
class A {
    long[] factors = new long[10];
    {
        factors[0] = 1;
        for (int k=1; k< factors.length; k++)
            factors[k] = factors[k-1]*k;
    }
}
```

Instance-initialization code is executed every time the class is instantiated but just before the constructor for that class is invoked. This can be very useful for putting in a class the initializing code that is used by all its constructors.

You will see other uses of instance initializers later on during the discussion of anonymous classes.

Creating & Using Objects

Defining classes and actually using them are two different things. Defining a class won't cause it to do anything but sit there and be defined. It is through the process of *instantiating* or *instancing*, wherein you call the class's constructor, that you actually get an object based on the class you defined. Instantiating also gives you a more specific representation of the defined class.

For an illustration of class instantiating, go back to the class Computer. A computer is defined by the *American Heritage Dictionary* as follows: "a device that computes, especially a programmable electronic machine that performs high-speed mathematical or logical operations or that assembles, stores, correlates, or otherwise processes information."

This definition could be the *class* for a computer. However, an *instance* of the definition could be the computer you have at home. In this case you have real-time information about its specifications (CPU speed, hard disk size, etc.), functionality (operating system running, etc.), and age. Thus, you have what could be considered an instance of a computer (as defined by the *American Heritage Dictionary*).

What if you have two objects that are exactly the same in every way? Technically speaking, if you have two objects instantiated separately, even though they are exactly the same, they are still considered different entities—the same way two computers of exactly the same make and model will still differ by their serial numbers.

One of the nice advantages Java has over C/C++ is what is happening on the inside when you instantiate an object. In Java, you call a class's constructor using the keyword new as you learned about in the "Constructors" section. Consider the following:

```
Computer myComputer = new Computer();
```

On the left, you are basically declaring an instance variable in the same manner that you would declare a primitive data type like you worked with in the last chapter. Also, notice the new keyword. Technically speaking, new is an operator that constructs the instance of the Computer class called myComputer.

Note: You can also specify variables when instantiating, depending on the constructor signature for a specified class. This variable information would go inside the parentheses. However, just like methods, if there are no parameters passed to this class, you still need to include the parentheses.

You now have an instance of Computer reflected specifically toward myComputer. However, it is extremely important to note that myComputer is *not* the actual object, but a reference to it. This is a very important implication because, when setting one variable to another, you actually are setting the reference so that both variables will point to the same object. Consider the following:

```
Computer c1;
Computer c2 = new Computer();

c1 = c2; //Both references now point to the same object c1
c2.setSpeed(500);
Int x = c1.getSpeed(); Will return 500 not 200!
```

Here, specifying the speed for c2 changes the speed for the object, so if you retrieve the speed for c1, it now will return 500.

Note: When comparing two variables using the == operator, it is important to understand that you are not comparing contents. Instead, you are comparing whether both operands point to the same object. If you wish to compare the actual contents of two objects, you should use the equals() method from the Object class (discussed in more detail in the "Inheritance," section of this chapter).

Another tool that you can use is the instanceof operator that lets you check to see if one object is an instance of another class. The following shows the syntax for using the instanceof operator:

```
Object instanceof Class
```

If the *Object* is an instance of *Class* on the right, then the expression returns true. Consider the following:

```
Computer myComputer = new Computer();
boolean test = myComputer instanceof Computer;
```

In the previous code, the first line creates myComputer, which is an instance of class Computer. The second line uses the instanceof operator to check to see if myComputer is an instance of Computer. In this case, the second-line-of-code test would be true.

Use of the instanceof operator allows you to avoid potentially dangerous problems with casting one object reference to another class (which you will have a chance to learn more about later on in the chapter). Right now, let's turn our attention back to understanding how to add functionality to classes.

Class Fields

Sometimes you may have a variable you wish to make available to the entire class (rather than to specific objects of the class). In such cases, you can create static variables.

```
static y = 25;
```

You declare this field like any other, except the keyword static prefixes it. Also, to use an instance field you have to have an instance of the class (for an example of trying to use a nonstatic member of a class without proper initialization, please see the next section); however, this is not so with static fields. You can use them any time you need them.

TIP

As you will learn later on, you can add combinations of keywords to a field declaration.

Class Methods

So far, you have looked at how to create classes and how to populate your classes with members. It is important to note that you cannot use any of the members in a class; you can use these members only from an *object* of that class. So, going to the `Computer` example, consider the following:

```
Computer myComputer;
int i = myComputer.getSpeed();

myComputer = new Computer(1000);
```

Based on the class definition for `Computer`, what is the value of `i`? Someone inexperienced may say 200, but this is wrong, because you would be referencing an object (`myComputer`) that has not been constructed yet. So, when you attempt to compile this code, you would get an error because `myComputer` has not been initialized yet.

Sometimes you may have a method (usually utility related) that is consistent among all instances of the class of which it is a member. In such cases, you can declare the method with the keyword `static` in front of it to specify that this method belongs to the class and not to any instance of it.

Note: It is important to understand that `static` methods cannot access nonstatic data; to do otherwise would defeat their static nature, and always precipitate a compile-time error.

The concept of static methods is something you have already been exposed to in the last chapter. The method `println()` from the `System` class used to display some specified text on the user's console is static, which is why you do not need to instantiate `System` to use it. For example:

```
System.out.println("Hello World!");
```

Discussing static methods also leads us to an important part of creating a stand-alone Java program, and that is the `main()` method. The `main()` method is a static method that is used in a very similar fashion to the `main()` method used in C/C++ programs. Effectively, this method acts as the central point where the program is to begin execution. When your application runs, it starts by executing any code inside this method, and when it reaches the end of this method, it signifies the end of execution for the program. Note that since `main()` is a static method, only one `main()` method can be present in a given Java class. The following shows the declaration for the `main()` method:

```
public static void main(String args[]) {
    //Body of the method
}
```

The public modifier will be talked about a little later on. Note that unless you declare your main( ) method (as shown in the previous code), Java will not recognize it as the main( ) method used for the execution of the Java program. The next section will give you a chance to execute your first Java application and will demonstrate how the main method works.

Class-Initialization Blocks

Similar to what you learned earlier about instance-initialization blocks, you also can specify a block of code to be static. This is done using brackets prefixed by the keyword static:

```
class A {
    static long[] factors = new long[10];
    static {
        factors[0] = 1;
        for (int k=1; k< factors.length; k++)
            factors[k] = factors[k-1]*k;
    }
}
```

Class- or static-initialization blocks are executed once when the class is loaded. As you can see in the preceding code, a static block is very useful for initializing a complicated set of static variables (usually involving a loop).

Example: My First Java Program

In this example, you are going to create your first real Java application using the Java Development Kit (JDK). I hope this isn't your first time. If it is, this section will show you step by step how to create and execute a Java application. Future examples will show a condensed version.

The application FirstTest that you will create demonstrates a simple example of declaring a variable, assigning it a value, and displaying your results on the screen.

Download the JDK from JavaSoft's home page at http://www.javasoft.com. Then, following the instructions shown in http://www.javasoft.com, install the JDK into a \java directory off the root of your hard disk. Make sure that java\bin and java\lib directories are included into search path.

Checking Your Installation of the JDK

You can check your installation of the JDK by executing the following command in the directory (or directories) where you are going to be doing Java development:

```
java -version
```

You should see something similar to the following:

```
java version "1.1.1"
```

If you don't, or if you get some sort of error, be sure to check the installation and verify the accuracy of your search path.

1. Using an ASCII-based text editor (such as Notepad), create the file FirstTest.java and enter the following code into it:

```
class FirstTest {

    public static void main(String args[]) {

        char X= 'Y';

        System.out.println("The literal for X is " + 'X' + "\nThe
value inside of X is " + X);

    }
}
```

In the previous code, you declare the char variable called X to contain the value Y. Then you use the println() method to print the value of X.

2. Save the FirstTest.java file.

3. From a command line, type **javac FirstTest.java** to compile the Java code (see Figure 3-2).

Figure 3-2: Compiling the FirstTest application.

The javac.exe compiler is part of the JDK. Compiling a Java source file (such as FirstTest.java) results in a corresponding executable class file to be created with the same name but ending with .class (i.e., FirstTest.class).

When the executable class file is created nothing will be displayed on the screen letting you know that it compiled properly.

4. From a DOS command line, type **java FirstTest** to execute the application. Notice that you do not specify the .class extension. The java.exe interpreter is part of the JDK. Once the application executes, you will see what appears in Figure 3-3.

TIP

In more serious solutions, you may need to compile, execute, and/or debug the program many times. In such situations you can create a batch file (or whatever is appropriate on your platform) and simply execute that batch file. For the example program above, we could have created an arbitrarily named FirstTest.bat batch file containing the following code:

```
c:\JavaJDK\bin\javac FirstTest.java
c:\JavaJDK\bin\java   FirstTest
```

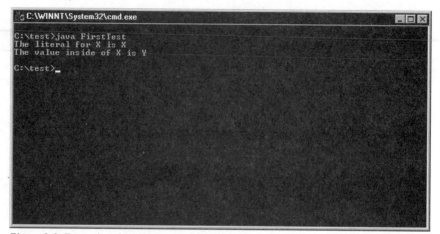

Figure 3-3: Executing the FirstTest application.

Note: Remember, any time you make a change to a Java source file, you need to follow the previous steps to compile it into a class file again. The newly compiled class file will overwrite the older one and contain the changes you made in the corresponding source.

Object-Based Data Types

In the last chapter, you were introduced to a variety of primitive data types. However, there are a few data types in Java not yet covered because they are represented as a sort of object/primitive hybrid or crossbreed. The two major data types not discussed until now are *arrays* and *strings*. Both of these are actually represented as Java classes.

Note: Java contains a set of built-in classes that represent all the primitive data types discussed earlier. Therefore, all data types in Java have a primitive and a corresponding object-based representation available. However, arrays and strings (discussed in detail in this section) do not have a primitive counterpart as they are objects with some uniquely primitive characteristics.

In C/C++, an array is basically a set of memory addresses set in sequential order. Furthermore, a C/C++ string is merely an array of characters. Unfortunately, without the direct use of pointers (or pointer arithmetic), you lose the functionality of arrays (and ultimately strings) that exists in the C/C++ languages. That is why Java must wrap these two data types in object-based classes and not have a primitive counterpart. In essence, you treat them just like any other class in Java.

Note: With all its OOP, why does Java bother with primitive data types? The answer: efficiency. Working with primitive types is much more efficient than working with their object-based counterparts.

Arrays

In C/C++, an *array* is a domain of allocated memory. To refer to a particular location or element in the array, you would specify the name of the array and/ or the position number. In C++, there is no data type for a string variable, so a programmer would utilize an array of characters instead.

However, because of Java's explicit pointerless environment and focus on simplicity, an array is represented as objects. And just like any other class in Java, it must be instantiated in order to be used. The following example shows the declaration of an array of five integers called group:

```
int group[] = new int[5];  // five elements
```

Now you have an array of five integer values that can be accessed by reference to the array name plus the location number of each value in the braces. The following example puts a value in the third element in the array:

```
group[2] = 10;
```

Note: In C/C++, the index of the array starts with 0. This is also true for Java. To illustrate, look at the array in the preceding example: group[0] would be the first index; the last is group[4].

An alternative way to declare an array group would be to put the brackets next to the keyword int as follows:

```
int[] group = new int[5];
```

You also can declare and assign values to an array all in the same line. The following example of this uses the group example:

```
int group[] = {10, 2, 27, 32, 33};
```

What if you wanted to access the value of the third element in the preceding array? That is done by referencing that element as follows:

```
int i = group[2]; //i equals 27
```

Note that all arrays have the instance variable length which is defined automatically. This field represents the integral length for its array (as measured by the number of elements). So, for example, the following would return the number 5 since there are five elements in the array:

```
int j = group.length; //j equals 5
```

TIP

In Java, you can declare an array and assign for it at a later time, using the new *operator (like you would to instantiate an object). The following shows a simple example:*

```
char c;
//Later on in the program
c = new char[] { 'a', 'b', 'c' }
```

One final note is that, in Java, you can create multidimensional arrays by declaring an array of arrays. Examine the following examples, which demonstrate how you would declare a two-dimensional array implicitly and explicitly:

```
int multigroup[][] = new int[10][20];
int multigroup[][] = {{1,2}, {2,4}, {4,8}};
```

Arrays are a very basic and useful part of programming in any language. The important thing to keep in mind, however, is that arrays that are built in Java are represented as classes.

Strings

The String class is a key class used in Java to represent a string of Unicode characters. One of the extra hooks that Java provides this class is that it will automatically initialize a String object any time it runs into straight double quotation marks ("). This means that you can declare a String as if it were a primitive data type (i.e., you don't need to use the new operator):

```
String s = "My test string.";
```

TIP

This also applies to string literals because they are represented as String objects as well.

The String class provides a variety of methods used to perform various string-based operations.

Note: This class uses functionality that is similar to that defined in the <string.h> header file used in C.

It is important to note that, when performing operations, the contents of the String instance cannot be changed after its creation (i.e., Strings are immutable). Instead, you must create new String objects in which to put the results of the String operations that will result from using the methods defined in this class.

Remember that when testing for the equality of two Strings, you do not use the ==
*operator, as Strings are objects and this will test only to see whether both operands
point to the same String object. Instead, you should use the* equals() *method
defined in the* Object *class.*

Notwithstanding, you can concatenate Strings using the + operator. Technically speaking, Java has overloaded the + operator so that any data type con-
catenated to a string will be promoted/converted to the string type.

One important note is that unlike other object types, Strings are passed by value.

You also can use the substring() method from the String class to extract a
specified portion of a given String, with the returning value being placed in a
new String object.

Note: It is possible to perform in-place modifications of a String using the
StringBuffer class, which also is available in the Java Class Library.

Packages

In Java you have the ability to group certain classes into a single collection,
which is known as a *package.* You also can include other packages so that a
given package will contain a set of classes and several other "subpackages."

You can nest packages in other packages as many times as you want.

Introducing the Java Class Library

A good part of the Java technology belongs to the Java Class Library. This library is distributed with the JDK and comprises much of the functionality
behind the capabilities of Java. Simply put, this library is nothing more than one
huge package containing an entire hierarchy of subpackages and so on. The Java
Class Library is named java (interestingly enough). The following table describes all of the packages contained in the Java Class Library (Table 3-1):

Package	Description
java.applet	Used for Java applets.
java.awt	Used for GUI Design.
java.awt.datatransfer	Used for data transfer (including clipboard operations).
java.awt.event	Used for event handling.
java.awt.image	Used for image processing.
java.awt.peer	Supporting package to java.awt. Not used directly.
java.beans	Used for Java Beans.
java.io	Used for creating and using I/O streams.
java.lang	Used for the default classes.
java.lang.reflect	Used for reflection.
java.math	Used for mathematical operations.
java.net	Used for communication.
java.rmi	Part of the Remote Method Invocation (RMI) API.
java.rmi.dgc	Part of the RMI API.
java.rmi.registry	Part of the RMI API.
java.rmi.server	Part of the RMI API.
java.security	Part of the Java Security API.
java.security.acl	Used for an Access Control List (ACL) in the Java Security API.
java.security.interfaces	Part of the Java Security API.
java.sql	Used for database connectivity.
java.text	Used for processing international texts.
java.util	Contains utility classes used in Java.
java.util.zip	Used for I/O operations of compressed archives.

Table 3-1: Packages contained in the Java Class Library.

Inside each of these packages are collections of classes, some of which—as you will learn later on—you can access, while other reside for "behind-the-scenes" purposes.

In this book, you will be introduced to several of these packages and the classes contained within. However, for a comprehensive listing of all these packages, look for *The Java 1.1 Programmer's Reference,* also published by Ventana.

Creating Packages

When you write a Java program, you can include it in a package by using the package keyword and specifying the name of the package to which you wish the class(es) in this source file to belong. Note that this declaration must be the first line of code in the file (not counting white spaces and comments). For example, imagine you had the file `Stuff.java` and you wanted to include it in a specific package. The following would be the first line of code in `Stuff.java`:

```
package coolstuff;

//Rest of the source file
```

This specifies that `Stuff.java` is a member of the `coolstuff` package. Let's consider another example of adding MoreStuff.java to the package `coolstuff.joshi`:

```
package coolstuff.joshi;
//Rest of the source file
```

> **TIP**
>
> *In situations (such as the `FirstTest` example you created earlier) in which a package is not explicitly stated, Java will automatically include the given class in an anonymous package based on the current directory.*

It is important to note that there is a one-to-one relationship between the subdirectory, the source file in which a class is to reside, and the package of which it is a member. For instance, `Stuff.java` would reside in the `\coolstuff` (`/coolstuff` for UNIX) subdirectory and `MoreStuff.java` would be located in the `\coolstuff\joshi` (`/coolstuff/joshi` for UNIX) subdirectory; otherwise, the compiler would not be able to locate the source files.

> **TIP**
>
> *You need to ensure your packages are found: After you have created a package and an appropriate set of subdirectories with source files, you then need to edit the CLASSPATH environmental variable specifying the directory where these classes can be located for every system that wishes to use that package. To illustrate, the following shows two example CLASSPATHs for specifying the `coolstuff.joshi` package:*
>
> ```
> CLASSPATH=c:\test;
> CLASSPATH=c:\prod\a\devteam;
> ```
>
> *Both of these CLASSPATH variables specify where the `coolstuff\joshi` subdirectories are located.*

Alternatively, you can create a single archive (be sure compression is off and the directory structure and long filenames are preserved). This approach (used by the JDK with its classes.zip archive) is a much easier and more effective way to deploy your packages.

When creating a package and deciding what to name it, it is important that your package name not be confused with those already available, particularly those belonging to the Java Class Library. In fact, JavaSoft has recommended a naming convention that uses the domain and network parts of your organization's Uniform Resource Locator (URL) along with the name of the package. So, for example, based on the URL www.joshipublishing.com and the coolstuff package, the proper package name would be:

```
com.joshipublishing.coolstuff
```

Importing Packages

When you wish to use a class from a particular package, you can simply reference it with its complete package name. For example, assuming you wish to use the class Stuff from the com.joshipublishing.coolstuff package, here is one way you can accomplish it:

```
com.joshipublishing.coolstuff.Stuff myStuff = new
com.joshipublishing.coolstuff.Stuff();
```

While this may be fine for onetime situations, it can quickly become tedious to type out the entire package name every time you wish to reference the Stuff class. Alternatively, you can import the class, making it available to the entire source file. This is done using the import keyword and the name of the class you wish to have imported. Notice that you no longer have to reference the package of which Stuff is a member:

```
import com.joshipublishing.coolstuff.Stuff;
//Later on in the program
Stuff myStuff = new Stuff();
```

Finally, in situations in which it is easier to import all the classes of a given package, you can use the * wildcard as opposed to a specific class reference in your import statement. For example:

```
import com.joshipublishing.coolstuff.*;
```

This imports all the classes in coolstuff. Using this approach does not add any unnecessary overhead and does not automatically import any subpackages that may be present.

Note: The java.lang package is the only package in the Java Class Library that is imported automatically to every Java program (whether you explicitly import it or not). It contains the key classes that are the backbone of Java and the rest of the library. Optionally, you can import this package, but it does not add any value to the program.

Inheritance

At this juncture, you should be familiar with building and using classes. However, that is only part of the object-oriented programming picture. The next step is to build a class that extends another class. This form of extending classes involves the idea of *inheritance*, a powerful part of object-oriented programming.

When you create a subclass, you are creating a more specific representation of the *superclass* from which it is inheriting. Inheritance got its name because the subclass (think of it as the child class) inherits functionality from the superclass (think of it as the parent class) with additions and/or differences of its own.

You have seen earlier that you can create your own classes, and in this section, you will learn how to create subclasses from these classes, and so on. Essentially, there are only two key points to extending classes in the Java language:

- Each subclass can extend from only one superclass. This means that Java supports the *single-inheritance model*.

- You can specify how much access each class or its members can have to other classes by using modifiers (discussed in more detail later in this section).

Note: In C++, a subclass can extend from more than one superclass. Unfortunately, once you have more than two parent classes in your subclass it can become very confusing to keep track of all the functionality each superclass brings to the subclass. Java's single-inheritance version is much simpler but compromises versatility. As you will learn later on, this compromise is offset by Java's concept of interfaces.

Let's go back to the class Computer discussed earlier in the chapter, and let's create a subclass Notebook. The assumption that not all computers are notebooks makes it a good example of inheritance (i.e., computers are the superset, and notebooks are the subset). In this logical relationship, the class Computer is the superclass, and class Notebook is the subclass. The following code shows how to create the subclass Notebook:

```
class Notebook extends Computer {

    String batteryType;

}
```

Notice the keyword extends and also notice the class name Computer following it. This is how you can subclass the functionality of Computer to class Notebook. You also created a variable batteryType in class Notebook that is specific to that class. Remember the variable speed (which is part of the Computer class created before) is available to class Notebook, but the variable batteryType is not available to class Computer.

The Root Object Class

To better understand inheritance, it is important to recognize that all classes in the Java Class Library and of your own design inherit from the root class java.lang.Object. Even classes that don't explicitly have an extends clause still implicitly extend from Object. So for example:

```
class A {
//Body of class
}
```

is the same as:

```
class A extends Object {
//Body of class
}
```

In the preceding example, extends Object is there for clarity only. If you are new to Java (or are working with junior programmers), for the sake of simplicity, you may want to extend Object explicitly for classes that normally would appear not to extend any class.

It is important to appreciate the implications of the Object root class. First, note that it is the only class that does not extend another. Second, methods in this class are available to all classes in Java. Some key methods are clone(), equals(), finalize(), and toString(). You have been introduced to some of these methods already. However, you will have a chance to learn more about them later in the book.

At this point, you should have a very basic handle on how inheritance works. Java, however, supports much more granularity than the simple relationships shown here, and that is done using a variety of modifying keywords (i. e., modifiers).

Modifiers

Modifiers help to regulate how much access you want to grant to a particular class or one of its members. Specifying how much access your classes, methods, and variables can have is one of the most useful parts of OOP and one of the principal factors behind OOP's improved organization.

You are familiar with adding the static modifier to methods and fields. However, you also can add various modifiers to Java classes. The following shows the syntax:

```
modifier[modifiers]class ClassName {
//Body of class
}
```

Notice that you can have one (or a combination of more than one) modifier in the declaration preceding the class keyword.

Note: Not specifying a modifier actually implies a default modifier in Java. The default modifier (sometimes referred to as "friendly") for a class, method, or variable makes it available to the class of which it is a member and to any other classes in the same package. Note that subclasses may or may not have access to the friendly entity (depending on the package to which the subclass belongs).

private

Use the private modifier for a method or variable declaration to allow it to be accessed only by the members of the original class that declared it. This is the most restrictive modifier you can use.

To illustrate, let's take a look at the following example:

```
class ABC {
    private int A;
    //Body of class
}
```

The modifier private in front of the variable declaration makes this variable private. Following is the class XYZ that extends ABC:

```
class XYZ extends ABC {
    //Body of class
}
```

Now the functionality from ABC is part of class XYZ. However, because A has been declared private, class XYZ will not inherit it. This simple example shows how to declare an access modifier and what one does.

public

This access modifier is the least restrictive, in the sense that it makes the class, variable, or method it modifies accessible by any class, regardless of which package it belongs to.

To illustrate, let's return to our ABC-XYZ example:

```
package test;

public class ABC {
    public int A;
    //Body of class
}
```

Notice that ABC is part of package test. Also, notice the modifier public in front of the class declaration makes this class available to everything. Following is the class XYZ that does not extend ABC, but imports the package of which ABC is a member:

```
import test.ABC;

class XYZ {
    //Body of class
}
```

Now even though it may not be apparent, class ABC and its public integer A is available to class XYZ. This simple demonstration shows that even though XYZ is not a subclass of ABC or belonging to the test package, it can still use class XYZ.

protected

This access modifier works specifically with variables and methods so that any subclasses inherited from the class to which the protected member belongs or any class that belongs to the same package can have access to it.

So, for example if we return to our ABC-XYZ example from the "private" section earlier and change A to be modified by protected, class XYZ (which is a subclass of ABC) will have access to A:

```
class ABC {
    protected int A;
    //Body of class  [
}

//Since A is protected XYZ can access it:
class XYZ extends ABC {
    //Body of class
}
```

final

This modifier is useful for specifying that the given class cannot be subclassed, the method cannot be overridden (see "Method Overriding," later in this chapter), and the fields are to be represented as constants.

> **TIP**
>
> *When working with fields,* `final` *is usually used in conjunction with* `static`, *making the given field a constant available to the class.*

Note that you do not have to initialize a constant in its declaration (you can leave it blank); rather, you can perform initialization (only once and unambiguously) in either a constructor or an instance initializer.

Note: A *constant* is a field with a specified value that does not change. For example, if you are writing a program that performs various trigonometric calculations, you would want to have a π constant representing pi:

```
final double PI = 3.1415926535;
```

Useful Keywords in Inheritance

The keywords `this` and `super` let you reference member variables or methods of certain classes (or their parents). They are used with the dot (.) operator, along with the variable or method they are referencing. These two keywords provide a powerful way to point indirectly to another part of a class or its parent.

this

With `this`, the reference points to the object itself. Consider the following:

```
class Sphere extends Circle {
    int dimensions;

    void properties() {
        this.dimensions = 3;
    }
    void displayProperties() {
        dimensions = 3;

    }
}
```

In this code, both of these methods reference the same variable. There also are times when `this` can be extremely useful, such as when you want to pass a reference of the current class to another class by passing it through a method, as in the following:

```
class ABC {
    TestClass.testMethod(this);
    //Body of class
}
```

Here, you are passing the reference of the current object to testMethod( ), which is part of class TestClass and requires a reference to class ABC. Once again, this is useful to the instance of that class.

Another usage for this goes back to the topic of scope (something that will be discussed in further detail later on), where you have two variables with the same name and you want to access both inside a certain block of statements. You can use this to specify the hidden variable. To illustrate, let's go back to our example from the section on scope:

```
void test() {
// Declaring the original a
int a = 5;

// A for loop containing another a
    for (int a = 1; a < 10; a++) {
        //Body of loop
        // The original a has been hidden

//Accessing and printing the original a
System.out.println("The hidden a is " + this.a);
    }
// The original a can now been seen
}
```

The boldfaced code shows the code we are most interested in. Explicitly stating this, you now can access the original variable that normally would be hidden by the one declared in the for loop.

Note: The this keyword in Java is the same as this in C++, except Java's this has added functionality that lets you use it to call another constructor (of the same class) from a given constructor (as discussed in the following paragraphs). Also, note that there is no analogue super in C++ as there is in Java.

Finally, this—when postfixed with ( )—can be used inside a constructor to reference another constructor and commonly is used to eliminate writing the same initialization code for each constructor. Consider the following:

```
class B {
    int theBuffer;
    String myName;

    //The default constructor
    public B() {
        //Pass default values since none were specified
        this(512, "myB");
    }

    //Another constructor
    public B(int buffer) {
```

```
        //Pass a default name along with the specified buffer size
        this(buffer, "myB");
    }

    //Third Constructor
    public B(String name) {
        //Pass a default buffer along with the specified name
        this(512, name);
    }

    //Fourth constructor
    public B(int buffer, String name) {
        theBuffer = buffer;
        myName = name;
    }
    //Rest of class
}
```

In the preceding code, this references are used so that all constructors point to one constructor (i.e., the one with two parameters), which contains the actual initialization code for the class B.

TIP

Note that this() *calls must be the first statement in a given constructor.*

super

You can use the keyword super to reference parts of the parent class, while the keyword this references parts of the class it is within. So, for example, let's look at the parent class Circle for class Sphere:

```
class Circle {
int dimensions = 2;
// Body of class
}

class Sphere extends Circle {
    int dimensions;

    void properties() {
        this.dimensions = 3;
        // Body of properties() method
    }
    void displayProperties() {
        dimensions = 3;
```

```
        // References the number of dimensions for class Circle.
        System.out.println("Num. of dimensions " + super.dimensions"); //
Displays 2

        // References the number of dimensions for class Sphere.
        System.out.println("Num. of dimensions " + this.dimensions); //
Displays 3

    }
}
```

The preceding shows boldfaced code added to the original class Sphere (introduced in the this section). Notice the first System.out.println() accesses the variable contained in the super (i.e., parent) class Circle and, as a result, prints out 2. The second System.out.println() accesses the variable from the class Sphere and prints out 3.

Note: Java does not support the use of multiple super references to access a supersuperclass (and so on).

Also, just like this, super—when postfixed with parentheses—can be used in a constructor to reference a superclass's constructor. For example:

```
super(a, b, c);
```

This snippet of code calls the parent constructor, which takes three parameters.

> ## TIP
>
> *Note that a* super() *reference must be the first statement in a given constructor.*

Constructor Discussion Returned

Earlier in the chapter you were introduced to the concept of constructors. However, an important part of the disscusion was saved until now—the concept that all constructors are linked.

In Java, whether you explicitly put it there or not, every constructor has a default super() reference at its beginning. In this way all constructors are linked together so that, when a class is instantiated, each constructor will reference its parent until the root Object is reached, and at that point, each superclass's constructor will be invoked all the way back down.

However there is one implication that should be mentioned: If a this() reference is present in a constructor, then Java does not put a default super() reference in that constructor. Instead, the implicit super() is called from the constructor referenced by this().

Reference Casting

In the last chapter, you learned that you can convert explicitly from one data type to another by entering the data type you want to cast to in parentheses in front of the current data type. For review, suppose you have a data type int, and you want to cast to a data type byte. The following shows an example of casting variable i to b:

```
//Declare and initialize the variables
int i = 50;
byte b;

//Perform the Cast
b = (byte) i;
```

As you learned in the last chapter, when performing primitive type casts, you must be wary of data truncation, which can occur when casting from a larger type to a smaller one. However, another more complex version of casting is the ability to cast between reference (i.e., object) types.

Note: Casting between primitive and reference types is strictly prohibited.

Casting between reference types can be done only in ancestor-to-descendant (and vice versa) or same-class relationships; all others precipitate a compile-time error. For instance, assuming two arbitrary and unrelated classes, A and X:

```
A a = new A();
X x = (X)a; //Not related; won't work

A a2 = a; //Both objects of the same class; this works
```

Implicit reference casts (i.e., assigning the types without using the parentheses) can be performed in a subclass-to-superclass situation.

Note: Later on in the chapter, you will learn about other types of Java classes (i.e., interfaces and abstract classes). Even though these classes may contain "definitions," you can use them to specify an expected type of object (or any of its descendants). That is, either an implementation of the expected interface type or an object of a concrete subclass to the expected abstract type can be used.

For instance, assuming you have defined class X and class Y (which is a subclass of X) and there is a method that has a Y type parameter:

```
class X {
}

class Y extends X {
}
```

```
//Method definition: public void myMethod(Y y) {}
//Method assignment example:
X x2 = new X();
Y y2 = new Y();
myMethod(x2); //This works
myMethod(y2); //This works
```

However, all superclass-to-subclass casts must be done explicitly, and the former must be an instance of the latter; otherwise what is known as an *exception* will be thrown (you will learn more about exceptions in the next chapter). For instance, using our X and Y class-subclass example:

```
X x;
Y y = (Y)x; //Might work
```

TIP

You should always use the instanceof *operator to reconcile whether an ambiguous cast will work.*

Variable Scope & Hiding

When you declare and use a variable, it exists within a limited range in your program. In other words, it has a specific scope in your program.

The rules for variable scope are fairly easy to understand. Basically, a variable exists inside the block within which it has been declared. An excellent example of this is when you declare the int i inside a for loop:

```
for (int i = 0; i < 10; i++) {
    //Body of Loop
}
```

In the preceding loop, the scope of the variable i is available only inside the block for this loop; you cannot access it outside of this for loop. Also, if you have a block that contains another block inside it, a variable declared in the outer block will be available to any inner blocks contained in that same block. To illustrate, look at the following example:

```
void test() {
int a=0;

    for (int i = 0; i < 10; i++) {
        //Body of loop
        a++;
    }
}
```

In the preceding example, notice that a is accessible inside the for loop because the for loop is inside the method block where int a resides.

Note: Variables declared in the initialization part of a loop cannot hide other variables.

One final idea to discuss is that of hiding a variable. In certain situations, you can declare a variable in a class and declare a variable of the same name inside a subclass, which, in effect, hides the first variable. For example:

```
class X {
    int a = 5;
    //Body of class
}


class Y extends X {
    int a = 10;
    //Body of class
}
```

In the preceding, notice that the original variable a (declared in the first class) replaces the one created inside the loop. However, the original a is not destroyed; it is only hidden from view, and you can access it using a *super* reference. For example, take a look at the revised class Y:

```
class Y extends X {
    int a = 10;
    int b = super.a; //b = a =5
    //Body of class
}
```

What about situations in which you wish to access a variable hidden in a supersuperclass? In these situations, you can access it by casting the subclass object to the supersuperclass object. For example, imagine you had three classes Dot, Circle, and Sphere, wherein Sphere is a subclass of Circle and Circle a subclass of Dot. All of these classes have an arbitrary variable x. The following shows how Sphere could access the value of Dot's x (i.e., its supersuperclass):

```
((Dot)this).x;
```

Note: This casting technique does *not* work with methods.

It is important that you are careful to make your programs easy to understand by not declaring ambiguous variables with the same name within different blocks so that they hide one another.

Method Overriding

Another interesting topic that follows inheritance is the idea of *method overriding*. Simply stated, method overriding is the ability for two methods—one located in the superclass and the other located in its subclass—to be declared exactly the same (unlike method overloading, discussed earlier), with the latter overriding the former. Keep in mind that each is implemented in different ways. When you override a method, you "hide" the superclass's method within a method in its subclass. This is somewhat similar to the idea of scope with variables, discussed earlier, but assuming that they are the same would be misleading. Consider the following:

```
class Fruit {

    void eat() {
    //Body of method
    }
}

class Oranges extend Fruit {
    void eat()
    //Body of method
}
```

Looking at the two preceding classes, you see that class Oranges extends class Fruit. Both of them have the same method, eat(). However, the method eat()in class Oranges overrides the method eat() in class Fruit.

TIP

Sometimes you may want to access the overridden method in the superclass. All you have to do is use super *with the method call, and you can access the overridden method in the superclass hidden by the method in the subclass. For example, if the following shows an example of accessing* Fruit's eat() *method from* Oranges:
super.eat(); //Accessing Fruit's eat() from Oranges

Example: Object Casting

In this tutorial, you will be creating application B, which will perform various casts between very simple classes A and B (B is a subclass of A):

1. Create a text file called B.java and enter the following code:

```
class B extends A {

    public static void main(String args[]) {

        B b = new B();
        //Implicit cast up always works
        A a = b;
        System.out.println("Cast: A a = b; worked");

        //This cast down works, since a is
        // actually an instance of B class

        if (a instanceof B) {
            b = (B)a;
            System.out.println("Cast: b = (B)a; worked");
        } else
            System.out.println("Cast: b = (B)a; did not work");

        A a2 = new A();
        //This cast down doesn't work, since a2
        // is not an instance of B class
    if (a2 instanceof B) {
            B b2 = (B)a2;
            System.out.println("Cast:  B b2 = (B)a2; worked");
        } else
            System.out.println("Cast: B b2 = (B)a2; did not work");

    }
}

class A { }
```

2. After you finish, save the text file as B.java.

3. Then, compile the code and execute the program.

The program executes showing three casts: one implicit that goes up the inheritance hierarchy, another going down (that works), and the third going down (that doesn't work). See Figure 3-4.

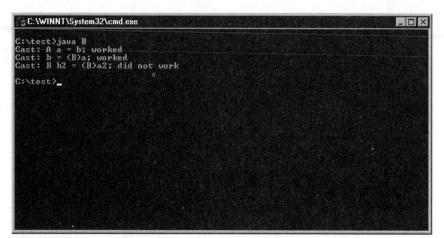

Figure 3-4: Executing Application B.

Advanced OOP in Java

In this section, you will be introduced to four concepts that are either new to Java or extend some of the key topics you learned about earlier in the chapter. The four concepts—abstract classes, interfaces, nested classes, and inner classes—deal with the class concept, except that there has been some distinct mutation for a specific purpose that will be explained a little later in this chapter.

Abstract Classes

As you work with larger and more sophisticated solutions in Java, you eventually will come across situations in which your program will evolve into an entire hierarchy of classes and subclasses and so forth. However, in order to maintain good OOP design, the top of any given hierarchy should be started with one or more *abstract classes*. Basically, you use abstract classes to build the infrastructure. Then, as you go down the hierarchy, methods become implemented and eventually you come to *concrete classes* (i.e., classes that have all their methods implemented and can therefore be instantiated). Finally, at the very bottom of the hierarchy will be situations in which earlier method implementations will be overridden by newer ones. An abstract class is one that has been modified with the keyword abstract. For example, the following shows the class Foo:

```
public abstract Foo extends Bah {
    //Body of class
}
```

Along these lines, it is important that you understand that methods also can be declared abstract, which is done using a special syntax. For example consider the abstract fooed( ) method:

```
abstract void fooed();
```

Notice that there are no brackets in the previous line of code; rather, there is a semicolon at the end. This means that this method has been defined here but will be implemented by a subclass later on down the hierarchy.

Note: Abstract methods are synonymous with pure virtual functions in C++. However, there is no = 0 appended to each function declaration.

The rules and ramifications of abstract classes/methods are very important:

- A class declared abstract cannot be instantiated.

- A class containing an abstract method also must be declared abstract itself (although the reverse is not necessarily true). Does this mean that abstract classes contain no implementations whatsoever? Not necessarily: It is entirely possible and quite probable that a class may contain a few abstract methods along with some real methods.

- A class extending an abstract one must either implement all the abstract methods in the superclass or be declared abstract itself. Note that the subclass can implement some of the methods and leave the rest abstract for its descendants to implement. But then it will inherit abstract methods and therefore must be declared abstract as well.

TIP

A common programming trick to block a class from being instantiated is to declare it abstract.

The whole concept of abstraction is hard to grasp if you do not have exposure to real implementations. The drawing in Figure 3-5 shows how abstraction fits into Java's OOP design.

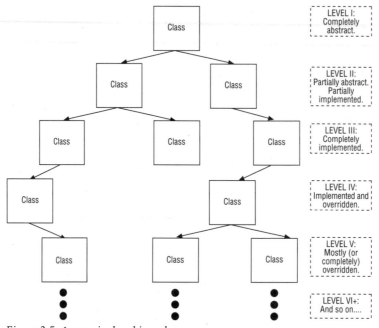

Figure 3-5: A generic class hierarchy.

Interfaces

Interfaces make up for the functionality lost when multiple inheritance was not included in the Java language. The last section introduced abstract classes; however, because a given class can extend only one superclass, there's a problem if you wish to define a set of abstraction that does not necessarily need to be at the top of the hierarchy. By definition, all interfaces exhibit the following properties:

- Interfaces are abstract classes even though the abstract keyword is not explicitly necessary.

- Unlike abstract classes, interfaces can contain no implementation code whatsoever.

- Methods in an interface are assumed to be public and abstract (even if you do not explicitly use the public and abstract keywords).

- Variables in an interface are assumed to be public, static, and final (even if you do not explicitly use the public, static, and final keywords). In other words, variables in a given interface are constants.

Interfaces behave in a very similar fashion to classes. They are declared and also can be extended within themselves, so you could feasibly have a superinterface parenting a subinterface. The following shows the syntax for declaring an interface:

```
interfaceModifier interface InterfaceName {
    //Body of interface
    //including method declarations and variables
}
```

The *interfaceModifier* can be either public or the default.

Note: Unlike classes, interfaces cannot be instantiated; however, like classes, variables of interfaces can be created. For example, assuming you have interface T, the following shows a variable declared for it, which is legal in Java:

```
T t;
```

You also can declare an interface to extend one or more other interfaces, and when a class implements the subinterface, it gets all the superinterfaces extended from the subinterface:

```
interfaceModifier(s) interface InterfaceName extends InterfaceName2
[, InterfaceName3...] {
    //Body of interface
    //including method declarations and constants
}
```

Notice in the preceding code that interfaces extend just as classes extend, only they do so using multiple inheritance rather than the single inheritance common with classes.

TIP

Inheritance between an interface and a class is not legal.

However, interfaces are only half the story; the other half is that of implementation in a real class. You can implement as many interfaces as you need in any given class, and you can use the same interface on several classes, even if they do not belong to the same package. This is really one of the fundamental purposes behind interfaces. The following shows the syntax for declaring a class with an interface implemented:

```
class ClassName implements InterfaceName [, InterfaceName2...] {
    //Body of class
}
```

or if this class has a superclass:

```
class ClassName extends SuperClassName implements InterfaceName
[, InterfaceName2..] {
    //Body of class
}
```

Notice the use of the implements keyword in the preceding syntax declaration. This is how you declare an interface in your class. Furthermore, implements is a fitting word, because that is exactly what you will be doing with the interface in this class. Additionally, as the preceding syntax shows, you can implement as many interfaces as needed.

Note: When one of your classes implements an interface, you must override and implement every method declared inside that interface and provide an implementation for it; otherwise, your class will be abstract.

Interfaces provide an excellent way to inherit multiple frameworks to one Java class. Consider the following; you have a class VCR and a class TV:

```
class VCR extends CassettePlayer {
    //Body of class
}


class TV extends Receiver{
    //Body of class
}
```

Now, assuming that you want the buttons for each of these electronic component Java classes to be the same, you want to create a similar set of methods and constants for each. One way would be to create two separate abstract classes and have each class (class TV and class VCR) extend and implement its corresponding abstract counterpart. However, not only does this not promote uniformity between the two implementations but also, if you want to add any other classes, you have to create more "dummy" abstract classes.

On the other hand, you could create one interface class that contains the abstract set of methods (e.g., play( ), stop( ), pause( ), etc.) and constants used on these two classes (TV and VCR). Furthermore, you could use this same interface on any other classes you may add or create later on. The following shows the interface UniversalButtons:

```
public interface UniversalButtons {
    //Body of interface
    //Including static final variables (constants)and method definitions
}
```

At this point, you have created the classes TV and VCR and the interface UniversalButtons. All that is left is that you implement the interface as follows:

```
class VCR extends CassettePlayer implements UniversalButtons {
    //Body of class

    //Implementation code for the interface
}

class TV extends Receiver implements UniversalButtons {
    //Body of class

    //Implementation code for the interface
}
```

Looking at the preceding code, you see that you have declared that you are implementing the interface and then actually implemented all the methods later on in each class. The fact that Java supports multiple interface implementations means that you have the added flexibility to implement other interfaces in the classes. Also, you have the added flexibility to use the interface you already created on other classes as well. Figure 3-6 shows a diagram of the preceding example and how interfaces connect to each of the classes.

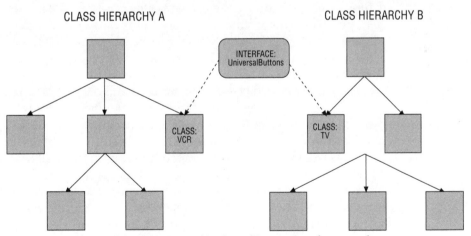

Figure 3-6: Diagram of the VCR, TV, and UniversalButtons interface example.

TIP

Interfaces provide an excellent way to take advantage of C++'s multiple inheritance without overcomplicating it.

Since interfaces can contain only definitions, they are similar to abstract classes. However, interfaces have a different functionality than abstract classes and can be implemented just about anywhere (not just at the top of a class hierarchy).

TIP

It is a common programming practice in Java to define empty interfaces and use them as programmatic markers, so that any class implementing that interface can be easily identified for whatever reason.

Nested Classes

Technically speaking, when you say "class" in Java, it is assumed that you are referring to a *top-level* class—since that is the assumed type for a Java class. This is because all classes are direct members of a given package (i.e., top-level classes). However, it is possible to define a class (or interface) as a *static* member of another top-level class.

Just like the class methods and variables you learned about earlier, a *class class* or *class interface* (so to speak) is a static member of the class in which it is defined. This also means nested classes cannot use any of the instance variables directly except for those contained in the class of which it is a member. In all other aspects, these nested classes behave like normal classes and also can contain nested classes (and so on to any level of nesting).

The primary advantage of nesting classes is that you are better able to organize closely related classes into one class and refer to all these classes the way you would a package. For instance, consider the class Widget, which defines a generic widget (whatever widgets happen to be) and uses the interface Gadget to define a standard set of methods all Widget objects use. Also, there is a class Tool that contains methods necessary to install or remove a Widget object from a given source. We could condense all this functionality to a single class (which would be poor OOP design), or we could create three separate classes (two classes and one interface). But because these classes are so dependent on one another, a good solution could be to nest these classes:

```
class Widget {

    public static interface Gadget {
        void function1();
        void function2();
    }
```

```
static class Tool {
    void installWidget() {
        //Body of method
    }
    void removeWidget() {
        //Body of method
    }
}
}
```

Note: You do not have to declare static in nested interface definitions; interfaces are always static by default in these situations.

Class Widget now has the nested class Tool and the nested interface Gadget. Now one would reference interface Gadget, for instance, in the following manner:

Widget.Gadget;

So, for instance, imagine you wish to implement the Gadget interface:

```
class MyGadget implements Widget.Gadget {
    void function1 {
        //Implementation here
    }
    void function2 {
        //Implementation here
    }
```

Alternatively, just like packages, a single nested class (or interface) or the reference the group as a whole can be imported. To illustrate, let's assume you want to extend the class Tool:

```
import Widget.*; //Imports the nested classes

class MyTool extends Tool {
    //Body of class
}
```

The important thing to understand about nested classes is that, due to their static nature, they are still top-level classes, with the main difference being that all nested classes have access to private members of the class in which they are defined. Technically speaking, nesting is only to the benefit of improving organization.

Note: The Java compiler will generate separate class files for each of the local classes. The filename will be constructed as a combination of the parent class's name and its nested class name separated by the $ symbol. (The filenames for inner classes, discussed in the next section, are handled the same way.) For anonymous classes, subsequent numbers (1, 2, etc.) will be used instead. In our example, the Java compiler will generate three class files for Widget.java, Widget.class, Widget$Gadget.class, and Widget$Tool.class.

Inner Classes

An *inner class* stands for a collection of new class types that all fall under the category of being defined inside another class, block, or expression. This means that, unless an inner class is given a qualified name, the class cannot be referenced outside its scope. Thus, you can use simple names to define these basic inner classes without having to worry about name conflicts elsewhere in your Java program.

Origins of the Inner Class Concept

Like almost everything else in the Java language, inner classes are borrowed from other more established languages. The concept of inner classes (a.k.a. defining a class inside another class, statement, or expression) is no exception. In fact, the inner class concept was pioneered in the Beta language, and the scoping rules are similar to that of procedure-oriented programming languages such as Pascal and Scheme.

Other languages have similar implementations to that of inner classes. C and Lisp enable a programmer to define a freestanding function anywhere: In a *function pointer,* a block of code (e.g., a function) can be referred to without having to reference the object (or class) to which it belongs. Smalltalk implements a more object-based example of inner classes wherein you can define something known as a *block*. These blocks are smaller self-contained objects that behave similarly to inner classes.

Java now gives programmers, in a fashion similar to other languages, the ability to use a kind of method pointer. However, inner classes go beyond just being a method pointer, because Java also gives you the ability to define and reference completely self-contained classes (somewhat like those in Smalltalk).

Note: Neither the inner classes nor nested classes implemented by the Java 1.1 compiler require any specific changes to the Java Virtual Machine. However, nested and inner classes are not supported by any Java 1.0 compilers. Inner classes can access variables or methods (including private members) of their parent class without any name extensions, as they would their own variables and methods.

Inner Class Inside Another Class

While nested classes give you the ability to better organize your program, all of the nested classes (or interfaces) are static members of the class in which they are defined. This means that they cannot access instance-related items. However, it is possible to define a class that is not static and can truly be inside another class.

An inner class has access to all members of the class that defined it (including private ones). Each instance of the inner class also has an instance of the class that defined it. This type of inner class is also useful in that it can be instantiated more than once in the class that defined it.

Note: An inner class cannot contain any static members and cannot have the same name as the class or package that contains it.

Defining instances of inner classes is very useful for smaller supporting classes. And, as you will see in Chapters 5 and 6, inner classes play a key role in the Abstract Window Toolkit (AWT) and event handling. To illustrate, the following code shows an example of class List, which uses Unit objects to keep track of each entry in itself:

```
class List {

    //Inner class Unit
    class Unit {
        private String name;
        Unit(String theName) {
            //Set the name
            name = theName;

        }


    }

    //Constructor for List
    public List(String name[]) {
        for (int i = 0; i <= name.length; i++) {
            display(new Unit(name[i]));
        }
    }

    void display(Unit u) {
        System.out.println((u.name + " has been added"));
    }
```

You see that in the constructor for List there is an instance of Unit created along with a method call to display(), which will display each Unit created. So, to demonstrate, the following instantiates List, passing three items to be added:

```
String names[] = {"One", "Two", "Three" };
List l = new List(names);
```

The preceding will, in turn, instantiate three `Unit` objects that display the following output to the user's console:

```
One has been added
Two has been added
Three has been added
```

This is just a simple example. But it should give you a feeling for the syntax for using inner classes.

TIP

> As inner classes are just like normal top-level classes, they can be modified with `public`, `protected`, `private`, or the default. However, based on the current inner class design, a protected inner class ends up with a public visibility, and a private inner class is actually shown with default visibility.
>
> An inner class can be declared as `final` or `abstract`, which also implies that inner classes can be extended. In fact, inner classes can be extended by normal top-level classes.

Before moving on, it is important to understand that inner classes must be referenced with the class that contains them. This puts a few wrinkles in how you would use `this` with inner classes. Technically speaking, `this` refers only to the current class, which means there is granularity between a given class and any of its inner classes.

For example, imagine you had two classes `Outer` and `Inner` (which is an inner class to `Outer`). If `Inner` has code that is using `this` to reference `Outer` (or explicitly a member of `Outer`), it will need to use the following syntax:

```
Outer.this;
```

Likewise, if `Outer` wishes to explicitly use `this` to reference `Inner`, it will need to do so in the following manner:

```
Inner.this;
```

Note: This remains true for any level of nesting, in that you must resolve to which class you are referring.

Along these lines, it is important to understand that when working with inner classes you can explicitly instantiate them to belong to a specific object for the class in which they are defined. For example, the following shows how you can explicitly specify the `Outer` instance `myOuter` to be associated to the `Inner` object that is being instantiated:

```
Inner i = myOuter.new Inner();
```

Inner Class Inside a Block of Code

Along the lines of inner classes discussed in the prior section, you can declare a class inside a given block of code, method, or initializer. This is commonly referred to as a *local class*. Like the inner classes described before, local classes are contained in the class that has the given of block of code in which the local class is defined, which implies that they can access the fields and methods in the defining class. A key point to understand is that a local class can reference only the final variables (or final variable parameters for that matter) declared in the same block as itself (i.e., local variables). This is due to the fact that it does not directly access a given local variable but actually accesses a copy of it; to avoid inconsistencies, any variable to be accessed by a local class must be final (i.e., unchanging).

Note: Local classes use the same `this` syntax discussed in the last section.

Unlike the inner classes described earlier, local classes are not accessible outside the block of code in which they were defined. Note that this scope cannot be changed since local classes cannot use `public`, `private`, `protected`, and `static`.

Note: Local classes can be extended from another class.

The following shows an example of a class X with a local class `LocalClass` defined in X's `test()` method. Notice that `LocalClass` is available only inside the `test()` method. Also notice that all of the members (only variables in this simple example) are available to `LocalClass` except for the nonfinal local variable y:

```
class X {
    private int x = 5;

    void test() {
        int y = 10;
        final int z = 15;

        //Local class
        class LocalClass {
        int a = 20;
            void display() {
                System.out.println(x); //OK
                System.out.println(y); //Not OK
                System.out.println(z); //OK
                System.out.println(a); //OK
            }
        }
        //Instance the local class and call its display() method
        LocalClass local = this.new LocalClass();
        local.display();

    }
```

Anonymous Inner Class Inside an Expression

In the previous section, you learned how a local class can be inside a given block of code (including a method or initializer). Java has taken this yet one step further and allowed you to declare a local class without a name; it will come as no surprise that these are referred to as *anonymous classes*.

Note: As anonymous classes do not have names, interfaces do not apply, they cannot have constructors, and they cannot explicitly extend from a given class using the extends clause.

The purpose of anonymous classes is for those situations that call for a simple and straightforward solution needing only a single instance of the given anonymous class. The following shows the syntax for declaring an anonymous class using the new operator:

```
new ABClass () { /*Anonymous subclass for ABClass here */ }
new GHInterface() { /* Anonymous implementation class for GHInterface here */ }
```

Note: The standard indentation for braces is not usually used for anonymous classes. Rather, the brackets should be part of the first and last lines of code for the anonymous class. This is to help spot anonymous class implementations.

So, wherever you need to use an instance for a given class, you can specify an anonymous class (which automatically becomes a subclass). Or, wherever you need to use an instance for a given interface, you can specify an anonymous class (which automatically becomes an implementation for that interface).

Note: Anonymous classes often are used in conjunction with instance initializers.

Moving On

In this chapter you had a vigorous overview of Java's OOP design and implementation. You also were introduced to some of the more advanced topics involved. However, OOP is a very broad and complex topic that can merit a book in and of itself, and this chapter only scratched the surface of most of these topics. Fortunately, the book *Principles of Object-Oriented Programming in Java 1.1* (published by Ventana) does just that.

So far, we have been laying foundations of the basics. However, in the next chapter you will start using Java, beginning with an overview of how to program threads at the linguistic level in Java.

Exceptions & Multithreading in Java

This chapter starts with an introduction to exceptions—what they are, how to use them, and what to do to handle them. The chapter also provides an overview of the classes and techniques needed to effectively program in threads. While to most people multithreading is synonymous with animations, multithreaded programming is an extremely valuable asset for many other areas.

Note: As you read through this chapter, you may notice terminology such as the following: "spawning a new thread," "killing a thread," or "invoking isAlive( )." In just about any programming language, thread discussion uses this "lifelike" terminology.

By the end of this chapter, you should have an understanding of exceptions in Java and how to handle them. You will also have an introduction to what threads are and how to use them in the Java language.

Exceptions

Java's exception handling lets you handle run-time issues easily, without having to write a lot of special code. In Java, an *exception* is defined by the class java.lang.Exception (or any of its derivatives of your own design). The concept behind an exception is that it is an "error" that can propagate if there is some circumstantial issue that arises during normal execution. An exception might halt program execution if it isn't dealt with; but, when an exception is properly dealt with, it is recoverable, allowing the program to continue.

Note: Java also defines *errors* based on the class `java.lang.Error`. This class (and any of its derivatives) is used to denote some sort of error that is always abnormal and precipitates a premature end to program execution.

The key root class for both `java.lang.Exception` and `java.lang.Error` is `java.lang.Throwable`. This key class signifies that any of its subclasses can be *thrown* inside a given method during program execution. Let's take a closer look at how this is done.

When some sort of issue arises, an exception should be thrown. It is at this point that one of two things can occur: Either the exception is *handled* in the method where it originated, or it is passed (i.e., rethrown) to the method that has called the current method. If left unhandled, this rethrowing will continue to occur until the exception gets handled or we reach the end of the line (i.e., the `main()` method). If `main()` does not handle the exception itself and simply rethrows it, then the program prematurely exits and the exception is displayed on the user's console.

How you deal with an exception depends on whether it should be handled (or even caught) to begin with. As you will see demonstrated a little later, most exceptions are expected to be either caught or rethrown. The only time this does not hold true is for errors (i.e., `java.lang.Error` and its subclasses) and run-time exceptions (i.e., `java.lang.RuntimeException`—a subclass of `Exception`—and its subclasses). These are exempt because they are highly abnormal in nature and/or have completely unexpected meanings, leaving you no choice but to halt execution anyway.

Throwing Exceptions

If you have not already noticed, exceptions are classes. So, it should be no surprise to realize that when you throw an exception, you are actually throwing an object that can contain data and methods. Technically speaking, you use the `throw` keyword to throw an exception. The syntax for `throw` is:

```
throw expression;
```

In the above, *expression* equates to some given exception object that is constructed as you would construct a normal Java class (using the `new` operator and a constructor). For example, the following shows how you might throw an instance of *Exception*:

```
throw new Exception();
```

Anytime you throw an exception and do not catch it (you will learn about catching in the next section), you must declare that exception in the signature of the corresponding method by using the `throws` keyword (save errors and runtime exceptions, of course). For example, the following method testMethod( ) throws the Exception exception.

```
public void testMethod( int x, int y) throws Exception {

//Body of method

}
```

Note: As mentioned earlier, an exception can be rethrown to the method that is calling the current method. It will then be up to the outer method to either catch or declare the exception in its throws clause.

You can throw more than one type of exception in the same method. When declaring these exception types in the throws clause of your method signature, you need simply to make sure they are separated by commas. For example the following testMethod( ) method throws two exceptions: SampleException1 and SampleException2:

```
public void testMethod(int x, int y) throws SampleException1,
SampleException2 {

}
```

Catching Exceptions

Throwing and/or rethrowing exceptions in Java is only half the story. There are also several blocks that are used to catch an exception. To catch an exception thrown by a method, you must place the questionable method call in a try block. The syntax for a try block is as follows :

```
try {
        //call the method here
    }
```

As you can see in the above, when you call a method that declares an exception in its throws clause, your method must either declare that same exception in its throws clause or put the calls to the original method in a try block.

Following the try block is the catch block, which catches the exception that is thrown by the method in the try block. The syntax for the catch block is:

```
catch ( Exception e ) {

//Catch exception here

    }
```

> **TIP**
>
> *Usually, you will want to use the* `System.err.print()` *and* `println()` *methods to display information to the user's console about what went wrong and why. Since all exceptions extend the* `Exception` *class, you can use the methods available from that class to extract more information about what exactly when wrong.*
>
> *Sometimes it may be to your advantage to simply try again or try doing an alternative path of action without ever bringing it up to the user that the program hiccuped.*

The exception specified inside the parentheses represents the exception that is to be caught and handled. The actual code used to handle the exception is located in the Catch exception. Above, the catch exception is block.

> **TIP**
>
> *When you specify an exception to be caught and handled, technically speaking you are now able to catch and handle that exception or any of its descendants. This can be very useful for generically handling a number of exception types all in one* `catch` *block. However, trying to handle too many exceptions in one* `catch` *block will cause you to lose the granularity of properly handling each respective exception.*

When any method in the try block throws an exception, execution of the try block stops. The control of the program is passed immediately to the corresponding catch block (if it exists). If it does not exist, the exception is rethrown to the outer method. A single try block may have multiple catch blocks, with each catch block specifying a different exception. The following is the syntax for a try block with multiple catch blocks:

```
try
    {
        //Method call here
    }
catch ( SampleException1 e1 )
    {
        //Handle SampleException1 here
    }
catch ( SampleException2 e2 )
    {
        //Handle SampleException2 here

    }
catch ( SampleException e3 )
```

```
    {
        //Handle SampleException3 here

    }
```

The finally Block

Optionally, you can add another block to the try-catch solutions shown above. This is called the `finally` block. This block of code is always executed, regardless of whether an exception is caught or no exception occurred at all. The following example shows the format for how the `finally` block is used:

```
try
    {
        //Method call here
    }
catch ( Exception e1 )
    {
        //Handle Exception1 here

    }
finally(){
    //Cleanup code here
    }
```

In the example above, if an exception is thrown, it is caught and the block of code in the `catch` expression is executed. This is followed by execution of code in the finally clause. On the other hand, if an exception is thrown that is not caught, the block of code in the `finally` clause is still executed. Even if no exception is thrown, the block of code in the `finally` block will still get executed immediately after the try block is executed.

Note: It is possible to nest try-catch blocks.

Exception handling is an important part of the Java language, and as you will see in the next part of this chapter, it is an integral part of the multithreading paradigm in Java.

The Multithreaded OS

Multithreaded operating systems represent the current model for how an operating system works. There are a number of operating systems on the market, and most of them now have support for Java. However, the ones discussed here cover the 32-bit Windows environment. Despite the fact that this discussion is Windows-centric, it should be generic enough to give you an understanding of how multithreaded operating systems work in general.

Note: Windows 95 and Windows NT look very similar on the outside. However, most of the differences between the two operating systems are on the interior architecture rather than the exterior user interface.

Windows NT is a completely *preemptive* operating system—the picture of what a multithreaded OS should look like. Windows 95 is an operating system hybrid or half-breed; it works as a preemptive operating system running 32-bit programs. Unlike Windows NT, however, Windows 95 reverts to a 16-bit *cooperative* model when it is working with 16-bit programs. The idea behind Windows 95 is to make it a 32-bit operating system for today's programs, which, nonetheless, has a fully backward-compatible design for older programs. While all 16-bit programs work in Windows 95, this is most certainly not always the case with Windows NT.

Understanding Preemptive Multitasking

Preemptive multitasking is the ability of the operating system (also known as the kernel) to interrupt a thread and assign the CPU to another waiting thread. Note that in certain situations, this is not always possible, so such operations are sent under a requesting pretense.

For example, if you are running a CPU-intensive process on program A, and in the middle of this process you decide to switch to program B to do something else, the thread for B effectively preempts the thread currently running (which is an A thread). This is how the modern desktop stays responsive, so to speak.

However, even this has limitations. If there are simply too many programs and not enough available resources, a bottleneck can be created, making the desktop appear slightly unresponsive or sluggish. Also, similar response deficits can be caused by poorly designed multithreaded programs.

Both Windows 95 and Windows NT operating systems are multithreaded. And because Java is inherently designed to use multiple threads (even if you do not explicitly use them in your program), it facilitates a powerful way to create modern application development solutions. When you start a program on a multithreaded operating system, you are effectively creating a process. A *process* is the technical term for a program loaded into memory and prepared for further execution.

Every time you load an application, it creates a new process. This is true for the OS as well. Each process can have one or more threads that execute under it. Threads are smaller, independently executing entities that a process or another thread can *spawn* (create). Once a thread has spawned, it goes into a queue. A thread scheduler that is part of the OS manages this queue, acting like a daisy wheel, giving each thread execution time with the CPU (albeit an extremely small amount). However, based on a thread's various attributes (e.g., priority, spawned by the kernel in the OS, etc.), it may receive more or less overall execution time than its peers.

The Car Analogy

One analogy that may make the idea of threads easier to understand is to think of them as cars on a highway. In one perspective, you have a finite number of different cars on the road, and each one can be categorized as belonging to Ford, Chevy, and so forth. On the other hand, every car is unique because if you attempt to look for exactly the same driver in two or more cars, you will quickly realize that each car is unique. Finally, some cars can have a higher priority over the road than others. For example, a police car with its lights flashing has the higher priority, causing the other cars on the road to stop and let it pass.

Threads are very similar in behavior. In one sense, threads all relate to one another and can be categorized as belonging to a parent process—or another thread. On the other hand, each thread spawned is a unique entity and has a completely unique identity. Preemptive multitasking and thread priorities can cause some threads (like the kernel belonging to the OS) to have priority over other threads that are executing. A higher priority thread can force another executing thread to stand down to let the higher priority thread execute.

The process contains the code from the program. Each process starts with a single thread, but additional independently executing threads can also be created. Each thread works as an independent entity and can be created and destroyed without ending the parent process (i.e., the program). Processes can create threads, and threads can create threads; but threads cannot create processes. The beauty of multithreaded operating systems is revealed when you realize that all of these threads can execute at the *same* time.

On a single processor system, however, a multithreaded operating system only gives the illusion that more than one thread is executing at one time. It is only on Symmetric Multiprocessing Systems (SMP)—also known as parallel processing—that true multitasking at the processor level takes place. On a single processor, the CPU cannot work with more than one thread at a time. What happens is that each of the active threads receives a time slice (usually an extremely small amount) of CPU time, and each of the available threads takes a turn.

Note: In the Windows NT environment, the time slice quantum is approximately 20 milliseconds.

Think of the process as a string of lights in which each bulb is a thread. Each of these bulbs lights up, one after the other, with only one bulb truly lit at any one point in time. Moreover, because these lights are blinking so fast and continually looping, it looks as if all the lights are on at the same time to the human eye. Figure 4-1 shows several threads sharing time and resources on a single machine.

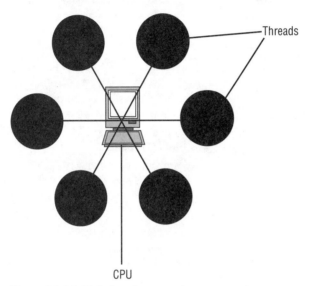

Figure 4-1: Multiple threads on a uniprocessor system.

Multithreaded operating systems can help create a better environment in which to develop. You can have more than one program executing at the same time, and you can have one program doing more than one thing at the same time, too.

The preemptive multithreaded operating system is not an easy topic to understand. However, it is a very powerful tool, and as you use threads to program in Java, you need to understand at least to some degree how the operating system works. This introduction to the multithreaded operating system remains high level so as not to hit upon points where Windows 95 and Windows NT differ. Also, since most multithreaded operating systems work in similar ways, this also will give you an understanding of how any multithreaded operating system works.

Linguistic Multithreaded Programming

Threads are the building blocks of multithreaded environments. However, it is Java's introduction, allowing programmers to use threads at the linguistic level, that is implied when someone makes the statement "Java is multithreaded." Although you have not programmed threads explicitly in the examples so far, all Java programs are multithreaded internally. Typically, Java creates a thread for the user interface and another for the main body of the program. You do not have to do anything; in terms of the programming, everything is done implicitly.

However, Java also gives you the ability to work directly with the creation (or spawning) and destruction (or death) of threads. Java has wrapped all this functionality into one class in the Java Class Library: java.lang.Thread. Table 4-1 lists methods available to the Thread class. You will have a chance to learn about many of these methods throughout the rest of this chapter.

Method	Description
activeCount()	Returns an integer value that represents the number of active threads in a particular thread group.
checkAccess()	Performs a check to see if the current thread is allowed to modify this thread.
countStackFrames()	Returns an integer value that represents the number of stack frames in this suspended thread.
currentThread()	References the currently executing thread.
destroy()	Removes an active thread. This is a last resort method, as it does not clean up after the thread.
dumpStack()	A debugging procedure to print a stack trace for this thread.
enumerate(Thread[] threadArray)	Copies, into the specified array, references to every active thread in this thread's group.
getName()	Returns a String that contains this thread's name.
getPriority()	Returns an integer value that represents the thread's priority.
getThreadGroup()	Returns a ThreadGroup object for this thread.
interrupt()	Sends an interrupt to this thread.
interrupted()	Returns a boolean based on whether the current thread has been interrupted.

➡

Method	Description
isAlive()	Returns a boolean indicating if the thread is active (i.e., the thread has been successfully started and has not been stopped).
isDaemon()	Returns a boolean that evaluates whether this thread is daemon.
isInterrupted()	Returns a boolean value based on whether a thread has been interrupted.
join(), join(long millisec), and join(long millisec, int nanosec)	Waits for this thread to die.
resume()	Resumes this thread's execution. This method is used only after a thread has been suspend()ed.
run()	The actual action code for the thread. This method usually is overridden.
setDaemon(boolean x)	Marks this thread as a daemon thread.
setName(String name)	Sets this thread's name.
setPriority(int Priority)	Sets this thread's priority.
sleep(long millisec) and sleep(long millisec, int nanosec)	This method will cause the currently executing thread to become inactive for a specified period of time.
start()	Starts the thread and calls the run() method.
stop() and stop(Throwable obj)	Stops a thread by throwing a ThreadDeath error.
suspend()	Causes a thread to be blocked and remain that way until it is resume()ed.
toString()	Returns a String that describes this thread, including the thread's name, priority, and thread group (if any).
yield()	Causes the currently executing thread to yield so other threads can execute.

Table 4-1: Class Thread methods.

Let's take a closer look at how threads live and die in Java.

Thread Life Cycle

You learned that applications have a single main( ) method that dictates program execution. However, unlike the single-method paradigm, a thread can be in any of several states. These states are referred to collectively as a thread's *life cycle*. Figure 4-2 shows a diagram.

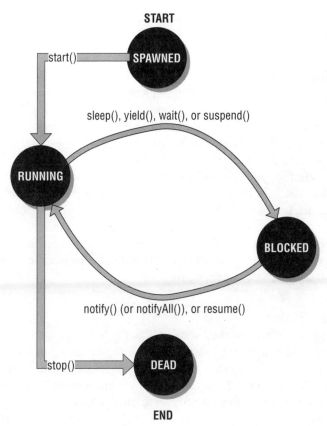

Figure 4-2: Thread life cycle.

Notice in Figure 4-2 that threads are in one of four states: spawned, running, blocked, or dead. Let's take a closer look at each of these states.

TIP

You can use the method isAlive() *from the* Thread *class to return a* boolean *determining the thread state (spawned, running, blocked, or dead).*

The Spawned State

Any time you spawn a thread in Java, you can recognize it by the new operator's presence. Typically, the spawn stage occurs in the main() method. The important thing to remember is that when you create a thread, it is sent to the system and does not execute immediately. The system then does some preparing before the thread can start execution and enter the running state.

The Running State

When a thread enters the running state, this does not mean that it actually runs. Technically, it means that it is spawned and accounted for by the OS and is now thrown into a queue with all the other threads waiting to execute. As you will learn, your thread may be bumped up to the front of the line or pushed to the back, depending on its priority.

It is important that you know the reality of multithreaded environments. (Recall the discussion of the multithreaded multitasking on a uniprocessor system.) In short, only one thread can execute at one time. The point is that just because your thread is in a running state does not necessarily mean it is executing. Your thread is one of many running threads "executing" at this stage. However, when your thread is in this state, it is running code in the run( ) method defined in your Java program.

The Blocked State

When your thread is in a blocked state, it is not able to run for several reasons. When a thread enters a blocked state, it is no longer in the queue of running threads; it does not return to the queue until it is put back in a running state.

Looking back at Figure 4-2, you see that there are several Thread methods you can invoke at the programmatic level to block a thread's execution. For most methods that cause a blocked state, there is another method that puts it back in the running state again.

Note: There are other reasons that a thread can be put in a blocked state that do not always come directly from the programmer. For example, during Input Output (I/O) operations, a thread can be put in a blocked state waiting for the I/O procedure to complete.

sleep()   Using the sleep( ) method causes the Thread to go to a blocked state for the specified number of milliseconds; then the Thread jumps back to a running state. The following shows an example of putting the current Thread to sleep for 500 milliseconds:

```
try {
    Thread.currentThread().sleep(500);
} catch (InterruptedException e) {}
```

TIP

The sleep() *method frequently is used in animations to pause between frames so that the animation will not go too fast.*

wait() & notify() or notifyAll()   The wait() and notify() methods defined in the java.lang.Object class are used to set up object monitors. A monitor can be any object that contains one (or more) *synchronized* method(s). You will learn more about synchronization a little later on in this chapter. In short, a synchronized method will block all threads except the current thread from executing. However, if for some reason during the operation, you wish to have the currently executing thread stand down, you can call the wait() method on the current thread, putting it into a blocked state. It will remain blocked until the thread that now owns the object monitor calls the notify() method and so causes the thread to be put back into a running state. You also can use the notifyAll() method to unblock all threads currently waiting.

suspend() & resume()   The suspend() method from the Thread class is similar to sleep(), except it causes the thread to remain blocked for an indefinite amount of time—until its counterpart method, resume(), is called to bring it back to a running state. To illustrate, the following code shows an example of suspending and resuming a Thread called theThread:

```
if (i < 100)
    theThread.suspend();
 else
    theThread.resume();
```

Notice that you are checking to see if i is less than 100. If so, you suspend() theThread. On the other hand, if theThread is not less than 100, then you resume() it.

yield()   The yield() method causes a thread to be put in a blocked state for an unspecified amount of time and to go to the back of the line (or queue) of running threads:

```
if (i < 100)
    theThread.yield();
```

In the preceding example, if the i is less than 100, the currently executing thread will yield().

TRAP

> *Using* yield( ) *on your threads may not be the smartest choice for all situations, because your thread does not execute again until the other threads that are now in front of it have finished. So, when you call* yield( ), *you do not really know when your thread will get a chance to execute again. Furthermore, if the thread has a high priority, it may force the other threads to lose control and start executing again anyway.*

State Exceptions   You can use all of the preceding techniques to block thread execution. If, for some reason, you invoke a method when it is in the wrong state for that method (i.e., calling resume() on a thread that has not had suspend() called), Java throws the exception IllegalStateExeception.

TIP

> *You can avoid these exceptions by using the* isInterrupted( ) *method from the* Thread *class to find out whether a given thread is blocked.*

The Dead State

The dead state is a thread's final cycle. A thread can die (or be killed) in the following ways:

- When it reaches the end of the run( ) method.
- If someone (or something) invokes stop( ) on it.
- If you call the destroy( ) method. Typically, the destroy( ) method is used as a last resort, because it kills the thread without cleaning up any resources used by the thread.

The important thing to know about thread death is that the death of a thread is *not* always immediate. (It is when destroy( ) is called.) Usually, what happens is a ThreadDeath error is passed to the thread before the thread can be sent to the OS to be unloaded from memory.

Note: There is a reason that the error ThreadDeath behaves like an exception (in the sense that it is a regular occurrence every time a thread dies); but it is not actually an exception: It has to reconcile itself from being caught in a try-catch block that catches the Exception objects. If ThreadDeath were declared as an exception, it would prove troublesome, since this object must be rethrown (by the program) so that the thread can actually die. Otherwise, it will be up to the program to clean up after the thread.

Multithreaded Programming Techniques

To use the Thread class, you need to instantiate it. The simplest way to construct a thread is to use the default constructor as follows:

```
Thread myThread = new Thread();
```

Another way that you can construct a thread is by passing it a name, thus giving your thread a readable name that you can reference throughout your Java program. The following shows an example of declaring a thread with a name:

```
Thread myThread = new Thread("Test");
```

> **TIP**
>
> *You can also use the* getName( ) *and* setName( ) *methods from the* Thread *class to get or set/change the name of a given thread.*

Usually when you create a new thread, you need to pass it an object. However, the object passed needs to implement the Runnable interface.

Note: The java.lang.Runnable interface contains one method—run( )—and is implemented by any class wishing to use threads.

In doing this, the given object will be part of the thread to which it is passed, and it will live as part of that thread, so to speak. The following shows an example of an instance of a class ABC that implements the Runnable class and how you would construct a thread with it:

```
ABC ABCInstance = new ABC();
Thread myThread = new Thread(ABCInstance);
```

or:

```
ABC ABCInstance = new ABC();
Thread myThread = new Thread(ABCInstance, "Test");
```

The second example shows the constructor that lets you pass a Runnable object and a name to construct the Thread.

Working with threads in your Java programs involves using one of two specific techniques—subclassing the Thread class or implementing the Runnable interface.

Note: If you intend to simply use threads, then you should implement Runnable. On the other hand, if you have some custom functionality you wish to add to Thread, then subclassing it is the better alternative.

Subclassing Thread

One method that can work only if your Java application does not need a superclass would be to subclass the Thread class direct so that it inherits all the functionality of the Thread object. The following shows an example of subclassing the Thread class:

```
class SomeThread extends Thread {
//Body of class
}
```

The next thing that you need to do in the main( ) method of your class (in this case SomeThread) is to construct an instance of your class. Then, you must construct an instance of a Thread class, passing a reference of the instance you just constructed:

```
public static void main(String args[]) {
    SomeThread a = new SomeThread();
    Thread h1Thread = new Thread(a);

//Rest of main()

}
```

The previous code snippet constructs a new thread, h1Thread.

Note: Earlier you learned that you can pass objects only to a Thread constructor that has implemented the Runnable interface. How does this jibe with the previous example?

Well, the reason it is legal stems from the fact that the Thread class itself implements the Runnable interface. Thus, when your own class inherits the Thread class, it also inherits the Runnable interface implementation.

A key factor in multithreading is the ability to create several threads that are based on the same object but which have individuality aside from just having a different name:

```
public static void main(String args[]) {
    SomeThread a = new SomeThread();
    Thread h1Thread = new Thread(a);
    Thread h2Thread = new Thread(a);

//Rest of main()

}
```

Notice that two threads—h1Thread and h2Thread—are created with the same a reference. The important thing to note here is that h1Thread and h2Thread are independently executing entities. For example, even though you constructed h2Thread after h1Thread, it could finish execution and die before h1Thread. This exemplifies one of the key concepts of concurrent programming and shows you the power of multithreaded programming.

Implementing the Runnable Interface

Another programming technique you can use to add multithread programming to your Java programs is to implement the Runnable interface. As you will learn later, implementing the Runnable interface provides you a much more versatile solution than subclassing the Thread class, discussed in the last section.

Remember that you can subclass only once, but you can implement as many interfaces as necessary. The following shows an example of a class declaration implementing the Runnable interface:

```
class MyApp extends SomeClass implements Runnable {

    public static void main(String args) {
        //Body of main
    }

    public void run() {
        //Body execution code for the thread(s)
    }

}
```

As you can see, implementing the Runnable interface is almost the same as extending.

Example: Implementing Runnable

In this example, you will create a very simple Java application to demonstrate subclassing Thread for multithreaded programming. You will create a subclass of Thread and pass it to two Thread instances, allowing them to execute independently:

1. Create a text file called ThreadTest.java and enter the following code (or you can copy it from the CD):

```
public class ThreadTest implements Runnable
{

    public static void main(String args[])
    {
```

```java
        //My code starts here
        ThreadTest a = new ThreadTest();
            System.out.println("a constructed\n");

            Thread h1Thread = new Thread(a, "h1Thread");
            System.out.println("h1Thread spawned");

            Thread h2Thread = new Thread(a, "h2Thread");
            System.out.println("h2Thread spawned\n");

            //Start each thread (which implicitly calls run())
    h2Thread.start();
            System.out.println("h2Thread started");

            h1Thread.start();
    System.out.println("h1Thread started\n");


            int i = 0;
    //As long as the threads are alive do some arbitrary function
        while (h1Thread.isAlive() && h2Thread.isAlive())
        i++;

            //Stop each thread
    System.out.println();
            h2Thread.stop();
    System.out.println("h2Thread stopped");

            h1Thread.stop();
    System.out.println("h1Thread stopped\n");


    }

    public void run()
    {

        System.out.println("Thread " + Thread.currentThread().getName()
+ " is running.");
    }

}
```

Before we move on to steps 2 and 3, however, let's analyze the preceding code. Underneath the class declaration is the `main()` method.

The `main()` method starts by constructing an instance of the `ThreadTest` class (a). Then, underneath it, are the constructors for two `Thread` objects—`h1Thread` and `h2Thread`—which both receive a. Following that is a call to start both threads. Note that even though you passed a to both `h2Thread` and `h1Thread`, they still are considered two separate entities.

TIP

Any time you invoke the `start()` method for a `Thread`, it automatically calls the `run()` method when the thread is ready to enter the runnable state.

Following that is a `while` loop that pauses execution long enough for both threads to access the method `run()` and return to `main()`. Notice that the `while` loop uses the `isAlive()` method contained in the `Thread` class to determine if `h1Thread` is still alive.

The next part of `main()` contains the code to stop both of the threads from executing. `stop()` is another method that is part of the `Thread` class. But it's important to note that `stop()` actually is more destructive than it sounds. `stop()` effectively kills the thread. Once you have stopped a thread, you must reinstantiate it to use it again.

The `run()` method that gets automatically called by `start()` uses a combination of methods to retrieve the name of the thread to print on the screen. As you will see in Table 4-1, the `currentThread()` method returns a `Thread` for the thread that is currently executing. Then, `getName()` returns the name of the currently running thread returned in the `currentThread()` method. Hence, you receive the name of the current thread executing.

TIP

The `currentThread()` method can be very useful because it can return the threads created by the Java Virtual Machine (JVM). The only stipulation is that it must be the currently executing thread.

2. After you finish, save the text file as `ThreadTest.java`.

3. Then compile the code and execute the program (See Figure 4-3.)

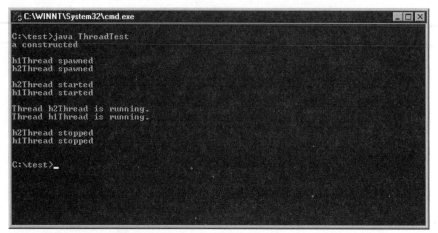

Figure 4-3: Executing the ThreadTest application.

Notice in the preceding example that h2Thread starts before h1Thread, proving that each thread behaves as its own entity. This is the power of multithreaded programming: having your Java program do more than one task at the same time.

Advanced Multithreaded Topics

The following sections discuss several topics that relate to multithreaded programming in the Java language:

- Specifying priorities giving one thread more (or less) CPU attention than its peers.

- Using synchronization to deal with concurrency conflicts when different threads attempt to access the same resource.

- Creating "behind-the-scenes" tasks that act as helper threads for other threads in a given program.

- Implementing thread management to organize collections of related threads into groups.

Thread Priorities

Threads are scheduled in a queue. In particular, the thread-scheduling queue utilizes the First In First Out (FIFO) logic. This logic allows the OS to manage all the threads related to the system and threads related to applications. When a program executes, it usually has several threads executing. Each thread is responsible for a specific task. For example, one thread handles mouse events and will have a higher priority in order to get immediate attention from the CPU when it asks for it. This helps ensure that the mouse will not be unresponsive every time a user starts a task that hogs CPU time.

By default, any time you create a thread, it automatically inherits the priority from its parent thread. However, you can increase or decrease the priority by using the setPriority( ) method defined in the Thread class.

Note: Another method related to thread priority is getPriority( ), which lets you get the priority for a given thread.

Setting the priority of a thread is based on a scale of 1 to 10 (10 being highest). There are also three constants defined in the Thread class: MAX_PRIORITY (equal to 10), NORM_PRIORITY (equal to 5), and MIN_PRIORITY (equal to 1). The following illustrates several examples of setting priority:

```
myFirstThread.setPriority(Thread.MAX_PRIORITY -2); //Set to 8
mySecondThread.setPriority(Thread.NORM_PRIORITY); //Set to 5
myThirdThread.setPriority(Thread.MIN_PRIORITY +3); //Set to 4
```

You can see that the first line sets the priority of myFirstThread to 8, the second sets mySecondThread to 5, and the third sets myThirdThread to 4.

Note: If two threads have the same priority, then they are put on the same level and share equal execution time based on their mutual priority status.

Example: Setting Thread Priorities

Setting the priority of a thread can make a big difference. To prove it, let's create a very simple Java application:

1. Create a text file called PriorityTest.java, and enter the following code:

```
public class PriorityTest implements Runnable
{


    public static void main(String args[])
    {

        PriorityTest P= new PriorityTest();

        Thread threadA = new Thread(P, "ThreadA");
        Thread threadB = new Thread(P, "ThreadB");

            threadA.setPriority(Thread.MIN_PRIORITY);
            threadB.setPriority(Thread.MAX_PRIORITY);

            threadA.start();
            threadB.start();
```

```
        //Pause execution so both threads can enter run()
        int i = 0;
        while (threadA.isAlive() || threadB.isAlive()) {
            i++;
        }

        threadA.stop();
        threadB.stop();

    }

    public void run()
    {

        //When did the thread enter run()?
        System.out.println(Thread.currentThread().getName() + " entered
    run() at " + System.currentTimeMillis());

    }

}
```

Before moving on to steps 2 and 3, let's investigate the preceding code. Notice that the class PriorityTest implements Runnable. Then, the main() method creates an instance of ThreadTest (P), and in the two lines following it, you create two Thread objects, threadA and threadB, both being passed P. After that, the next two lines set the priority for the threads. Notice that threadA is set with the minimum priority, MIN_PRIORITY (1), and threadB has the highest, MAX_PRIORITY (10).

Below the priority-setting lines are the two lines to start both of the threads. Then, you have a while loop cycling until either of the threads die. This gives both threads time to start() and run() before main() executes the last two lines of code, which call stop() and kill both threads.

In the run() method, you have one long statement that basically retrieves the current Thread executing and the current time (in Universal Time Coordinated UTC).

2. After you finish, save the text file as PriorityTest.java.

3. Then compile the code and execute the program (Figure 4-4).

Figure 4-4: Executing the PriorityTest application.

You see in Figure 4-4 that threadB (set with a priority of MAX_PRIORITY) entered run( ) at 871589876902 milliseconds since epoch, and threadA (set with a priority of MIN_PRIORITY) entered at 871589880768 milliseconds since epoch. Subtracting those two numbers and dividing by 1,000 gives you a 3.9-second time lapse before the lower priority thread was allowed to run( ).

Note: You could argue that the preceding test is inaccurate, because, technically speaking, you are constructing and starting the two threads at different times. However, if you look at the code, you'll notice that threadA is constructed and started *before* threadB. Yet, threadB, with its higher priority ranking, got to run( ) *before* threadA. So, even after giving threadA a head start, threadB still beat it to the punch.

TIP

Try commenting out the following two lines of code from PriorityTest:

```
//ThreadA.setPriority(Thread.MIN_PRIORITY);
//ThreadB.setPriority(Thread.MAX_PRIORITY);
```

By not specifying a priority, Java will have both threads assume the same default priority. Recompile and execute the program, and this time—with both threads on equal footing—you will see threadA *enter* run( ) *about .01 seconds before* threadB*!*

Thread Synchronization

All threads in a given program share the same resources. Because of this, several threads sometimes try to access the same resource at the same time. This can result in concurrency issues. One answer is *thread synchronization*. Thread synchronization queues up all of the threads wanting to access the same resource, making each one take a turn with the resource, and thus removing any possibility for conflicts.

As you continue to work with threads, you may run across a situation in which you have several threads attempting to access more than one object at the same time. In certain situations, this can be a big problem, especially since you cannot always be certain when and in what order these threads will execute.

Note: Java supports modifying a variable as volatile. By specifying a variable volatile, you are telling the Java compiler that this variable may be accessed in an asynchronous fashion (that is, accessed by more than one thread) and should not be optimized.

Java's solution to the problem of several threads attempting to access more than one object at the same time: it allows you to synchronize the operation (using the synchronized keyword). This tells Java to set up a monitor that blocks a method, letting only one thread enter and execute at a time, while the rest are put in a queue. The following shows an example of a method declared with synchronized:

```
synchronized void test() {

    //Body of method

}
```

wait() & notify(), or notifyAll() Revisited

Sometimes you may want to stop the current thread executing inside a synchronized method. You can do this by using wait(), notify(), and notifyAll(), discussed earlier.

For example, you have two threads called x and y. Thread x enters a synchronized method and, part of the way through it, you realize that you need thread y to execute in this same method (or you simply do not want thread x to continue execution). What you can do is invoke wait(), causing the current thread to be blocked. In this case thread x will stop executing and let thread y execute.

Then, later on, the synchronized method calls notify() (or notifyAll() if more than one thread is waiting) and thread x will continue to execute.

It also is important to note that your wait() and notify() calls must be balanced, unless, of course you are using notifyAll().

Thread Groups

The `java.lang.ThreadGroup` class is part of the Java Class Library. It lets you define a sort of management class for your threads. As your programs become more sophisticated, you may find it useful to be able to invoke some action on a group of related threads in one simple action.

There are several advantages to utilizing `ThreadGroup` to manage your threads. For example, you can specify things with one `ThreadGroup`, and that will, accordingly, make the changes to all the threads that belong to it. This is much more efficient than the alternative of making the changes to each and every thread. Basically, implementing a `ThreadGroup` is a two-step process:

1. Construct an instance of a `ThreadGroup`. The following shows an example of a constructor:

   ```
   ThreadGroup threadGrp = new ThreadGroup("Manager");
   ```

   This constructs a `ThreadGroup` called `threadGrp` with the name `Manager`.

2. Use a special constructor from the `Thread` class that has not been introduced before now. This constructor, `Thread`, is like all the others you have worked with in this chapter, except it has one extra input parameter in front for passing a `ThreadGroup` object to which it will belong:

   ```
   Thread xThread = new Thread(threadGrp, "Employee1");
   Thread yThread = new Thread(threadGrp "Employee2");
   ```

   You have constructed two threads: `xThread`, labeled "Employee1," and `yThread`, labeled "Employee2." Both of these threads belong to the `ThreadGroup threadGrp`.

Note: The `ThreadGroup` class supports the ability to be nested inside other thread groups. You can add a `subThreadGroup` to a given `ThreadGroup` by passing it as you would a normal `Thread` object:

```
ThreadGroup threadGrp2 = new ThreadGroup(threadGrp, "Assistant Manager");
```

Daemon Threads

Daemon threads (a.k.a. user threads) are threads with a specific purpose: to support other threads that are executing.

Note: When the only threads left executing in your Java program are daemon threads, your program exits. Note that daemon threads are destroyed when the program exits.

To understand daemon threads, let's look at a simple example. When you print a large document from your word processor, the program normally creates a daemon thread that executes the print job. Then, even if the word processing program is no longer open, the daemon thread (which has been passed to the OS in this case) will continue to live. Hence, your document will continue to print.

In the Thread class, there are two methods that deal with daemon threads. The first method, setDaemon( ), lets you set or unset a thread with a daemon status based on the boolean you pass to it:

```
myThread.setDaemon(true); //myThread is a daemon thread
myThread.setDaemon(false); //myThread is not a daemon thread
```

This shows two examples—one setting the thread myThread to a daemon thread, and the other unsetting myThread as a daemon thread. The second method, isDaemon( ), lets you check to see if a particular thread has daemon status.

Moving On

In this chapter, you were introduced to exception handling and learned about multithreading and how a multithreaded program works. You were introduced to the Thread and ThreadGroup classes with related discussions including topics such as the thread life cycle. You also had a chance to try threading in a few simple example programs.

In the next chapter, you will learn how to create graphical user interfaces (GUIs) in Java, using one of its largest packages: java.awt. You also will be introduced to event handling, which will be fully explained in Chapter 6.

The AWT

One of the most significant parts of Java is the AWT (Abstract Window Toolkit). The AWT represents the java.awt package, which happens to be the largest package in the Java Class Library. It is used to design graphical user interfaces (GUIs), the event handling to make your GUIs responsive, and other graphics-related technologies.

Note: Throughout this book, the abbreviations GUI and UI have the same meaning.

When thinking of the AWT, you must understand that it is a relatively primitive GUI environment. However, the key strength in the AWT is that it provides a compatible and transparent GUI environment for all platforms supported by Java. Java developers need to create only one UI (user interface) that will be displayed in essentially the same manner on any platform supported by Java. From a multiplatform developer's perspective, this is a blessing, because it reinforces the cross-platform compatibility that has made Java famous. On the flip side, many of the UI bells and whistles simply are not present. A Windows developer, for example, most certainly will be familiar with several UI components (sometimes referred to as *widgets* in Java) that are either not present, are present in a watered-down state, or simply are harder to implement in Java.

JFC to Enhance the Java User Interface

The next version of Java (the version following 1.1) is due to include the first installment of the Java Foundation Classes (JFC), available for preview at JavaSoft's site. This GUI environment is going to contain all the functionality from the AWT as well as functionality from Netscape's Internet Foundation Classes (IFC).

In short, the JFC will facilitate Java's first GUI development environment that will be up to par with the more traditional, native GUI environments (such as Windows and Motif). See Chapter 11 for more information.

TIP

If you cannot find a tool from the AWT package to match your needs, you can always create your own class that subclasses a component that comes closest to matching your needs. You also can use the AWT's lightweight interface to create and add a custom component that you design.

Unfortunately, the AWT package is extremely large, so this chapter is geared to be more of an introduction to various parts of the AWT than a complete overview. The next chapter will show you how to use various technologies in the AWT with numerous examples.

The AWT Package

The GUI foundations of the AWT can be divided up into the following classes: components (i.e., widgets), layout managers, containers, and menus. Most of these classes subclass off java.awt.Component, the "root" class of the AWT package. The few that subclass off other classes in the java.awt package will be so noted in the text.

Introducing the AWT Components

Throughout the chapter, you will notice that Java uses a specific UI terminology. For example, Java jargon refers to a UI object as a component (or widget). Button, Canvas, Checkbox, CheckboxGroup, Choice, Label, List, Scrollbar, TextComponent, and TextArea (among others) are Java components that belong to the AWT.

Note: All of the previously mentioned classes subclass from `java.awt.Component`. `CheckboxGroup`, however, extends from `java.lang.Object` directly.

The key to designing UIs in Java is the ability to understand and use all of the components mentioned previously. However, Java has defined a class called `java.awt.Container` that subclasses `Component`. The idea behind containers is extremely simple: they are used to hold components. Let's take a closer look.

Introducing the AWT Containers

Technically speaking, a *container* is a sort of hybrid AWT component used to house other components. Probably the easiest way to think of containers is to imagine them as windows and panels in the Windows 95 and Windows NT environments. The primary difference between a window and a panel in the Windows environment is that a panel is a sort of subcontainer for a window. Furthermore, a window can contain several panels, giving you increased flexibility for how components are displayed. Figure 5-1 shows a Java program with a window with several components in a single window container.

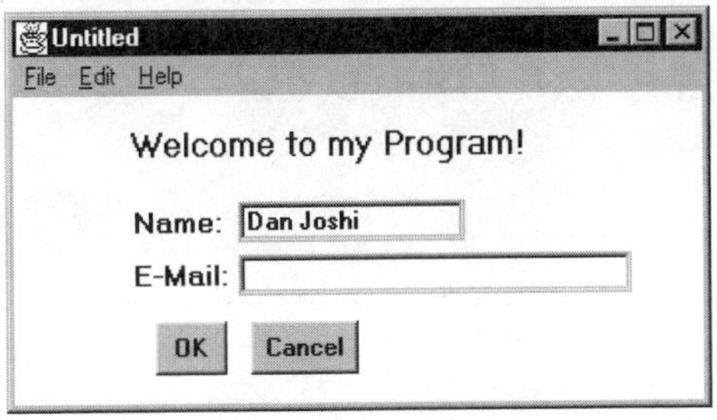

Figure 5-1: A Java program with a container showing several components.

The `Panel`, `Frame`, `Dialog`, and `FileDialog` containers have roots that go back to `java.awt.Container`. Furthermore, most containers can use menus. This functionality is supplied by the classes `Menu`, `MenuBar`, `MenuItem`, and `CheckboxMenuItem`, which all derive from the abstract class `java.awt.MenuComponent`.

Introducing the AWT Layout Managers

When working with components and containers, it is important to understand that, unlike other programming languages, Java uses a special set of classes from the AWT package to oversee GUI layout. These are called *layout managers* (or *layouts* for short), because they oversee how components are displayed in a container. A layout does pretty much what it says, in the sense that it manages where components are displayed in the given container. You can choose from several styles of layout managers to get the right look and feel for your Java programs.

At this point, you may be wondering what advantage there is to utilizing a layout manager. Simple. The layout manager is very useful in Java's heterogeneous environment. If you have ever compared Motif, Mac, and Windows UI formats, you will have noticed that each has its own set of standards and different versions of standards within itself. With the layout manager, layouts adapt to the platform and desktop of the user who's executing the program.

Note: You may ask: Do I have to use a layout manager? The answer is no. Later in the chapter, you will have a chance to learn about programming techniques that can circumvent the use of layouts.

BorderLayout, CardLayout, FlowLayout, GridLayout, and GridBagLayout are the currently available layouts. All of these layouts implement the java.awt.LayoutManager interface. BorderLayout, CardLayout, and GridBagLayout, however, implement the java.awt.LayoutManager2 interface (used specifically for layouts that utilize specific constraints).

Note: You can create your own layout managers that will do just about anything you want them to do. All you need to do is to create a class that implements the LayoutManager interface (or the LayoutManager2 interface if it is constraints-based) and to override the methods defined in that interface.

Including Components

Adding components to a given container is a very simple process. Essentially, you have a layout manager specified for a given container, and you have component(s) that you add to the layout manager. Consider the following example:

```
Button myTestButton = new Button("Test");
add(myTestButton);
```

This snippet of code creates an instance of the component you want to use. Here, you are constructing a Button with a label of "Test." Second, you use the method add() (inherited from the Container class) to add the specified component to the given container.

The AWT Components

Let's consider the first set of tools—components. The following paragraphs will provide you with a complete description of each component, the constructors available to it, a table of useful methods for the class, and a figure showing you what it looks like on the Windows 95/NT platform. Let's take a closer look at the components available to the AWT:

Button

A Button represents nothing more than a box that looks like a button on the computer screen. When pushed, it sends a message to its owner. The owner then can execute a block of code in response.

Syntax

The following shows two examples of instantiating the Button class:

```
Button myOKButton = new Button("OK");
Button = myButton = new Button();
```

Looking at the preceding constructors, the first one should not be new to you. It creates an instance of Button with the label "OK." The second one shows the default constructor for a button that does not have a label.

Example

Figure 5-2 shows an example of what buttons look like. Remember, the button shown here represents what a Java button looks like on the Windows 95/NT platforms. These same buttons will look slightly different on a UNIX or Mac platform.

Figure 5-2: An example of a button in Java.

The following shows a snippet of code for the button shown in Figure 5-2:

```
setLayout(new FlowLayout());
Button myOKButton = new Button("OK");
add(myOKButton);
setVisible(true);
```

Useful Methods

Table 5-1 shows useful methods that are members of the Button class:

Method	Explanation
getLabel()	Returns a String object containing the label of the button.
setLabel(String name)	Sets the label for the button to the specified String object.

Table 5-1: java.awt.Button methods.

Canvas

Canvas is a component with little functionality that allows you to both draw something from the Graphics class (you will learn more about the Graphics class in Chapter 7) and include it as a component. Instead of drawing directly to the pane of the program, you can use a canvas to treat the whole thing as a component (which is very beneficial for effective layout management).

Syntax

The only constructor for Canvas is the default constructor shown in the following example:

```
Canvas myCanvas = new Canvas();
```

Typically canvases are not instantiated; rather, they are subclassed with custom functionality.

Example

The following shows an example of a Canvas subclass:

```
class CanvasTest extends Canvas {
    public void paint(Graphics g) {
        g.fillOval(0, 0, 100, 100);

    }
```

Figure 5-3 shows how the preceding code looks when CanvasTest is added to a frame.

Figure 5-3: Example of a canvas with an oval drawn.

Useful Methods

The only useful method included in the Canvas class is the paint() method; it accepts a Graphics object reference parameter used for drawing purposes. Canvases also are useful because they can catch and handle events. You will learn more about event handling in the next chapter.

Checkbox

Checkboxes are used to set to a state of true or false for a given option. Usually, checkboxes are best suited for a particular user preference because they provide an option for the user to toggle "on" or "off."

Syntax

Following are several examples of instantiating a Checkbox class:

```
Checkbox myCheck = new Checkbox();
Checkbox myEarthCheck = new Checkbox("Earth Inhabitant");
```

The first example represents the default constructor for a Checkbox object with no label. The second example represents another constructor for a Checkbox, allowing you to specify a label of "Earth Inhabitant." Note that, on the inside, checkboxes retain their state with a boolean value of true or false. On the outside, the user sees a corresponding "on" or "off" for the Checkbox.

TIP

The default value for a Checkbox object is false or off.

Example

The following snippet of code shows how to use a checkbox:

```
setLayout(new FlowLayout());
Checkbox myRedCheck = new Checkbox("Red");
Checkbox myWhiteCheck = new Checkbox("White");
Checkbox myBlueCheck = new Checkbox("Blue");
add(myRedCheck);
add(myWhiteCheck);
add(myBlueCheck);
setVisible(true);
```

Figure 5-4 shows three checkboxes based on the preceding code.

Figure 5-4: Example of three checkboxes.

Useful Methods

Table 5-2 lists the useful methods available in the Checkbox class:

Method	Explanation
getCheckboxGroup()	Returns a reference to the CheckboxGroup to which this Checkbox object belongs.
getLabel()	Returns a String object that contains the label of this Checkbox.
getState()	Returns a boolean for the current state of this Checkbox.
setCheckboxGroup (CheckboxGroup mygroup)	Sets the CheckboxGroup to which this Checkbox object is to belong.
setLabel(String txt)	Sets the label of this Checkbox to the specified String object.
setState(boolean state)	Sets state of this Checkbox to the specified state.

Table 5-2: java.awt.Checkbox methods.

CheckboxGroup

A checkbox group is a collection of checkboxes that are grouped together using the CheckboxGroup class. The CheckboxGroup class allows you to group several checkboxes, only one of which has the ability to be true (i.e., checked) at any one time.

Syntax

Consider the following:

```
CheckboxGroup myCheckGroupRank = new CheckboxGroup();

Checkbox myHighCheck = new Checkbox("High", myCheckGroupRank, false);
Checkbox myMeduimCheck = new Checkbox("Medium", myCheckGroupRank, false);
Checkbox myLowCheck = new Checkbox("Low", myCheckGroupRank, true);
```

Notice that the first constructor builds the CheckboxGroup object myCheckGroupRank. Then, using a special constructor from the Checkbox class, the next three lines construct a Checkbox but pass the object for the CheckboxGroup to which this Checkbox will belong.

Example

The following is a (pseudo) example of a checkbox group:

```
setLayout(new FlowLayout());
CheckboxGroup myCheckGroupNumbers = new CheckboxGroup();

add(new Checkbox("00-10", myCheckGroupNumbers, false));
add(new Checkbox("11-20", myCheckGroupNumbers, false));
add(new Checkbox("21-30", myCheckGroupNumbers, true));
add(new Checkbox("31-40", myCheckGroupNumbers, false));
add(new Checkbox("41-50", myCheckGroupNumbers, false));
setVisible(true);
```

Figure 5-5 shows the preceding snippet of code in action.

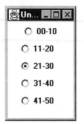

Figure 5-5: Example of a CheckboxGroup.

Notice that the checkboxes that are part of a group have a cosmetic difference—they are round rather than square like the checkboxes discussed in the last section. Second, also unlike ungrouped checkboxes, a checkbox group can have only one item checked at a time.

> **TIP**
>
> *Here's how to construct a* checkbox *that does not belong to a group but would be toggled initially to true:*
>
> ```
> Checkbox myTestCheck = new Checkbox("Test", null, true);
> ```

Useful Methods

Table 5-3 lists the useful methods available in the CheckboxGroup class:

Method	Explanation
getSelectedCheckbox()	Returns a reference to the Checkbox that is currently toggled in this CheckboxGroup.
setSelectedCheckbox(Checkbox chxbx)	Sets toggles for the specified Checkbox object for this CheckboxGroup.

Table 5-3: java.awt.CheckboxGroup methods.

Choice

The Choice component allows you to create a drop-down list of items from which the user may choose. However, it does not take up much space on the screen because it can hide its list.

Syntax

The default constructor is the only constructor for Choice:

```
Choice myChoice = new Choice();
```

Example

Unlike other components, just constructing an instance of this class is not enough to use it. You now need to populate it with items, using the addItem() method. The following shows an example of how you would add items to myChoice, constructed previously:

```
myChoice.addItem("Windows NT");
myChoice.addItem("Windows 95");
myChoice.addItem("PowerMac");
myChoice.addItem("Unix");
add(myChoice);
```

Each of the items added will appear as items in the drop-down list for the Choice myChoice. The last line uses the add() method to add it to the current container. Figure 5-6 shows two instances of the same Choice component created from the preceding code.

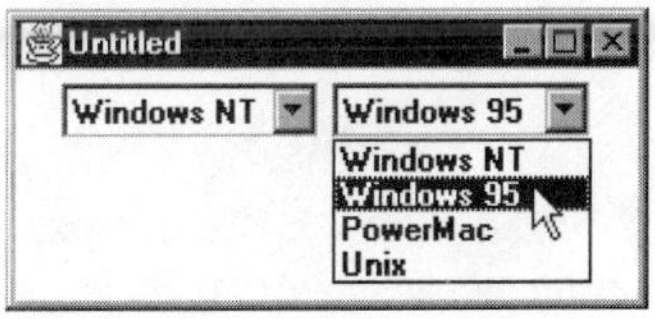

Figure 5-6: Left, an example of a Choice that is closed. Right, an example of a Choice that is open.

Useful Methods

Table 5-4 lists useful methods for the Choice class.

Method	Explanation
addItem(String item)	Adds the specified item.
countItems()	Returns the number of items.
getItem(int index)	Returns a String that represents the specified index.
getSelectedIndex()	Returns an integer representing the index of the currently selected item. (Note that this index starts at 0.)
getSelectedItem()	Returns a String that represents the currently selected item.
select(int index), select(String value)	Selects the item in this Choice.

Table 5-4: java.awt.Choice methods.

Label

A Label component is a string of text displayed as a component in a container of your Java program. In essence, using it is the same as using the drawString() method you will work with later on in the book. However, Label has an advantage over drawString(): Label is a component and can be housed with other UI components, thus making it much more versatile.

Syntax

Here are two examples of constructing instances of the Label class:

```
Label myHelloLabel  = new Label("Hello World");
Label myHelloAgainLabel = new Label ("Hello again", Label.LEFT);
```

The first example constructs a label object with the parameter "Hello World." Using the default, the first label constructs to be left justified. The second label uses the constructor that lets you also define the justification for the label. Table 5-5 shows all of the available justifications for the Label class.

Justification	Explanation
Label.CENTER	Specifies center alignment (integer value of 0).
Label.LEFT	Specifies left alignment (integer value of 1).
Label.RIGHT	Specifies right alignment (integer value of 2).

Table 5-5: Constants for java.awt.Label.

Example

Consider the following:

```
setLayout(new FlowLayout());
Label myWelcomeLabel = new Label("Welcome to Java");
add(myWelcomeLabel);
setVisible(true);
```

Figure 5-7 shows what the preceding code looks like in Java.

Figure 5-7: An example of a label in Java.

A label looks very similar to the text you could print directly on the program's container pane. However, remember that labels *are components and can belong to a layout manager, which is very important to maintain your GUI designs between different platforms.*

Useful Methods

Table 5-6 lists the useful methods for the Label class.

Method	Explanation
getAlignment()	Returns an integer for the alignment.
getText()	Returns a String for this label.
setAlignment(int align)	Sets the alignment.
setText(String label)	Sets the text to be displayed for this label to the specified String.

Table 5-6: java.awt.Label methods.

List

A List displays a list of items in a scrolling format. The functionality of lists is very similar to the choices described earlier. However, a list is always in a drop-down state. What makes lists unique is that they can be configured to have more than one selection in one box at one time.

Syntax

The following shows examples of constructing two List objects:

```
List myList = new List();
List myMultiList = new List(5, true);
```

The first example uses the default List constructor that builds the myList reference with no lines or items. The second constructor for the List class takes two parameters—one for the number of lines, and the second to indicate whether multiple selection is enabled.

Example

Just as in Choice, you must use the addItem() method to populate your List:

```
myMultiList.addItem("CD-ROM");
myMultiList.addItem("Sound Card");
myMultiList.addItem("modem");
myMultiList.addItem("SCSI controller");
myMultiList.addItem("EIDE controller");
myMultiList.addItem("16 MB RAM");
myMultiList.addItem("32 MB RAM");
myMultiList.addItem("64 MB RAM");
add(mylist);
setVisible(true);
```

As you can see, you are adding various items using the addItem() method from the List class. Figure 5-8 shows how the list constructed from the preceding code looks.

Figure 5-8: An example of a list with multiple selections set to true.

Useful Methods

Table 5-7 shows all the useful methods for the class List.

Method	Explanation
addItem(String item), addItem(String item, int index)	Adds the specified item.
allowsMultipleSelections()	Returns a boolean representing whether multiple selection is available.
delItem(int index)	Removes the specified item.
delItems(int startIndex, int endIndex)	Removes the specified series of items.
deselect(int index)	Deselects the specified item.
getItem(int index)	Returns a String representing the item of the specified index.

Method	Explanation
getItemCount()	Returns an integer representing the number of items in this List.
getRows()	Returns an integer representing the number of visible lines.
getSelectedIndex()	Returns an integer representing the selected item (-1 if no item was selected).
getSelectedIndexs()	Returns an array of integers that represents the selected items.
getSelectedItem()	Returns a String containing the selected item.
getSelectedItems()	Returns an array of String objects that contain all of the selected items.
getVisibleIndex()	Returns an integer representing the index value for the last item that was made visible by the method makeVisible( ).
isIndexSelected(int index)	Returns a boolean for the specified index's state.
makeVisible(int index)	Makes the specified item visible.
getMinimumSize(), getMinimumSiz(int numofRows)	Returns a Dimension object containing the minimum dimensions needed for this List.
paramString()	Returns a String that contains the parameters of this List.
getPreferredSize(), getPreferredSize(int numofRows)	Returns a Dimension object holding the preferred dimensions for this List.
removeAll()	Clears this List.
replaceItem(String item, int index)	Replaces the item at the specified index with the specified String.
select(int index)	Selects the item at the specified index.
setMulipleMode(boolean bool)	Specifies the state of multiple selection for this List.

Table 5-7: java.awt.List methods.

Scrollbar

A scrollbar lets a user scroll through a continuous range of predetermined integer values. You can create stand-alone scrollbars. You can also create scrollbars that are dependent on other components in your UI, just like the ones that appear on the corner of your word processor document when it grows larger than one page.

Syntax

The following shows several examples of constructing a Scrollbar object:

```
Scrollbar myScroll = new Scrollbar();
Scrollbar myHScroll = new Scrollbar(Scrollbar.HORIZONTAL);
Scrollbar myVScroll = new Scrollbar(Scrollbar.VERTICAL, 500, 50, 10, 1000);
```

Above, we have three constructors for the Scrollbar class. The first is the default constructor for the scrollbar, which builds a vertical scrollbar. The second constructor for Scrollbar lets you specify whether the scrollbar is horizontal or vertical, using the constants Scrollbar.HORIZONTAL and Scrollbar.VERTICAL. The final constructor takes several parameters. Table 5-8 describes what each parameter does:

Input Variable	Explanation
orientation	Specifies if this scrollbar will be VERTICAL or HORIZONTAL.
value	The initial value for this scrollbar.
visible	The size of the visible scrollable area.
minimum	The minimum value for this scrollbar.
maximum	The maximum value for this scrollbar.

Table 5-8: Scrollbar constructor parameters.

Example

Figure 5-9 shows an example of a scrollbar.

Figure 5-9: An example of a scrollbar in Java.

Useful Methods

Table 5-9 lists useful methods for the Scrollbar class.

Method	Explanation
getBlockIncrement()	Returns an integer value of the page increment for this scrollbar. (*Note*: This value is fired when the user clicks in the area between the thumb, i.e., the gray box in the scrollbar, and the arrows.)
getMaximum()	Returns an integer that represents the maximum value for this scrollbar.
getMinimum()	Returns an integer that represents the minimum value for this scrollbar.
getOrientation()	Returns an integer value representing this scrollbar's orientation.
getUnitIncrement()	Returns an integer of the incremental value for this scrollbar. (*Note*: This value is fired when the user clicks on one of the arrows.)
getValue()	Returns an integer representation for the value of this scrollbar.
getVisibleAmount()	Returns an integer of the visible size for this scrollbar.
setBlockIncrement(int value)	Sets the page increment.
setUnitIncrement(int value)	Sets the line increment.
setValue(int value)	Changes the value of this scrollbar to the specified value.
setValues(int value, int visible, int min, int max)	Changes the values for this scrollbar.

Table 5-9: java.awt.Scrollbar methods.

TextComponent

This class is a superclass for two component-based subclasses: TextField and TextArea. TextField and TextArea are discussed in the following two sections. These classes are extremely similar and share some common behavior, which is currently present in this class.

TRAP

You do not use TextComponent *directly in your Java UI. Instead, you can use the two subclasses* TextField *and* TextArea, *which are discussed in the next two sections.*

Useful Methods

Table 5-10 shows available methods for the TextComponent class.

Method	Explanation
getSelectedText()	Returns a String object representing the selected text contained in this TextComponent.
getSelectionEnd()	Returns an integer with the selected text's end position.
getSelectionStart()	Returns an integer with the selected text's start position.
getText()	Returns a String object representing the text contained in this TextComponent.
isEditable()	Returns a boolean indicating whether this TextComponent is editable.
paramString()	Returns a String containing a list of parameters for this TextComponent.
select(int selstart, int selEnd)	Selects the text specified by the starting and ending locations.
selectAll()	Selects all the text in this TextComponent.
setEditable(boolean txtbool)	Sets whether this TextComponent can be edited.
setText(String txt)	Sets the text of this TextComponent to the specified String.

Table 5-10: java.awt.TextComponent methods.

TextField

A text field is an area designated for a user to type in data. A text field could be considered as an editable label designed for input. Note that a text field can be only one row in height. However, the number of columns (i.e., width) of a text field is customizable.

Syntax

Consider the following code:

```
TextField myField1 = new TextField();
TextField myField2 = new TextField(20);
TextField myField3 = new TextField("This is my TextField!");
TextField myField4 = new TextField ("This is my TextField!", 20);
```

As you can see, you have four different ways to construct a TextField object. The first uses the default constructor wherein you can use methods from this class to design the text field to your specifications (see Table 5-11). The second lets you specify the number of columns that this TextField object can have. The third constructor example constructs a text field with the specified string as default text to be typed in it. Finally, the fourth TextField constructor shows how to implement a combination of the first two constructs, giving you maximum extendability right from the constructor.

Example
Here's an example of code using a text field. Figure 5-10 shows how it looks.

```
setLayout(new FlowLayout());
TextField myField1 =new TextField("This is a text field.", 18);
add(myField1);
setVisible(true);
```

Figure 5-10: An example of a text field.

Useful Methods
Table 5-11 lists methods available for the TextField class.

Method	Explanation
echoCharIsSet()	Returns a boolean based on whether this TextField has a character set for echoing.
getColumns()	Returns an integer that represents the number of columns for this TextField.
getEchoChar()	Returns the character that is being used for echoing.
getMinimumSize(), getMinimumSize(int cols)	Returns the Dimension object that contains the minimum dimensions needed for this TextField.
getPreferredSize(), getPreferredSize(int cols)	Returns the Dimension object that contains the preferred dimensions for this TextField.
setEchoChar(char c)	Changes the echo character for this TextField.

Table 5-11: java.awt.TextField methods.

Note: Several methods involve echoing characters. Echoing characters gives you the capability to build text fields that do not display the user's text. Instead, it echoes the characters with one placeholder character. This is useful for password text fields that need echoing of this sort.

TextArea

A text area is nothing more than a text field that can have more than one row for inputting information.

Syntax

There are four constructors for the TextArea class:

```
TextArea myTextArea1 = new TextArea();
TextArea myTextArea2 = new TextArea(10, 30);
// TextArea
TextArea myTextArea3 = new TextArea("User input goes here.");
// TxtArea, rows, cols
TextArea myTextArea4 = new TextArea("User input goes here.", 20, 40);
```

The first example uses the default constructor, wherein the text area has no size or default text. The second example (myTextArea2) is constructed with 10 rows, 30 columns, and no initial text. The third example (myTextArea3) constructs a text area wrapped around the size of the default text passed to it. The final constructor builds a text area with 20 rows, 40 columns, and the initial text "User input goes here."

These four constructors for TextArea give you the flexibility to create a text area best suited to your needs. The constructs for TextArea are almost the same as the ones for TextField, except that there is one more parameter available to specify the number of rows in a TextArea instance.

Example

Here's example code for the text area shown in Figure 5-11:

```
setLayout(new FlowLayout());
TextArea myFirstTextArea =new TextArea("This is an example of \n a
multilined text area.", 5,18);
add(myFirstTextArea);
setVisible(true);
```

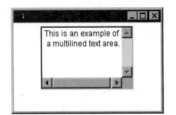

Figure 5-11: An example of a text area.

Note: Unlike other GUI environments, text areas in Java do not have word wrapping capabilities. This functionality may be added in future updates, but in the meantime it will be left to the programmer to implement such functionality.

Useful Methods

Table 5-12 lists available methods for TextArea.

Method	Explanation
appendText(String text)	Adds the specified text to the end.
getColumns()	Returns an integer that represents the number of columns in this TextArea.
getRows()	Returns an integer that represents the number of rows in this TextArea.
insertText(String text, int pos)	Inserts the specified text at the specified point.
minimumSize()	Returns the Dimension object that contains the minimum dimensions.
minimumSize(int rows, int cols)	An overloaded method that returns the Dimension object.
preferredSize()	Returns the Dimension object that contains the preferred dimensions for this TextArea.
preferredSize(int rows, int cols)	An overloaded method that returns the Dimension object that contains the dimensions for a text area with the specified number of columns.
replaceText(String text, int start, int end)	Replaces text from the indicated start to end position with the new text specified.

Table 5-12: java.awt.TextArea methods.

AWT Layout Managers

By now, you have been introduced to the components available in the AWT. At this point, we are going to turn our attention to layout managers. Layout managers are used to define how a component is to be displayed (in relation to other components around it and the container to which it belongs). By using layout managers, you can place components relative to other components in your program. This provides more flexibility, especially considering that it is extremely difficult to anticipate all of the screen formats used in the different environments supported by Java.

You can use several types of layouts when developing UIs. When dealing with all of the UI components discussed in the last section, you need to form some kind of structure to define how they will be put on the screen. The idea behind the layout manager is that it handles the components inside a container.

BorderLayout

BorderLayout places UI components in relation to geographical locations (i.e., North, South, East, West, and Center).

Syntax

Consider the following:

```
setLayout(new BorderLayout());
add(new Button("OK"), "North");
setVisible(true);
```

The default BorderLayout constructor merely adds components with no spaces either above or beside each component. The add( ) method for BorderLayout is specialized in the sense that you need to specify to what region this component belongs: "North," "South," "East," "West," or "Center."

Note: The specification of a location (e.g., "North," "South," etc.) in a BorderLayout object is case sensitive.

You also can determine which insets (if any) you want the layout to use for each component. Consider the following:

```
setLayout(new BorderLayout(10,15));
//Add components here
```

This constructor for BorderLayout specifies 10 points of inset space for the width and 15 points for the height of each component that you add.

Note: BorderLayout is the default layout manager for Frame objects. If you do not explicitly state a layout manger, Java uses an anonymous BorderLayout instance.

Example

As you can see, BorderLayout orients UI components on relative geographical locations in the container. The following code shows five command buttons, all created and displayed using the BorderLayout format:

```
setLayout(new BorderLayout(10, 10));
    Button myButton1=new Button("One");
    add(myButton1, "North");
```

```
Button myButton2=new Button("Two");
add(myButton2, "South");
Button myButton3=new Button("Three");
add(myButton3, "East");
Button myButton4=new Button("Four");
add(myButton4, "West");
Button myButton5=new Button("Five");
add(myButton5, "Center");
setVisible(true);
```

Figure 5-12 shows several examples of the preceding snippet of code with various sizes for the frame.

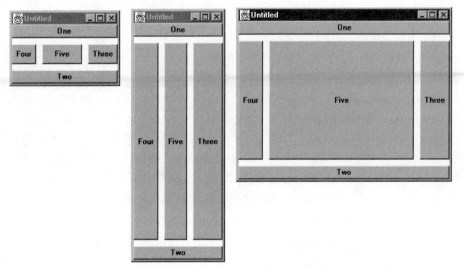

Figure 5-12: Several examples of BorderLayout using the same five-button example.

Each item is separated by 10 points on each side as defined in the constructor for BorderLayout in the preceding code. Furthermore, each component maintains its relative position as the frame is set to various sizes from one example to the next.

Note: The five-button example shown in Figure 5-12 will be modified and used with all the layout managers in this section. This will give you a better understanding of the similarities and differences between the layout managers.

Useful Methods

Table 5-13 shows useful methods for the BorderLayout class.

Method	Explanation
getHgap()	Returns an integer for the horizontal gap between set components of this BorderLayout.
getVgap()	Returns an integer for the vertical gap between components of this BorderLayout.
maximumLayoutSize(Container)	Returns a Dimension object specifying the maximum dimensions for this BorderLayout and its components in the specified Container.
minimumLayoutSize(Container)	Returns a Dimension object specifying the minimum dimensions for this BorderLayout and its components in the specified Container.
preferredLayoutSize(Container)	Returns a Dimension object specifying the preferred dimensions for this BorderLayout and its components in the specified target Container.
setHgap(int)	Sets the horizontal gap between components to the specified integer for this BorderLayout.
setVgap(int)	Sets the vertical gap between components to the specified integer for this BorderLayout.

Table 5-13: java.awt.BorderLayout methods.

CardLayout

CardLayout is unique among layout managers because it does not show all of the UI components on the screen at any one time. An easy way to understand CardLayout is to think of a stack of cards: Only one component is on top at any one time. However, the other components reside underneath and can be brought to the top. This is very similar to the use of tabular windows in other GUI environments.

Syntax

The following shows examples for the two constructors for CardLayout:

```
setLayout(new CardLayout());
setLayout(new CardLayout(10, 10));
```

The constructors for CardLayout are very similar to that of BorderLayout. The first is obviously the default, and the second takes two integers that represent the space between the components themselves and the borders of the frame.

Example
The following shows the five-button example using the CardLayout class:

```
CardLayout cLayout;
setLayout(cLayout = new CardLayout(10, 10));
    Button myButton1=new Button("One");
    add(myButton1);
    Button myButton2=new Button("Two");
    add(myButton2);
    Button myButton3=new Button("Three");
    add(button3);
    Button myButton4=new Button("Four");
    add(myButton4);
    Button myButton5=new Button("Five");
    add(myButton5);
    setVisible(true);
```

Figure 5-13 shows several examples of the preceding snippet of code.

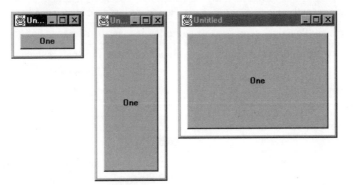

Figure 5-13: Notice that the first button is on the "top of the stack."

Figure 5-14 shows several instances of the preceding example, with the following line of code used each time to both move between cards and display respective buttons:

```
cLayout.next(this);
```

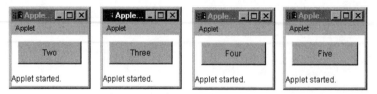

Figure 5-14: Moving between cards in the five-button example.

What about adding more than one component to a card? Usually, CardLayout is used in conjunction with a Panel object, wherein each of several panels will contain a set of components (you will learn more about panels later on in this chapter). Each panel will then be added to the CardLayout object so that each card will represent a sheet of components rather than a single component (as demonstrated previously).

Useful Methods

Table 5-14 lists useful methods for the CardLayout class.

Method	Explanation
first(Container cont)	Flips to the first card in the specified Container.
last(Container cont)	Flips to the last card of the specified Container.
layoutContainer(Container cont)	Performs a layout in the specified Container.
minimumLayoutSize(Container cont)	Returns a Dimension object specifying the minimum size for the specified Container.
next(Container cont)	Moves to the next card in the specified Container.
preferredLayoutSize(Container cont)	Calculates the preferred size for the specified Container.
previous(Container cont)	Moves to the previous card of the specified Container.
removeLayoutComponent (Component comp)	Removes the specified Component from the layout.
show(Container cont, String txt)	Flips to the specified component name in the specified Container.

Table 5-14: java.awt.CardLayout methods.

FlowLayout

FlowLayout is one of the easiest containers to use. Its logic is based simply on the fact that as components are displayed, the container moves in a left-to-right fashion, laying out UI components until it comes to the border of the container. Then it continues on the next line.

Syntax

Here is an example of constructing several FlowLayout objects:

```
setLayout(new FlowLayout());
setLayout(new FlowLayout(FlowLayout.LEFT));
setLayout(new FlowLayout(FlowLayout.RIGHT, 10, 10));
```

Aside from the default constructor, you can specify all of your components to be right or left justified or centered using the integer constants FlowLayout.RIGHT (2), FlowLayout.LEFT (0), and FlowLayout.CENTER (1). Also, just like all the other layout managers discussed thus far, you also can specify horizontal and vertical insets (as shown in the third constructor in the preceding code).

Note: Unless otherwise specified, CENTER is the default alignment for FlowLayout objects.

Example

The following is the code for the five-button example used for the previous layout mangers. In this example, however, the code has been modified to utilize FlowLayout:

```
setLayout(new FlowLayout());
    Button myButton1=new Button("One");
    add(myButton1);
    Button myButton2=new Button("Two");
    add(myButton2);
    Button myButton3=new Button("Three");
    add(button3);
    Button myButton4=new Button("Four");
    add(myButton4);
    Button myButton5=new Button("Five");
    add(myButton5);
    setVisible(true);
```

Figure 5-15 shows several examples of the preceding snippet of code.

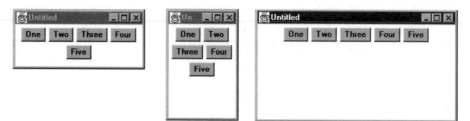

Figure 5-15: Several examples of FlowLayout with a five-button example.

Notice in Figure 5-15 that as the frame is resized from one example to the next, the components dynamically reorient themselves to always be visible.

Useful Methods
Table 5-15 lists the useful methods for FlowLayout.

Method	Explanation
layoutContainer(Container cont)	Lays out components in the specified Container.
minimumLayoutSize(Container cont)	Returns a Dimension object containing the minimum size needed to lay out this flow layout's components for the specified Container.
preferredLayoutSize(Container cont)	Returns a Dimension object that contains the preferred size needed to lay out this flow layout's components for the specified Container.

Table 5-15: java.awt.FlowLayout methods.

GridLayout

GridLayout gives you one of the more precise ways to actually specify a pixel-by-pixel location for your UI components. Hence, GridLayout gives you the most control over where to place your components. When you construct a GridLayout object, you specify rows and columns to allocate locations for your UI components. So, for instance, you can design a GridLayout to have two components on each row for two rows.

Syntax
Here are several examples of constructing a GridLayout object:

```
GridLayout grid1 = new GridLayout();
GridLayout grid2 = new GridLayout(4, 2);
GridLayout grid3 = new GridLayout(4, 2, 10, 10);
```

First is an example of the default constructor, which contains no specifications or insets. The second example specifies the number of rows (4 in this case) and columns (2 in this case). Finally, the third example shows two added parameters for the horizontal and vertical insets (respectively).

Example

Let's take a look at the five-button example using a 3 x 2 GridLayout object:

```
setLayout(new GridLayout(3,2));
    Button myButton1=new Button("One");
    add(myButton1);
    Button myButton2=new Button("Two");
    add(myButton2);
    Button myButton3=new Button("Three");
    add(myButton3);
    Button myButton4=new Button("Four");
    add(myButton4);
    Button myButton5=new Button("Five");
    add(myButton5);
    setVisible(true);
```

Figure 5-16 shows several examples of the preceding snippet of code.

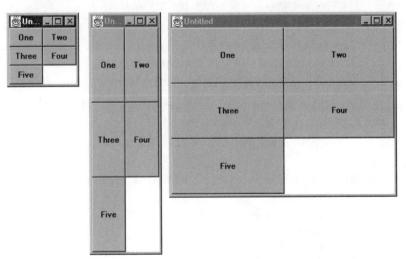

Figure 5-16: Several examples of a GridLayout with three rows and two columns.

You can see that no matter how the frame is resized, the components always reset themselves back to a 3, 2 grid format.

GridBagLayout

GridBagLayout is a more versatile and much more complex version of GridLayout. It allows you to allocate several blocks on a grid for a particular component. GridBagLayout is beyond the scope of this book. For more information, consult the Java application programming interface (API) specification at JavaSoft's site (http://www.javasoft.com).

No Layout Manager

You do not *have* to use any layout manager. Basically, you can specify manually how components are going to be laid on the screen.

Syntax

To avoid using a layout manager, you need to do several things:

1. Tell your container that you do not want to use a layout manager:

   ```
   setLayoutManager(null);
   ```

2. Declare the component and add to the container using the add( ) method:

   ```
   TextField myNameField = new TextField(10);
   add(myNameField);
   ```

3. Use the setBounds( ) method (inherited from the Component class) to specify the given component's location and size:

   ```
   myNameField.reshape(5, 10, 20, 10);
   ```

Notice that the setBounds( ) method takes integers for the x, y, width, and height of this component (respectively).

Example

Consider our five-button example without a layout manager:

```
setLayout(null);
    Button myButton1=new Button("One");
    add(myButton1);
    myButton1.setBounds(30, 30, 50, 25);

    Button myButton2=new Button("Two");
    add(myButton2);
    myButton2.setBounds(80, 60, 50, 25);
```

```
Button myButton3=new Button("Three");
add(myButton3);
myButton3.setBounds(130, 100, 50, 25);

Button myButton4=new Button("Four");
add(myButton4;
myButton4.setBounds(180, 140, 50, 25);

Button myButton5=new Button("Five");
add(myButton5);
myButton5.setBounds(230, 180, 50, 25);

setVisible(true);
```

Figure 5-17 shows several examples of the preceding code in action.

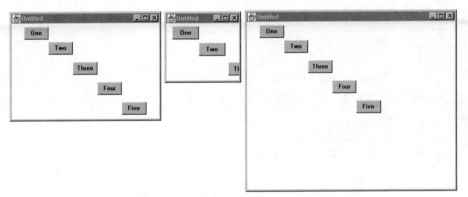

Figure 5-17: Five-button example using no layout manager.

Notice that because you do not have a layout manager to dynamically handle how the components are laid out if the window changes size in any way, the components can be cut or clipped off. While using no layout manger probably gives you the most control over how your components are laid out, it does limit you by not ensuring that your UI will maintain its integrity between different platforms.

AWT Containers

The AWT package includes several classes that you can instantiate or subclass to best fit your needs for containing the components discussed earlier. The Frame, Panel, Dialog, and FileDialog classes give you the ability to add components quite easily.

Frame

The Frame class comes from the abstract class java.awt.Window, which creates the primary window in all of your UI-based Java applications. Frame includes a top-level window, a title, and a border that you can customize yourself or disable altogether, depending on your needs.

Syntax

The Frame class contains two constructors, exemplified as follows:

```
Frame myFrame = new Frame();
Frame myNewFrame = new Frame("This is a new Window");
```

First, the default constructs the Frame object with no title; the second takes a String for the title.

Example

Consider the following:

```
Frame frame = new Frame("Sample Frame");
frame.setBounds(150, 50, 220, 120);
frame.setLayout(new FlowLayout());
frame.add(new Label("This is a Sample Frame"));
frame.add(new Button("OK"));
frame.setResizable(false);
frame.setVisible(true);
```

Here, a new Frame object with the title "Sample Frame" is created. Then, the program sets the position and size for the new frame on the user's desktop, using the setBounds() method. After that, you specify FlowLayout to be the layout manager for this frame and add two components to the frame. Finally, the resizable property is false (the default is true) and the frame displayed using the setVisible() method. (Using setVisible() to show the frame is required for any frame you wish to have displayed, as the visibility for Frame objects always defaults to false.) This example is demonstrated in Figure 5-18.

Figure 5-18: A basic instance of a frame.

Another way that you can incorporate Frame functionality into your Java solutions is to subclass it and then add any customizations you want to the frame:

```
class TestFrame extends Frame {
    public void TestFrame() {
        setBounds(150, 50, 220, 120);
        setLayout(new FlowLayout());
        add(new Label("This is a Sample Frame"));
        add(new Button("OK"));
        setResizable(false);
        setVisible(true);

    }
    public static void main(String args[]) {
     new TestFrame();
    }
}
```

The first line constructs the class TestFrame that inherits from the Frame class. The method located under the class declaration is the default constructor for the TextFrame class. Essentially, the only thing you are doing for the constructor is resizing the frame, adding a few arbitrary components, and setting resizability to false and visibility to true. The next method is the main() method, which creates an instance of TestFrame called myTestFrame, causing the constructor to be invoked. The preceding will produce the same frame as that shown in Figure 5-18.

Useful Methods

Table 5-16 lists the most used methods for the Frame class.

Method	Explanation
dispose()	Unloads this Frame.
getIconImage()	Returns an Image object for the icon image of this Frame.
getMenuBar()	Returns a MenuBar object for the menu belonging to this Frame.
getTitle()	Returns a String object representing the title of this Frame.

➡

Method	Explanation
isResizable()	Returns a boolean representing the resizability of this Frame.
paramString()	Returns a String of parameters documenting the name (if available), location, width, height, whether this Frame has been laid out, whether it is visible, what layout is being used, the Frame's resizability status, and its title (if available).
remove(MenuComponent menuCom)	Removes the specified menu component from this Frame.
setIconImage(Image img)	Sets the icon image for this Frame to the specified Image reference.
setMenuBar(MenuBar menuBar)	Sets the menubar for this Frame to the specified MenuBar.
setResizable(boolean bool)	Sets the resizability flag.
setTitle(String txt)	Sets the title for this Frame to the specified String.

Table 5-16: java.awt.Frame methods.

Panel

Unlike a Frame object, a Panel object does not create a separate window for itself. Instead, the Panel object usually is added to another Container (e.g., a Frame or Panel). This makes Panel objects very useful for designing specific areas or parts of your GUI to contain certain components and/or use a specific layout manager in some way. In short, Panel allows you to better customize the look and feel of your GUI.

Syntax
The following code demonstrates using the two constructors available to the Panel class:

```
Panel myPanel1 = new Panel();
Panel myPanel2 = new Panel(new CardLayout());
```

The first line exemplifies the default constructor wherein the default layout manager of FlowLayout is used. The second lets you explicitly specify a layout manager (CardLayout in this case). Once you have constructed your panel, you then add components to it and finish up by adding that (now populated) panel to the given frame as if it were a component in and of itself.

Example

The following shows an example of using two Panel objects:

```
Panel pn1 = new Panel(new GridLayout(3, 2, 20, 20));

pn1.add(new Label("First name:"));
pn1.add(new TextField(15));
pn1.add(new Label("Last name:"));
pn1.add(new TextField(15));
pn1.add(new Label("Telephone:"));
pn1.add(new TextField(15));

pn1.setSize(200, 100);
add(pn1, "North");

Panel pn2 = new Panel(new FlowLayout());

pn2.add(new Button("Add new record"));
pn2.add(new Button("Edit record"));
pn2.add(new Button("Delete record"));

pn2.setSize(200, 30);
add(pn2, "South");

setVisible(true);
```

Panel pn1 uses GridLayout and contains some arbitrary components. Panel pn2 uses FlowLayout. When both panels are added to a frame (remember that all frames use the default layout manager of BorderLayout), they produce the result shown in Figure 5-19.

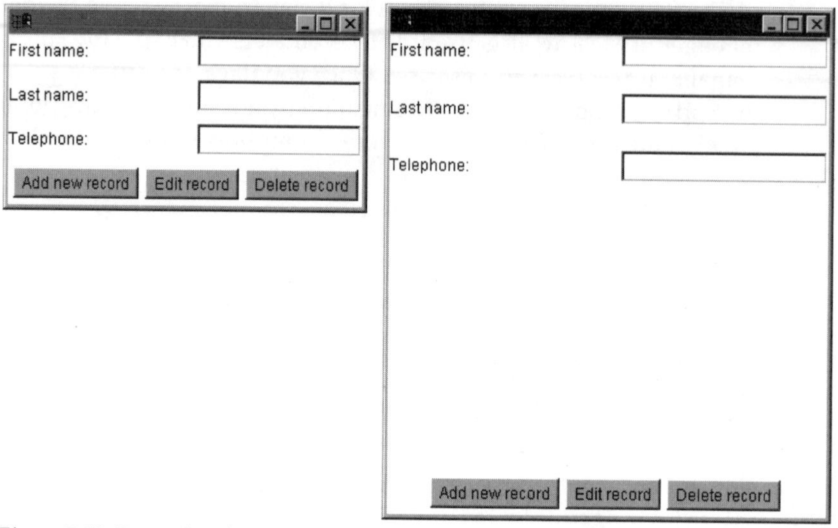

Figure 5-19: Examples of Panel.

Useful Methods

All of the functionality for Panel is inherited from its parent (Container) and the parent's parent (Component) to add components to and customize the Panel (similar to what we learned about for List objects earlier in the chapter).

Dialog

The Dialog class represents a tool that you can use to create dialog boxes. Dialogs are temporary windows that display an important message or perform specific tasks for the user of your Java program.

TIP

The default layout for Dialog is BorderLayout.

Syntax

The following shows several examples of constructing a dialog:

```
Dialog myDialog = new Dialog(myFrame, true);
Dialog mySecondDialog = new Dialog(myFrame, "WARNING!", false);
```

Looking at the previous code, notice that the first constructor requires you to pass a Frame object, and the second is a boolean specifying whether this dialog is modal. *Modal* means that the user must finish with the dialog (usually pressing an OK or Cancel button) before continuing in that Java program. The second constructor for Dialog is the same as the first, except that this constructor adds another parameter specifying a title for this dialog.

Note: Whenever you construct a Dialog instance, you must attach it to a Frame object. Thus, there is no default Dialog constructor, and you cannot pass null.

TIP

As with frames, a common solution is to subclass Dialog and add your own custom functionality.

Example

The following shows an example of using Dialog:

```
Frame frame = new Frame("Parent");
Dialog dialog = new Dialog(frame, "Dialog");
dialog.setSize(120, 100);
dialog.setLayout(new FlowLayout());
dialog.add(new Label("Are you sure ?"));
dialog.add(new Button("Yes"));
dialog.add(new Button("No"));
dialog.setResizable(false);
dialog.setVisible(true);
```

After constructing the frame, the example constructs a modal Dialog object called dialog, specifying frame as the parent frame to which this dialog will be attached. Then we set the dialog's size to 120, 100. Following that, FlowLayout is specified to manage the following components that are added to the dialog: one label and two buttons labeled "Yes" and "No." Last, the resizable property for the dialog is set to false, and the dialog is displayed using the setVisible() method (see Figure 5-20).

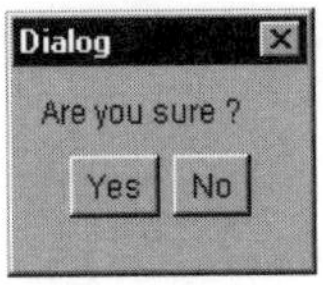

Figure 5-20: An example of a dialog.

Useful Methods

Table 5-17 lists useful methods for the Dialog class.

Method	Explanation
getTitle()	Returns a String for the title of this Dialog.
isModal()	Returns a boolean that will be true if this Dialog is modal.
isResizable()	Returns a boolean that will be true if this Dialog is resizable.
paramString()	Returns a String of parameters documenting the name (if available), location, width, height, whether this Dialog has been laid out, whether it is visible, what layout is being used, whether it is modal, and the Dialog's title (if available).
setResizable(boolean bool)	Sets the resizable flag to the specified boolean.
setTitle(String title)	Sets the title for this Dialog based to the specified String.

Table 5-17: java.awt.Dialog methods.

FileDialog

FileDialog is another type of dialog that you can use in Java. This dialog is actually a link to the set of system dialogs that are part of the operating system (OS). In Windows 95 and Windows NT, the two system dialogs with which you can interact are the Open dialog, as shown in Figure 5-21, and the Save As dialog, shown in Figure 5-22.

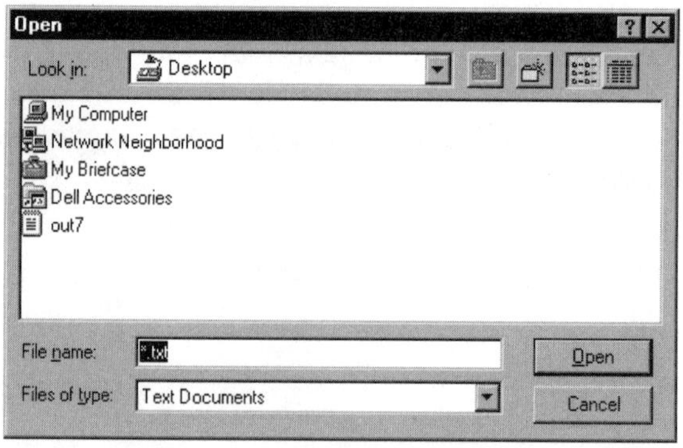

Figure 5-21: Open dialog in Windows 95/NT.

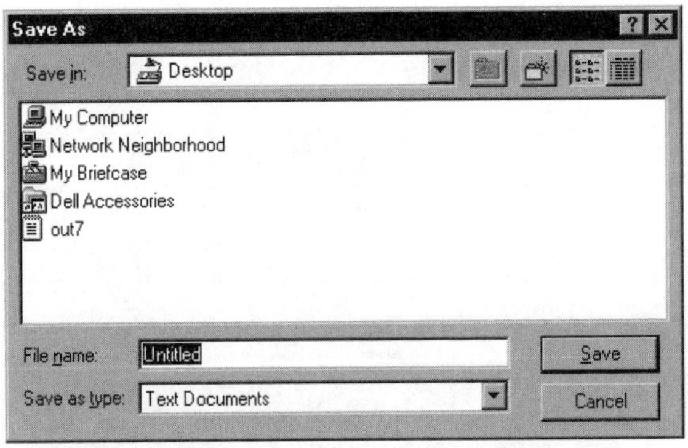

Figure 5-22: Save As dialog in Windows 95/NT.

Note: If you tried these exact examples of FileDialog on a Mac- or UNIX-based platform, you would see different dialogs based on the respective operating system even though it is the identical Java program. All FileDialog objects are modal.

Syntax

The advantage of using a system-based dialog is that it changes with each platform, but the functionality is essentially the same. This lets the user spend less time trying to understand a new interface and more time being productive with your Java program. The following shows three examples of the two constructors for the FileDialog class:

```
FileDialog myOpenDialog = new FileDialog(myFrame, "Please choose a File.");
FileDialog mySaveAsDialog = new FileDialog(myFrame, "Save As Dialog",
FileDialog.SAVE);
FileDialog myOpenDialog2 = new FileDialog(myFrame, "Please chose Another
File.", FileDialog.LOAD);
```

Notice that you need to pass all of the constructor examples a Frame object reference. In particular, the first constructor (constructing myOpenDialog) defaults to a FileDialog.LOAD (integer 0) state, using the specified String as its title. The second constructor (constructing mySaveAsDialog) acts just like the first except that there is another boolean parameter specifying that you want a FileDialog.SAVE (integer 1) state for this FileDialog. The final example (building myOpenDialog2) is like the one before it except it explicitly specifies a FileDialog.LOAD state for its FileDialog object.

Note: The third constructor example is redundant in specifying the FileDialog.LOAD state. If you do not specify a state for a file dialog, it defaults to FileDialog.LOAD.

Example

The following code shows an example of using the `FileDialog` class:

```
Frame frame = new Frame();
FileDialog OpenDlg = new FileDialog(frame, FileDialog.LOAD);
OpenDlg.setFile("*.gif;*.jpg");
OpenDlg.show();

String sFileName = OpenDlg.getFile();
if (sFileName == null)
    System.out.println(
        "No file has been selected");
else
    System.out.println("File "+sFileName+
        " has been selected");
```

To construct a `FileDialog` object, you need a reference to a constructed `Frame` object. Then you can construct a `FileDialog` specifying the dialog's title and type (`LOAD` in this case). The method `setFile()` is used to set the initial selection in the `FileDialog` object, and the `show()` method is invoked to display the dialog.

After the `FileDialog` dialog is finished, you use the `getFile()` method to retrieve the filename selected by the user. If the resulting String is `null`, that indicates that the user made no selection. Figure 5-23 shows the previous code in action.

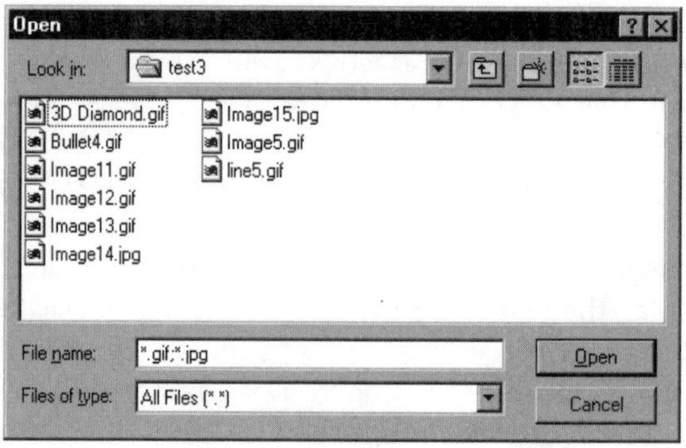

Figure 5-23: Example of a file dialog.

Useful Methods

When using file dialogs, you must use the methods in Table 5-18 to retrieve the information and specify certain options for your `FileDialog` class.

Method	Explanation
getDirectory()	Returns a String for the current directory to which this FileDialog points.
getFile()	Returns a String representing the actual file for this FileDialog.
getFilenameFilter()	Returns a FilenameFilter object containing the filter(s) used in this FileDialog.
getMode()	Returns an integer for the mode of this file dialog. If 0, then it is in the mode LOAD. If 1, then it is in the mode SAVE.
paramString()	Returns a String of parameters documenting the name (if available), location, width, height, whether this dialog has been laid out, whether it is visible, what layout is being used, the current directory, and what mode the dialog is in (i.e., LOAD or SAVE).
setDirectory(String dir)	Sets the directory of this FileDialog to the specified directory.
setFile(String file)	Sets the file for this FileDialog to the specified file.
setFilenameFilter(FilenameFilter filter)	Sets the filter for this FileDialog to the specified filter.

Table 5-18: java.awt.FileDialog methods.

ScrollPane

Using the Scrollbar class to add scrolling functionality to a Java component/ container can be extremely cumbersome because you need to explicitly program the Scrollbar functionality and have the proper code to catch and handle its events (you will learn more about event handling later on in the chapter). However, the ScrollPane class is useful in this area because it enables automatic, always, or never scrolling options for any Component or Container subclass object. Furthermore, all events are handled internally, thus making it very easy to implement scrolling capabilities.

TIP

Only one object can be added to a given ScrollPane object. The best candidate is probably a Panel object, which can hold any number of your components.

Syntax

The following shows two examples of constructing a ScrollPane object:

```
ScrollPane myScrollPan1 = new ScrollPane();

ScrollPane myScrollPan2 = new ScrollPane(
    ScrollPane.SCROLLBARS_ALWAYS);
```

First is an example of the default constructor that sets the myScrollPan1 object to use scrollbars on an as-needed basis. The second shows an example of the constructor in which you explicitly specify what scrolling functionality myScrollPan2 is to use (in this case, ALWAYS has been specified). Table 5-19 shows the three constants you can pass to a ScrollPane constructor.

Constant	Explanation
ScrollPane.SCROLLBARS_AS_NEEDED	Specifies scrollbars to be displayed only if necessary (integer value of 0).
ScrollPane.SCROLLBARS_ALWAYS	Specifies scrollbars to be displayed all the time (integer value of 1).
ScrollPane.NEVER	Specifies scrollbars to never be displayed (integer value of 2).

Table 5-19: java.awt.ScrollPane class constants.

Note: Using the default constructor is the same as specifying SCROLLBARS_AS_NEEDED.

Example

The following example shows how to use the ScrollPane class:

```
Panel panToScroll = new Panel();
panToScroll.setLayout(null);
panToScroll.setSize(300, 200);

Button btn1 = new Button("North-West");
btn1.setBounds(10, 10, 80, 20);
panToScroll.add(btn1);
Button btn2 = new Button("South-East");
btn2.setBounds(210, 170, 80, 20);
panToScroll.add(btn2);
```

```
ScrollPane m_ScrollPan = new ScrollPane();

m_ScrollPan.setSize(200, 150);
m_ScrollPan.add(panToScroll);
add(m_ScrollPan);
setVisible(true);
```

This example starts by creating a Panel object (containing two buttons) called panToScroll to be added to a ScrollPane object. Then, you create a ScrollPane object using the default constructor. Finally, you add the panToScroll to the ScrollPane object. Since the Panel object has a larger size (300 x 200) than the ScrollPane (200 x 150), it forces the ScrollPane object to display scrollbars. Notice in Figures 5-24 and 5-25 that only one button is visible at once; to see the other, you need to scroll to it.

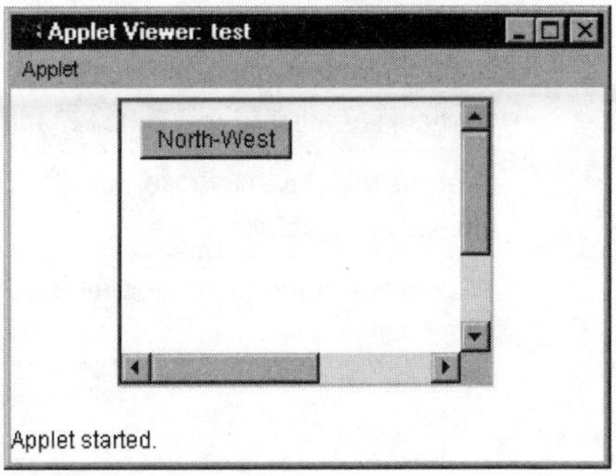

Figure 5-24: ScrollPane with the North-West button displayed.

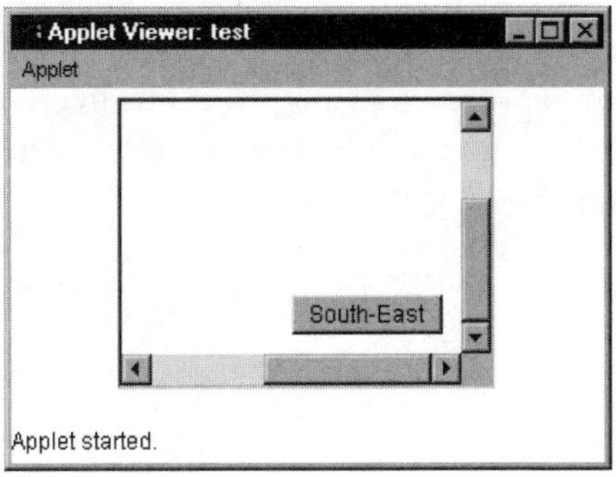

Figure 5-25: ScrollPane with the South-East button displayed.

Useful Methods

Table 5-20 lists the several methods available for the ScrollPane class.

Method	Explanation
doLayout()	Lays out this Container using its preferred size specifications.
getHAdjustable()	Returns an Adjustable object that represents the various attributes and current values for the horizontal scrollbar of this ScrollPane object.
getScrollbarDisplayPolicy()	Returns an integer specifying whether this ScrollPane object is set to scroll as needed (0), always (1), or never (2).
getScrollPosition()	Returns the current coordinates.
getVAdjustable()	Returns an Adjustable object that represents the various attributes and current values for the vertical scrollbar of this ScrollPane object.
getViewPortSize()	Returns the dimensions for this ScrollPane object's viewable size.
setScrollPosition(int x, int y)	Moves to the specified coordinates (scrolling if necessary).

Table 5-20: java.awt.ScrollPane methods.

Menus

Java contains several classes that you can use to create menus for your frames or dialogs. You know from your experience using programs like WordPad how to use and work with menus. For example, File I Save lets you save the current file in a WordPad session. See Figure 5-26.

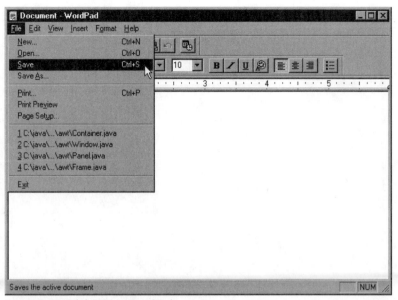

Figure 5-26: File | Save in WordPad.

Let's take a closer look at the terminology. If the menu used in Figure 5-26 were created in Java, you would use the MenuBar class to create the main menu bar. Then, you would use the Menu class for each of the menus in the menu bar. Finally, you can add MenuItem objects and CheckboxMenuItem objects to the menus along with an appropriate MenuShortcut object to specify a shortcut. So, for example, the cursor in the figure is positioned on the Save menu item in the File menu. However, you also can access that Save command by pressing Ctrl+S.

Figure 5-27 shows an example of a CheckboxMenuItem in WordPad. In the View menu is a list of various toolbars; their visibility can be toggled. The unchecked item (Status Bar) specifies that this option will not be displayed, while the other checkbox menu items (Toolbar, Format Bar, etc.) will be.

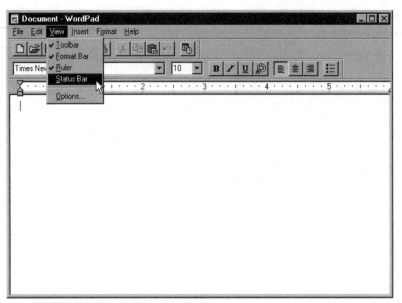

Figure 5-27: View | Status Bar in WordPad.

Note: The menu View has a separator (i.e., a line) that creates a distinct division within the menu. This, too, is functionality that you can do in Java-created menus. Let's take a closer look at each class to see how to implement each to create a menu in your Java programs. Following the introductions to each of these classes will be a combined example that shows each of the classes in action.

MenuBar

The MenuBar class is used as the "container" to which menus belong. Note that only one menu bar can be attached to a given Frame object at a time.

Syntax

The first class that you need to work with is MenuBar. Declare a MenuBar and add it to a Frame object using the setMenuBar() method from the Frame class. MenuBar contains only a default constructor, shown as follows:

```
MenuBar myBar = new MenuBar();
myFrame.setMenuBar(myBar);
```

This constructs a MenuBar object called myBar and—using setMenuBar( )—adds it to the specified Frame. You now have a menu bar, but there is no default functionality such as menus or menu items. All of these components need to be built and added to the menu bar with the add( ) method from the MenuBar class.

Useful Methods

Table 5-21 lists the useful methods for MenuBar.

Method	Explanation
add(Menu menuitem)	Adds the specified Menu to this MenuBar.
deleteShortcut(MenuShortcut shortcut)	Removes the specified MenuShortcut from this MenuBar.
getHelpMenu()	Returns a Menu object reference representing the help menu of this MenuBar.
getMenu(int menuloc)	Retrieves the menu specified by the integer.
getMenuCount()	Returns an integer for the number of menus in this MenuBar.
remove(int menuloc), remove(MenuComponent menu)	Removes the specified Menu.
setHelpMenu(Menu menu)	Sets the help menu to the specified Menu for this MenuBar.

Table 5-21: java.awt.MenuBar methods.

Notice that most of the methods in Table 5-21 are those that you will use to add menus to and remove menus from the menu bar. Let's now take a closer look at how to create and add menus to your menu bars.

Menu

A Menu represents the actual entry on a given menu bar. For instance, a very common menu is "File." Inside menus are a collection of various menu items with (optionally) corresponding menu shortcuts. So, in essence, menus are also containers.

Syntax

The Menu class lets you create objects that represent the actual menus that you add to your menu bar. For example:

```
Menu myFileMenu = new Menu("File");
myMenuBar.add(myFileMenu);
Menu myHelpMenu = new Menu("Help");
myMenuBar.add(myHelpMenu);
myMenuBar.setHelpMenu(myHelpMenu);
```

Starting from the top, you are constructing an instance of Menu labeled "File" that you add() to myMenuBar in the next line. The third line is the constructor for another instance of Menu called myHelpMenu. Just like the first Menu object, you use the add() method to add it to the MenuBar myMenuBar. The last line shows how you could use the setHelpMenu() method to set myHelpMenu as the application's standard help menu.

Tear-off Menus

There are constructors for Menu that let you pass a boolean parameter specifying whether this menu is allowed to be torn off (i.e., containing the ability to be "torn" from the menu and placed elsewhere). Since tear-off menus are not supported by all environments, they will not be discussed here.

Useful Methods

Table 5-22 lists the useful methods for MenuItem.

Method	Explanation
add (MenuItem item), add(String label)	Adds the specified item to this Menu.
addSeparator()	Adds a separator line, or a hyphen, to this Menu at the current position.
getItem(int loc)	Returns a MenuItem reference for this Menu.
getItemCount ()	Returns an integer representing the number of elements in this Menu.
remove(int loc), remove(MenuComponent menuItem)	Deletes the specified item from this Menu.

Table 5-22: java.awt.MenuItem methods.

You have been introduced to creating a menu bar and adding it to a frame. And you just saw how to add menus to the menu bar. The final section discusses how to populate your menus with items (and even other menus).

MenuItem & CheckboxMenuItem

MenuItem and CheckboxMenuItem represent the two menu items that can be added to a given Menu object.

Syntax

There are several types of menu items that you can add to a menu. The first and easiest is adding a basic menu item. The following is an example of constructing and adding a menu item to the menu myMenu:

```
Menu myMenu = new Menu("File");
MenuItem mySaveItem = new MenuItem("Save");
myMenu.add(mySaveItem);
```

Notice that the first line of code constructs myMenu. The second line constructs mySaveItem, and the final line uses the add( ) method from the Menu class to add mySaveItem to myMenu.

Note: MenuItem has a default constructor and another constructor that let you specify a shortcut for this item. You will have a chance to learn more about shortcuts a little later on in the chapter.

Useful Methods

Table 5-23 lists useful methods for the MenuItem class.

Method	Explanation
deleteShortcut()	Deletes the MenuShortcut object (if any) for this MenuItem.
getLabel()	Returns a String containing the label for this MenuItem.
getShortcut()	Returns a MenuShortcut object reference for this MenuItem.
isEnabled()	Returns a boolean based on the evaluation of whether this MenuItem is enabled.
paramString()	Returns a String of parameters documenting its label and shortcut (if available).
setEnabled(boolean)	Uses the specified boolean to enable/disable this MenuItem.
setLabel(String)	Sets the label for this MenuItem to be the specified String.
setShortcut(MenuShortcut)	Sets the specified MenuShortcut to this MenuItem.

Table 5-23: java.awt.MenuItem methods.

Adding a CheckboxMenuItem instance is almost the same as adding a menu. You construct an instance of CheckboxMenuItem; then you add it to the current menu:

```
Menu myMenu = new Menu("File");
CheckboxMenuItem myCheckItalicsItem = new CheckboxMenuItem("Italics");
myMenu.add(myCheckItalicsItem);
CheckboxMenuItem myCheckBoldItem = new CheckboxMenuItem("Bold", true);
myMenu.add(myCheckBoldItem);
CheckboxMenuItem myCheckUnderlineItem = new CheckboxMenuItem("Underline",
false);
myMenu.add(myCheckUnderlineItem);
```

Essentially, the logic for this segment of code is very similar to the last example, except that here you are constructing three CheckboxItem objects and adding them to myMenu. The first (myCheckItalicsItem) simply specifies its name and defaults to false. The second (myCheckBoldItem) specifies its name and its initial state (true in this case). Finally, the third (myCheckUnderlineItem) does the same as the second except it explicitly sets itself to false.

TIP

When creating a checkbox menu item, you can decide whether you want it to be checked by using the setState() *method contained in the* CheckboxMenuItem *class. Alternatively, you can use the* getState() *method (from the same class) to find out the state of a given* CheckboxMenuItem *object.*

Useful Methods

Table 5-24 lists useful methods for the CheckboxMenuItem class.

Method	Explanation
getSelectedObjects()	Returns the an array of Object objects (with only one el.ement) with the label of this CheckboxMenu item (if available).
getState()	Returns a boolean giving the state of this CheckboxMenuItem.
paramString()	Returns a String of parameters documenting the label, shortcut (if available), and current state for this CheckboxMenuItem.
setState(boolean)	Sets the state of this CheckboxMenuItem based on the specified boolean.

Table 5-24: java.awt.CheckboxMenuItem methods.

Another "item" you can add to a menu is a separator. Adding a separator lets you define certain sections in your menus. You can add a separator to your menu in one of two ways:

```
MenuItem myFileItem = new MenuItem("File");
myMenu.add(myFileItem);
MenuItem mySaveItem = new MenuItem("Save");
myMenu.add(mySaveItem);

myMenu.add(new MenuItem("-");

MenuItem myRunItem = new MenuItem("Run");
myMenu.add(myRunItem);
```

or:

```
MenuItem myFileItem = new MenuItem("File");
myMenu.add(myFileItem);
MenuItem mySaveItem = new MenuItem("Save");
myMenu.add(mySaveItem);

myMenu.addSeparator();

MenuItem myRunItem = new MenuItem("Run");
myMenu.add(myRunItem);
```

The preceding two snippets of code create the same menu. However, the first uses a constructor for the menu item, passing a label of "-" that tells Java to make this a separator. The second technique simply uses the method addSeparator( ) to do the job. Both techniques work equally well. It is up to you to choose which one you prefer.

TIP

You can disable a menu item in a menu by using the disable( ) *method contained in the* MenuItem *class:*

```
MenuItem myItem = new MenuItem("Run");
myItem.disable();
```

Our last topic for this section is the creation of a submenu. A submenu is essentially another menu inside a current menu. In Java, you can create a submenu through a very straightforward recursive process of creating a menu and adding a `Menu` instance, instead of a menu item, to it. Thus, you are creating a menu in a menu. Consider the following:

```
Menu mySubTestMenu = new Menu("Testing");
MenuItem myFirstItem = new MenuItem("First");
mySubTestMenu.add(myFirstItem);
myMenu.add(mySubTestMenu);
```

Notice that you constructed a `Menu` `mySubTestMenu` and added `MenuItem` `myFirstItem` to it. Then, on the last line, you added the `Menu` `mySubTestMenu` to the `Menu` `myMenu`. Hence, it is a menu in a menu.

MenuShortcut

A menu shortcut lets users press an assigned key or keys to invoke a specific menu item. This makes accessing a menu more efficient and less mouse-dependent.

Syntax

Menu shortcuts are made possible by the class `MenuShortcut`. The following shows two basic examples. The first specifies Ctrl+S to be a shortcut for the menu item Save, and the second example specifies Ctrl+Shift S for the menu item Send:

```
// Specify an 'Ctrl-S' shortcut for Save
myMenu.add(new MenuItem("Save...", new MenuShortcut('s')));

// Specify an ' Ctrl-Shift-S' shortcut for Send
myMenu.add(new MenuItem("Send...", new MenuShortcut('s', true)));
```

In the preceding, you use a special add method from the given `MenuBar` `myMenu` to specify an anonymous `MenuItem` object and an anonymous `MenuShortcut` object. There are only two constructors for `MenuShortcut`: The first specifies the actual key to be pressed (as defined by a defined integer value in the `java.awt.event.KeyEvent` class that you will learn more about in the next chapter). The second adds a `boolean` parameter stating whether the Shift key needs to be pressed as well. Now aside from being able to navigate the menu via the mouse, a user can accomplish the same menu-related tasks with these keyboard shortcuts.

Useful Methods

Table 5-25 lists useful methods in the MenuShortcut class.

Method	Explanation
equals(MenuShortcut)	Returns a boolean based on the evaluation of whether this MenuShortcut uses the same keys as the specified one.
getKey()	Returns an integer specifying the raw key code for this MenuShortcut.
paramString()	Returns a string documenting the keys used by this MenuShortcut.
usesShiftModifier()	Return a boolean based on the evaluation of whether this MenuShortcut uses the SHIFT mask.

Table 5-25: java.awt.MenuShortcut methods.

Example

You've learned a lot about creating menus in Java, including how to construct menu bars and how to add them to frames. You've also learned how to construct menus and add all sorts of menu items (or even other menus) to them. Take a look at the following code sample:

```
//Create the File menu
Menu myFileMenu = new Menu("File");
myFileMenu.add(new MenuItem("New"));
myFileMenu.add(new MenuItem("Open..."));
myFileMenu.add(new MenuItem("Save", new MenuShortcut('s')));
myFileMenu.add(new MenuItem("Save As...", new MenuShortcut('s', true)));
myFileMenu.addSeparator();
myFileMenu.add(new MenuItem("Exit", new MenuShortcut('x')));

//Add File to the menu bar
myMenubar.add(myFileMenu);

//Create the Execute menu
Menu myExecuteMenu = new Menu("Execute");
```

```
//Create the Options sub menu
Menu mySubOptionsMenu = new Menu("Options");
mySubOptionsMenu.add(new CheckboxMenuItem("Debug Mode"));
mySubOptionsMenu.add(new CheckboxMenuItem("Normal Mode "));
mySubOptionsMenu.add(new CheckboxMenuItem("Optimized Mode"));

//Add Options to Execute
myExecuteMenu.add(mySubOptionsMenu);

//Add Execute to the menu bar
myMenubar.add(myExecuteMenu);

//Set the menu bar to this Frame
this.setMenuBar(myMenubar);
```

The first line constructs the MenuBar instance myMenuBar. The second line constructs the Menu myFileMenu. The next several lines use the myFileMenu.add() method to add MenuItem objects and one separator to myFileMenu. Finally there is a line of code calling the myMenuBar.add() method to add the newly populated and constructed myFileMenu Menu to myMenuBar.

```
//Create the File menu
Menu myFileMenu = new Menu("File");
myFileMenu.add(new MenuItem("New"));
myFileMenu.add(new MenuItem("Open..."));
myFileMenu.add(new MenuItem("Save", new MenuShortcut('s')));
myFileMenu.add(new MenuItem("Save As...", new MenuShortcut('s', true)));
myFileMenu.addSeparator();
myFileMenu.add(new MenuItem("Exit", new MenuShortcut('x')));
```

The following constructs another menu—myExecute:

```
//Create the Execute menu
Menu myExecuteMenu = new Menu("Execute");
```

The line under it constructs the menu (which will be a submenu to myExecuteMenu) called mySubOptionsMenu. The next lines add three CheckboxMenuItem objects to it. The following line uses myExecuteMenu.add() to add the populated menu mySubOptionsMenu to the menu myExecuteMenu. Thus, it becomes a submenu to myExecuteMenu:

```
//Create the Options sub menu
Menu mySubOptionsMenu = new Menu("Options");
mySubOptionsMenu.add(new CheckboxMenuItem("Debug Mode"));
mySubOptionsMenu.add(new CheckboxMenuItem("Normal Mode "));
mySubOptionsMenu.add(new CheckboxMenuItem("Optimized Mode"));
```

Next, the code adds `myExecuteMenu` to `myMenuBar`. Finally, the last line of code uses `this` to refer to the given frame, and the `setMenuBar()` method to pass it to `myMenuBar`:

```
//Add Execute to the menu bar
myMenubar.add(myExecuteMenu);

//Set the menu bar to this Frame
this.setMenuBar(myMenubar);
```

Hence, you constructed a menu bar with two menus populated with menu items, separators, checkbox menu items, and submenus. Figures 5-28 and 5-29 show the previous snippet of code in action.

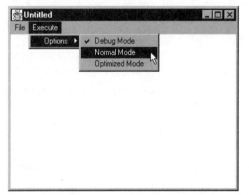

Figure 5-28: Menu example with File expanded.

Figure 5-29: Menu example with Options expanded.

Notice in Figure 5-29 that the three choices are checkbox menu items and that item Debug Mode is checked.

As you can see, creating menus can be a time-consuming process.

PopupMenu

Before moving on, let's touch on the concept of popup menus. Popup menus give you the ability to add a temporary menu that appears next to the user's cursor after he or she right-clicks (mouse button two for Windows or three for Motif) the mouse.

Syntax

Popup menus are made possible by the class `java.awt.PopupMenu`, which is subclassed from `java.awt.Menu`. You use three methods: `add()`, `remove()`—both inherited from `Menu`—and `show()`. The `add()` and `remove()` methods behave just like the `add()` and `remove()` methods that you learned about in the `Menu` class. The following shows a simple example:

```
PopupMenu popup = new PopupMenu("Edit");
MenuItem mItem = new MenuItem("Test");
popup.add(mItem);
```

Here we construct the `PopupMenu` instance `popup` and the `MenuItem` `mItem` and then add `mItem` to `popup`.

The `show()` method from `PopupMenu` invokes the popup menu and takes three parameters: The first parameter takes the component or container to which the popup menu belongs, and the second and third parameters represent the x and y locations (relative to the object passed in the first parameter) for the popup:

```
protected void activatePopup(int x, int y)
{
    popup.show(testFrame, x, y);
}
```

This method passes the x and y integers to the method `activatePopup()`. The method, when invoked, calls `show()`, passing the frame and the x and y integers specifying the coordinates where the popup menu should be located.

Moving On

In this chapter, you learned about the tools needed to construct a UI in Java. This included a description of all the available components, containers, and layout managers. While you now know how to layout a user interface, you have not learned how to make it responsive to user input. You'll learn how to do that beginning in the next chapter.

Chapter 6 discusses event handling in Java and making the UIs that you learned about in this chapter functional. It also delves into some of the functionality-based parts of the AWT such as printing and copying and pasting in Java.

Using the AWT

In this chapter, you are going to learn about the more functional parts of the Abstract Window Toolkit (AWT). In the last chapter, you were introduced to components, layouts, and containers. However, while they worked visually, they were not functional. In this chapter, you will learn how to make your graphical user interface (GUI) Java designs responsive to user input through event handling. You will also learn about other AWT topics, such as setting the colors of your Java GUI to the user's system colors, tabbing between components, and printing in Java.

Event Handling

Java is an event-driven language. This means that your Java program remains idle until an "outside source" sends it a message (i.e., an event). This event is then passed to and processed by your program, either being ignored or precipitating an action of some sort (based on the timing, type, and origination of this event).

Obviously, the most common "outside source" responsible for events comes from the user via a keyboard or mouse. However, in the event-driven programming model, your programs can be responsive to other types of events (such as those generated by the system kernel, internally, or by another Java program).

With event handling, a Java program will be responsive to user input. As you will learn in the next section, you will be able to design a program to have a designated object respond to a certain event.

Event Handling in Java

The event-handling model (redesigned for Java 1.1) allows for good object-oriented design (OOD) by letting an event be passed to the object best suited to handle the event (as opposed to the object from which the event originated, as was the case in Java 1.0). Further, an event is represented as an object of one class in a complete hierarchy of event classes (all extending in some way from the `java.util.EventObject` class). Figure 6-1 shows a diagram of the event-type classes.

Figure 6-1: Diagram of event types in Java.

Each of the event classes represents a group of sibling events. For example, a `MouseEvent` object can be used to represent the events originating from the user's mouse.

TIP

As you can see in Figure 6-1, Java provides a special `java.beans.PropertyChangeEvent` *class that is used by a Bean component. It also provides a* `sunw.util.EventObject` *class, used as a placeholder for backward compatibility with Bean components created using the Java Development Kit (JDK) 1.0.X. For more information on Java Beans, please refer to Chapter 10.*

Listeners

Any object that wishes to receive notification must implement one of the `Listener` interfaces (the actual interface implemented depends on the type of events this object needs to process). Just as there is a complete hierarchy of event classes, there is a corresponding hierarchy of listener interfaces that extend (in some way) from the `java.util.EventListener` interface. The methods implemented from a listener interface have the corresponding event object passed to the interface as a method parameter. Furthermore, these methods define the code that will be fired in response to this event.

TIP

Usually, it is proper event-handling design in Java for a listener class to be an inner class of the class from which the events that the listener is to handle originate. Inner classes are explained in Chapter 3.

The "glue" needed to assign a listener to a given object from which events might originate is created from an appropriate `addXXXListener()` method that specifies the listener object to listen to events. Consider the following:

```
TextArea myTextArea = new TextArea(30);
myTextArea.addKeyListener(new TextListener(id));
add(myTextArea);
```

First, you instantiate `myTextArea`. Then, you use the method `addKeyListener()`, passing it an instance of the `TextListener` Listener class that you would need to implement or extend along with a unique ID. Finally, you use the `add()` method to add `myTextArea` to the current container.

This represents only a very simple example. You can also add several listeners to one component, container, or whatever. However, it is important to note that the order in which the event will be passed to its listeners is not always consistent. You can also remove a listener by using a corresponding `removeXXXListener()` method.

Can an object listen and respond to its own events? Yes, this is a very common programming practice for simpler event-handling solutions. The class from which events would originate (e.g., a component) would implement the appropriate listener interface and respond to its own events by assigning itself to listen for events from itself. You will see several examples of this a little later on.

Adapters Java provides a number of empty adapter classes that implement particular listener interfaces with matching names. For instance, the WindowAdapter class implements the WindowListener interface. Extending your listener from WindowAdapter saves you the trouble of implementing unneeded methods (i.e., windowActivated( ), windowClosed( ), windowClosing( ), windowDeactivated( ), windowDeiconified( ), windowIconified( ), and windowOpened( )) from WindowListener. Remember, when implementing an interface, you must override all methods defined therein. Note that a given adapter class does nothing more than override each method in the corresponding listener interface that it is implementing without adding any real functionality.

Some listener interfaces have corresponding adapters and others do not: A listener with only one method makes the need for an adapter superfluous; so only listeners that have defined more than one method will have a corresponding adapter class.

Example: Event Handling First Example
In this example, you will create a button that will toggle its title from ON to OFF and vice versa. This is a very simple example of the new delegation event-handling model:

1. In a text editor, create a new file called EventTest.java. Enter the following code, or you may copy and paste it from this book's Companion CD-ROM:

```
import java.awt.*;
import java.awt.event.*;

public class EventTest extends Frame implements ActionListener
{

    Button m_Button;

    public EventTest() {
        setLayout(new FlowLayout());
        m_Button = new Button("ON");
        m_Button.addActionListener(this);
```

```
        add(m_Button);
        setSize(200, 100);
        setVisible(true);
    }


    // Handle the button click
    public void actionPerformed(ActionEvent event)    {
        if (m_Button.getLabel().equals("ON"))
            m_Button.setLabel("OFF");
        else
            m_Button.setLabel("ON");
    }

    public static void main(String args[]) {
        EventTest t = new EventTest();
    }
}
```

2. After you finish, save the text file as EventTest.java.

3. Compile the code and execute the program. See Figure 6-2.

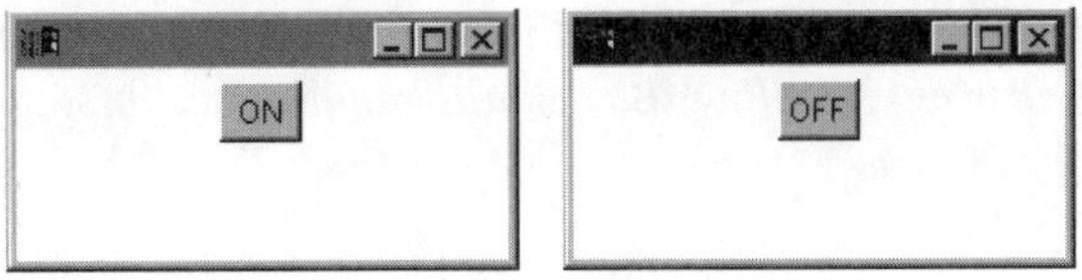

Figure 6-2: Executing the EventTest application.

With EventTest loaded, click on the button labeled ON; it should toggle to OFF. Click on the button again to toggle back to ON.

Note: Since we have not included any event-handling functionality to handle the destruction of a Java frame, you may find that the frame in the example is unresponsive to efforts to close it. To end this Java program, go to the DOS box where the program was invoked, and press Ctrl+C. You will learn a little later on about how to make your Java programs responsive to window-based events.

Event Handling & AWT Components

We'll now return to each of the components and containers introduced in the chapter, highlighting the necessary listeners (and/or adapters) and programming techniques to handle events for each component or container.

Note: Labels do not have any vehicle that directly precipitates an action, so they are not discussed in the following subsections. However, Label objects do come in handy to display the text to a user as the result of some action.

Component

To handle events from a Component object, you need to have an object that has implemented the ComponentListener interface. In this interface, the following methods must be implemented: componentHidden( ), componentMoved( ), componentResized( ), and componentShown( ) passing a ComponentEvent reference to each.

ComponentListener lets you handle generic component events; since all Java components subclass the Component class, ComponentListener can be implemented in any of them.

TIP

It is necessary to implement this event handling for components only if you wish to add your own custom event handling. By default, handling for these types of events has been provided for in Java.

Alternatively, you can subclass the empty ComponentAdapter class. As mentioned earlier, doing so allows you to concern yourself only with the methods that you are interested in using.

Since the basic functionality for handling these events is already provided for in Java, no example will be shown.

Button

To handle events from Button objects, you need to have an object that has implemented the ActionListener interface. In this interface, the actionPerformed( ) method must be implemented, passing an ActionEvent reference to the method.

In this method, you use the following programming technique to find out exactly which button was clicked:

```
public void actionPerformed(ActionEvent event)
if(event.getSource() == button1) {
    //Put code here
}
```

You use the getSource() method from the ActionEvent class and the equality operator to check the references, verifying that both the event and component reference identifiers originate from the same object.

Note: All event objects have the getSource() method because the method is defined in the root java.util.EventObject class. This method returns a reference to the object from which the event originated.

Example   The following shows an example of handling events from two Button objects:

```java
import java.awt.*;
import java.awt.event.*;

public class ButtonEvent extends Frame implements ActionListener {

    Button myButton1, myButton2;

    //The Constructor
    public ButtonEvent() {

        setLayout(new FlowLayout());

        myButton1 = new Button("Here");
        myButton1.addActionListener(this);
        add(myButton1);
        myButton2 = new Button("There");
        myButton2.addActionListener(this);
        add(myButton2);


        setSize(200, 100);
        setVisible(true);
    }

    public void actionPerformed(ActionEvent event) {
        if(event.getSource() == myButton1)
            System.out.println("Here was clicked.");
        else if(event.getSource() == myButton2)
            System.out.println("There was clicked.");
    }

    public static void main(String args[]) {
        ButtonEvent b = new ButtonEvent();
    }
}
```

Figures 6-3 and 6-4 show examples of the preceding code in action.

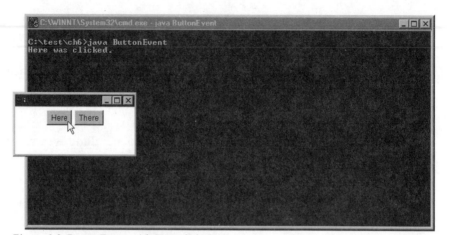

Figure 6-3: ButtonEvent with Here clicked.

Figure 6-4: ButtonEvent with There clicked.

Checkbox

To handle events from the Checkbox objects, you need to have an object that has implemented the ItemListener interface. In this interface, the itemStateChanged() method must be implemented, passing an ItemEvent reference to the method.

In this method, you use the following programming technique to find out exactly which button was clicked:

```
public void itemStateChanged(ItemEvent event)
if(event.getItemSelectable() == checkbox1) {
    //Put code here
}
```

You use the getItemSelectable() method from the ItemEvent class and the equality operator to check the references, verifying that both the event and component reference identifiers originate from the same object.

Event Handling CheckboxGroup Objects

You cannot handle events coming from CheckboxGroup objects directly because the class does not have an appropriate addXXXListener() method defined. Rather, you handle events for the individual Checkbox objects that belong to the group. Therefore, the event-handling techniques for CheckboxGroup items are the same as the techniques shown for regular Checkbox objects, except that in your actual event-implementation code, you also can use methods from the given CheckboxGroup.

Example   The following shows an example of handling events from three Checkbox objects:

```
import java.awt.*;
import java.awt.event.*;

public class CheckboxEvent extends Frame implements ItemListener {

    Checkbox myCheckbox1, myCheckbox2, myCheckbox3;

    //The Constructor
    public CheckboxEvent() {

        setLayout(new FlowLayout());

        myCheckbox1 = new Checkbox("Red");
        myCheckbox1.addItemListener(this);
        add(myCheckbox1);
        myCheckbox2 = new Checkbox("White");
        myCheckbox2.addItemListener(this);
        add(myCheckbox2);
        myCheckbox3 = new Checkbox("Blue");
        myCheckbox3.addItemListener(this);
        add(myCheckbox3);

        setSize(200, 100);
        setVisible(true);
    }
```

```
    public void itemStateChanged(ItemEvent event) {
        if(event.getItemSelectable() == myCheckbox1)
            System.out.println("Red is now " + myCheckbox1.getState());
        else if(event.getItemSelectable() == myCheckbox2)
            System.out.println("White is now " + myCheckbox2.getState());
        else if(event.getItemSelectable() == myCheckbox3)
            System.out.println("Blue is now " + myCheckbox3.getState());
    }

    public static void main(String args[]) {
        CheckboxEvent c = new CheckboxEvent();
    }
}
```

Figure 6-5 shows an example of the preceding code in action.

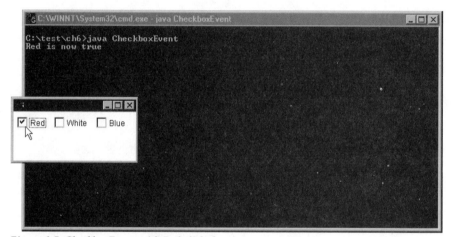

Figure 6-5: CheckboxEvent with Red clicked.

Choice

To handle events from Choice objects, you need to have an object that has implemented the ItemListener interface. In this interface, the itemStateChanged() method must be implemented, passing an ItemEvent reference to the method.

In this method, you use the following programming technique to find out exactly which button was clicked:

```
public void itemStateChanged(ItemEvent event)
if(event.getItemSelectable() == choice1) {
    //Put code here
}
```

You use the getItemSelectable() method from the ItemEvent class and the equality operator to check the references, verifying that both the event and component reference identifiers originate from the same object.

Example The following shows an example of handling events from a Choice object:

```java
import java.awt.*;
import java.awt.event.*;

public class ChoiceEvent extends Frame implements ItemListener {

    Choice myChoice1;

    //The Constructor
    public ChoiceEvent() {

        setLayout(new FlowLayout());

        myChoice1 = new Choice();
        myChoice1.add("Dell");
        myChoice1.add("Gateway2000");
        myChoice1.add("Micron");
        myChoice1.add("Compaq");
        myChoice1.addItemListener(this);
        add(myChoice1);

        setSize(200, 100);
        setVisible(true);
    }

    public void itemStateChanged(ItemEvent event) {
        if(event.getItemSelectable() == myChoice1)

System.out.println(((Choice)event.getItemSelectable()).getSelectedItem() + "
was selected.");
    }

    public static void main(String args[]) {
        ChoiceEvent ch = new ChoiceEvent();
    }
}
```

Figure 6-6 shows an example of the preceding code in action.

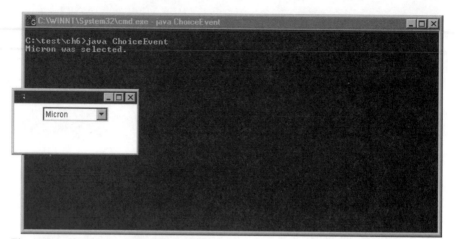

Figure 6-6: ChoiceEvent with Micron clicked.

List

To handle events from List objects, you need to have an object that has implemented the ActionListener interface. In this interface, method actionPerformed() must be implemented, passing an ActionEvent reference to the method.

In this method, you use the following programming technique to find out exactly which button was clicked:

```
public void actionPerformed(ActionEvent event)
if(event.getSource() == list1) {
    //Put code here
}
```

You use the getSource() method from the ActionEvent class and the equality operator to check the references, verifying that both the event and component reference identifiers originate from the same object.

Example   The following shows an example of handling events from the List class:

```
import java.awt.*;
import java.awt.event.*;

public class ListEvent extends Frame implements ActionListener {

    List myList1;
```

```
//The Constructor
public ListEvent() {

    setLayout(new FlowLayout());

    myList1 = new List(5);
    myList1.add("apples");
    myList1.add("peaches");
    myList1.add("oranges");
    myList1.add("melons");
    myList1.add("grapes");
    myList1.addActionListener(this);
    add(myList1);

    setSize(200, 150);
    setVisible(true);
}

public void actionPerformed(ActionEvent event) {
    if(event.getSource() == myList1)
        System.out.println(((List)event.getSource()).getSelectedItem());
}

public static void main(String args[]) {
    ListEvent l = new ListEvent();
}
}
```

Figure 6-7 shows an example of the preceding code in action.

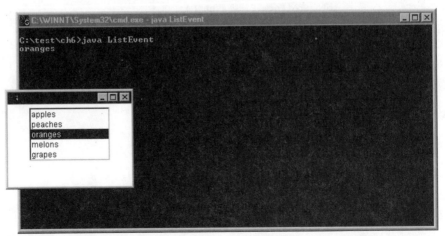

Figure 6-7: ListEvent with oranges chosen (i.e., double-clicked).

Scrollbar

To handle events from Scrollbar objects, you need to have an object that has implemented the AdjustmentListener interface. In this interface, method adjustmentValueChanged() must be implemented, passing an AdjustmentEvent reference to the method.

In this method, you use the following programming technique to find out exactly which button was clicked:

```
public void adjustmentValueChanged(AdjustmentEvent event)
if(event.getAdjustable() == scollbar1) {
    //Put code here
}
```

You use the getAdjustable() method from the AdjustmentEvent class and the equality operator to check the references, verifying that both the event and component reference identifiers originate from the same object.

Example   The following shows an example of handling events from a Scrollbar object:

```
import java.awt.*;
import java.awt.event.*;

public class ScrollbarEvent extends Frame implements AdjustmentListener {

    Scrollbar myScrollbar1;

    //The Constructor
    public ScrollbarEvent() {

        setLayout(new FlowLayout());

        myScrollbar1 = new Scrollbar(Scrollbar.HORIZONTAL, 50, 10, 1, 100);
        myScrollbar1.addAdjustmentListener(this);
        add(myScrollbar1);

        setSize(200, 100);
        setVisible(true);
    }
```

```
    public void adjustmentValueChanged(AdjustmentEvent event) {
        if(event.getAdjustable() == myScrollbar1)
            System.out.println("myScrollbar1 is now " +
myScrollbar1.getValue());
    }

    public static void main(String args[]) {
        ScrollbarEvent s = new ScrollbarEvent();
    }
}
```

Figures 6-8 and 6-9 show examples of the preceding code in action.

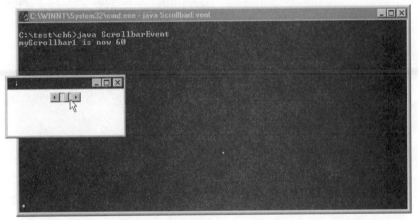

Figure 6-8: ScrollbarEvent paged to the right.

Figure 6-9: ScrollbarEvent incremented to the left.

TextComponent

To handle events from TextComponent objects (i.e., a TextField or TextArea), you need to have an object that has implemented the TextListener interface. In this interface, method textValueChanged() must be implemented, passing a TextEvent reference to it.

In this method, you use the following programming technique to find out exactly which button was clicked:

```
public void textValueChanged(TextEvent event)
if(event.getSource() == text1) {
    //Put code here
}
```

You use the getSource() method from the TextEvent class and the equality operator to check the references, verifying that both the event and component reference identifiers originate from the same object.

Example The following shows an example of handling events for changes made in TextField and TextComponent:

```java
import java.awt.*;
import java.awt.event.*;

public class TextComponentEvent extends Frame implements TextListener {

    TextField myTextField;
    TextArea myTextArea;

    //The Constructor
    public TextComponentEvent() {

        setLayout(new FlowLayout());

        myTextField = new TextField("Hello", 10);
        myTextField.addTextListener(this);
        add(myTextField);

        myTextArea = new TextArea("World", 5, 10);
        myTextArea.addTextListener(this);
        add(myTextArea);

        setSize(200, 150);
        setVisible(true);
    }
```

```
public void textValueChanged(TextEvent event) {
    if(event.getSource() == myTextField)
        System.out.println("Text was changed in myTextField.");
    else if (event.getSource() == myTextArea)
        System.out.println("Text was changed in myTextArea.");
}

public static void main(String args[]) {
    TextComponentEvent t = new TextComponentEvent();
}
}
```

Figures 6-10 and 6-11 show examples of the preceding code in action.

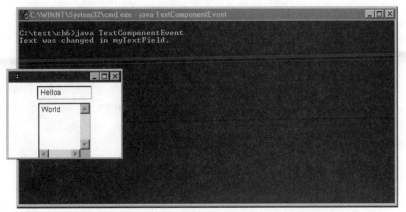

Figure 6-10: TextComponentEvent with text changed in its TextField.

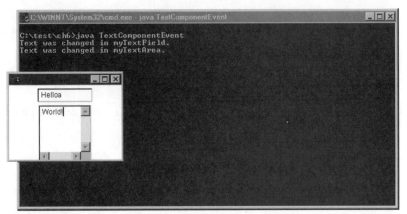

Figure 6-11: TextComponentEvent with text changed in its TextArea.

TextField

To handle events from TextField objects, you need to have an object that has implemented the ActionListener interface. In this interface, method actionPerformed() must be implemented, passing an ActionEvent reference to the method.

Reconciling TextEvent & ActionEvent Events With the TextField Component

The TextEvent that you learned about in the last section is used specifically for any change in a given TextComponent (i.e., every character typed precipitates a TextEvent). However, an ActionEvent is generated when a user has finished entering text in a given TextField. Java determines this when either the TextField loses focus or the Return/Enter key is pressed inside the TextField.

Note that there is no corresponding ActionEvent for TextArea objects, which is why they have not been discussed here.

In this method, you use the following programming technique to find out exactly which button was clicked:

```
public void actionPerformed(ActionEvent event)
if(event.getSource() == textfield1) {
    //Put code here
}
```

You use the getSource() method from the ActionEvent class and the equality operator to check the references, verifying that both the event and component reference identifiers originate from the same object.

Example The following shows an example of handling ActionEvent events from a TextField:

```
import java.awt.*;
import java.awt.event.*;

public class TextFieldEvent extends Frame implements ActionListener {

    TextField myTextField;

    //The Constructor
    public TextFieldEvent() {

        setLayout(new FlowLayout());
```

```
        myTextField = new TextField(10);
        myTextField.addActionListener(this);
        add(myTextField);

        setSize(200, 100);
        setVisible(true);
    }

    public void actionPerformed(ActionEvent event) {
        if(event.getSource() == myTextField)
            System.out.println(((TextField)event.getSource()).getText() + "
was entered in the TextField.");
    }

    public static void main(String args[]) {
        TextFieldEvent tf = new TextFieldEvent();
    }
}
```

Figure 6-12 shows an example of the preceding code in action.

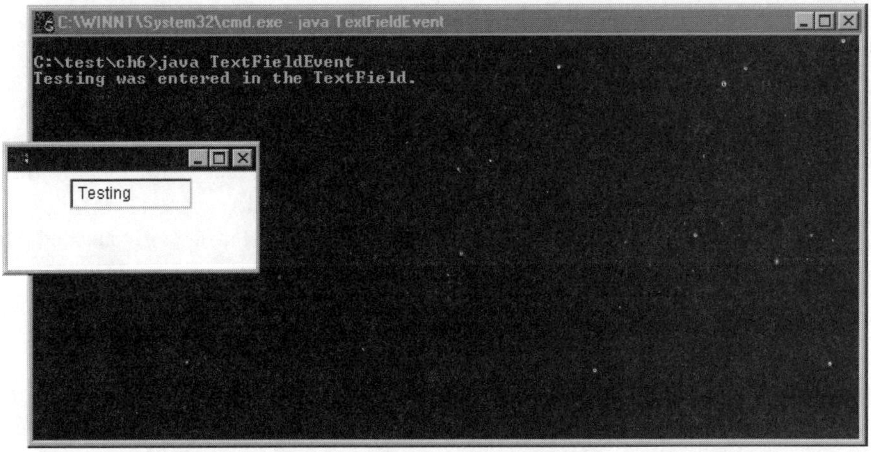

Figure 6-12: TextFieldEvent with text entered in its TextField.

Event Handling & AWT Containers

At this point, you have been introduced to the events and listeners that you would use to handle events from the various components in the AWT. This section details handling events from containers, starting with the generic Container events.

Container

To handle events from a `Container` object, you need to have an object that has implemented the `ContainerListener` interface. In this interface, methods `componentAdded()` and `componentRemoved()` must be implemented, passing a `ContainerEvent` to each.

`ContainerListener` lets you handle generic container events; since all Java containers subclass the `Container` class, `ContainerListener` can be implemented in any of them.

TIP

It is necessary to implement this event handling for containers only if you wish to add your own custom event handling. By default, handling for these types of events has been provided for in Java.

Alternatively, you can subclass the empty `ContainerAdapter` class. As mentioned earlier, doing so allows you to concern yourself only with the methods that you are interested in using.

Since the basic functionality for handling of these events is already provided for in Java, no example will be shown.

Window

To handle events from `Window` objects (i.e., a `Frame` or `Dialog`), you need to have an object that has implemented the `WindowListener` interface. In this interface, the following methods must be implemented: `windowActivated()`, `windowDeactivated()`, `windowClosing()`, `windowClosed()`, `windowIconified()`, `windowDeiconified()`, and `windowOpened()`, passing a `WindowEvent` to each method.

TIP

When a window is opened/closed, it is effectively added/removed from the user's desktop. When a window receives/loses focus, it is activated/deactivated. Finally, when a window is maximized/minimized, it is iconified/deiconified. As you can see in the list of methods in this section's introduction, Java provides for event handling in all of these areas.

Example   The following shows an example of handling events from a frame so that the frame will close like a normal Windows program:

```java
import java.awt.*;
import java.awt.event.*;

public class FrameEvent extends Frame implements WindowListener {

    //The Constructor
    public FrameEvent() {
        super("Test Window");

        addWindowListener(this);
        setSize(200, 150);
        setVisible(true);
    }

    public void windowClosing(WindowEvent event) {
        //Get rid of the current window and exit gracefully
        event.getWindow().dispose();
        System.out.println("Test Window is closed.");
        System.exit(0);
    }

    public static void main(String args[]) {
        FrameEvent f = new FrameEvent();
    }

    //These methods are not used but must be provided for.
    public void windowActivated(WindowEvent event) {}
        public void windowDeactivated(WindowEvent event) {}
        public void windowClosed(WindowEvent event) {}
        public void windowIconified(WindowEvent event) {}
    public void windowDeiconified(WindowEvent event) {}
    public void windowOpened(WindowEvent event) {}

}
```

Figures 6-13 and 6-14 show the preceding example in action.

Figure 6-13: FrameEvent with the program loaded.

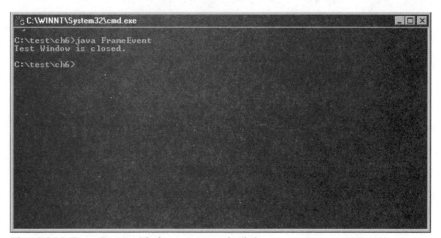

Figure 6-14: FrameEvent with the program unloaded.

The WindowAdapter Alternative   Alternatively, you can create an inner class that subclasses WindowAdapter to override only the methods that you need. In the example shown in the text for Window, it is not possible to have the application itself subclass WindowAdapter because it already subclasses Frame. The following shows the code for that example:

```
import java.awt.*;
import java.awt.event.*;
```

```
public class FrameEvent extends Frame {

    //The Constructor
    public FrameEvent() {
        super("Test Window");

        addWindowListener(this.new WndAdapter());
        setSize(200, 150);
        setVisible(true);
    }

    public static void main(String args[]) {
        FrameEvent f = new FrameEvent();
    }

    //Inner Event Handling class
    class WndAdapter extends WindowAdapter {

        public void windowClosing(WindowEvent event) {
            //Get rid of the current window and exit gracefully
            event.getWindow().dispose();
            System.out.println("Test Window is closed.");
            System.exit(0);
        }
    }
}
```

Event Handling & AWT Menus

In this section we will briefly touch upon how to handle menu events. Technically speaking, there is nothing new here. You have been introduced to all of the listeners as well as the events that are pertinent to handling menu-related events. The only missing piece is actually applying the event handling to a menu—and that is what this section will do.

When looking at event handling with menus, only two items actually do anything: MenuItem and CheckboxMenuItem. The others (Menubar and Menu) merely define the locations where these menu components are to reside.

MenuItem

To handle events from MenuItem objects, you need to have an object that has implemented the ActionListener interface. In this interface, method actionPerformed() must be implemented, passing an ActionEvent reference to the method.

In this method, you use the following programming technique to find out exactly which button was clicked:

```
public void actionPerformed(ActionEvent event)
if(event.getSource() == menuitem1) {
    //Put code here
}
```

You use the getSource() method from the ActionEvent class and the equality operator to check the references, verifying that both the event and component reference identifiers originate from the same object.

Example   The following shows an example of handling events from three MenuItem objects:

```
import java.awt.*;
import java.awt.event.*;

public class MenuItemEvent extends Frame implements ActionListener {

    //Declare the menu components
    MenuBar myMenuBar;
    Menu myMenu;
    MenuItem myMenuItem1, myMenuItem2, myMenuItem3;

    //The Constructor
    public MenuItemEvent() {

        setLayout(new FlowLayout());

        myMenuBar = new MenuBar();
        myMenu = new Menu("File");

        myMenuItem1 = new MenuItem("Open", new MenuShortcut('o'));
        myMenuItem1.addActionListener(this);
        myMenu.add(myMenuItem1);


        myMenuItem2 = new MenuItem("Save", new MenuShortcut('s'));
        myMenuItem2.addActionListener(this);
        myMenu.add(myMenuItem2);

        myMenu.addSeparator();

        myMenuItem3 = new MenuItem("Exit", new MenuShortcut('x'));
```

```
        myMenuItem3.addActionListener(this);
        myMenu.add(myMenuItem3);

        myMenuBar.add(myMenu);
        setMenuBar(myMenuBar);

        setSize(200, 100);
        setVisible(true);
    }

    public void actionPerformed(ActionEvent event) {
        if(event.getSource() == myMenuItem1)
            System.out.println("Open was clicked.");
        else if(event.getSource() == myMenuItem2)
            System.out.println("Save was clicked.");
        else if(event.getSource() == myMenuItem3)
            System.out.println("Exit was clicked.");
    }

    public static void main(String args[]) {
        MenuItemEvent b = new MenuItemEvent();
    }
}
```

Figures 6-15 and 6-16 show an example of the preceding example in action.

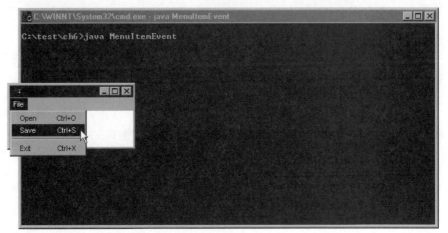

Figure 6-15: MenuItemEvent with the menu open.

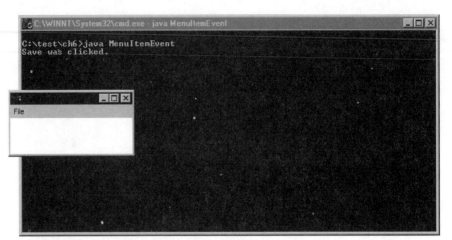

Figure 6-16: MenuItemEvent with the Save menu item selected.

CheckboxMenuItem

To handle events from CheckboxMenuItem objects, you need to have an object that has implemented the ItemListener interface. In this interface, method itemStateChanged() must be implemented, passing an ItemEvent reference to the method.

Note: Handling the events of a CheckboxMenuItem object is very similar to handling events from Checkbox, which you learned about earlier.

In this method, you use the following programming technique to find out exactly which button was clicked:

```
public void itemStateChanged(ItemEvent event)
if(event.getItemSelectable() == checkboxmenuitem1) {
    //Put code here
}
```

You use the getItemSelectable() method from the ItemEvent class and the equality operator to check the references, verifying that both the event and component reference identifiers originate from the same object.

Example   The following shows an example of handling events from three Checkbox objects:

```
import java.awt.*;
import java.awt.event.*;

public class CheckboxMenuItemEvent extends Frame implements ItemListener {

    //Declare the menu components
    MenuBar myMenuBar;
    Menu myMenu;
```

```java
    CheckboxMenuItem myCheckboxMenuItem1, myCheckboxMenuItem2,
myCheckboxMenuItem3;

    //The Constructor
    public CheckboxMenuItemEvent() {

        setLayout(new FlowLayout());

        myMenuBar = new MenuBar();
        myMenu = new Menu("Test");

        myCheckboxMenuItem1 = new CheckboxMenuItem("One");
        myCheckboxMenuItem1.addItemListener(this);
        myMenu.add(myCheckboxMenuItem1);


        myCheckboxMenuItem2 = new CheckboxMenuItem("Two");
        myCheckboxMenuItem2.addItemListener(this);
        myMenu.add(myCheckboxMenuItem2);

        myCheckboxMenuItem3 = new CheckboxMenuItem("Three");
        myCheckboxMenuItem3.addItemListener(this);
        myMenu.add(myCheckboxMenuItem3);

        myMenuBar.add(myMenu);
        setMenuBar(myMenuBar);

        setSize(200, 100);
        setVisible(true);
    }

    public void itemStateChanged(ItemEvent event) {
        if(event.getItemSelectable() == myCheckboxMenuItem1)
            System.out.println("One is now " +
myCheckboxMenuItem1.getState());
        else if(event.getItemSelectable() == myCheckboxMenuItem2)
            System.out.println("Two is now " +
myCheckboxMenuItem2.getState());
        else if(event.getItemSelectable() == myCheckboxMenuItem3)
            System.out.println("Three is now " +
myCheckboxMenuItem3.getState());
    }

    public static void main(String args[]) {
        CheckboxMenuItemEvent b = new CheckboxMenuItemEvent();
    }
}
```

Figure 6-17 shows an example of the preceding code in action.

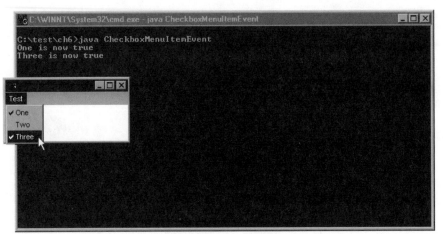

Figure 6-17: CheckboxMenuItemEvent with Three clicked.

Other Event Handling With the AWT

The last types of event handling to discuss are those that come directly from the user's input channels (i.e., the keyboard and mouse). Java provides event handling that you can use to respond to a user's mouse click or movement and keyboard actions.

Keyboard Events

To handle events from a keyboard, you need to have an object that has implemented the KeyListener interface. In this interface, the following methods must be implemented: keyPressed( ), keyReleased( ), and keyTyped( ), passing a KeyEvent to each method.

Alternatively, you can subclass the empty KeyAdapter class. As mentioned earlier, if you subclass the KeyAdapter class, you need to concern yourself only with the methods that you are interested in using.

Example The following shows an example of handling keyboard events from a TextField object:

```
import java.awt.*;
import java.awt.event.*;

public class KeyboardEvent extends Frame implements KeyListener {

    TextField myTextField;
```

```
//The constructor
public KeyboardEvent() {

    setLayout(new FlowLayout());

    myTextField = new TextField(20);
    myTextField.addKeyListener(this);
    add(myTextField);

    setSize(200, 100);
    setVisible(true);
}

public void keyTyped(KeyEvent event) {
    System.out.println(event.getKeyChar());
}

public static void main(String args[]) {
    new KeyboardEvent();
}

//Not used but must be provided for
public void keyReleased(KeyEvent event) {}
public void keyPressed(KeyEvent event) {}

}
```

Figure 6-18 shows the preceding example in action.

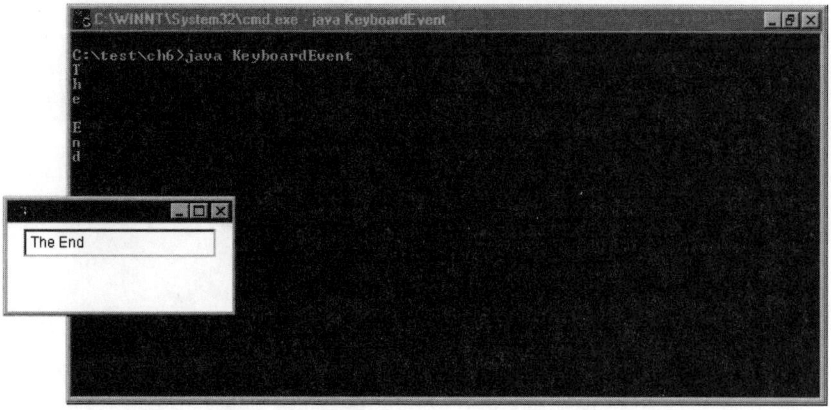

Figure 6-18: KeyboardEvent example.

Mouse Events

To handle events from a mouse, you need to have an object that has implemented the MouseListener interface. In this interface, the following methods must be implemented: mouseClicked( ), mouseEntered( ), mouseExited( ), mousePressed( ), and mouseReleased( ), passing a MouseEvent reference to each method.

Alternatively, you can subclass the empty MouseAdapter class. As mentioned earlier, doing so allows you to concern yourself only with the methods that you are interested in using.

Example The following shows an example of handling mouse events for an empty Frame object:

```
import java.awt.*;
import java.awt.event.*;

public class MyMouseEvent extends Frame implements MouseListener {

    //The constructor
    public MyMouseEvent() {

        addMouseListener(this);
        setSize(200, 100);
        setVisible(true);
    }

    public void mouseEntered(MouseEvent event) {
        System.out.println("The mouse entered the application.");
    }

    public void mouseExited(MouseEvent event) {
        System.out.println("The mouse exited the application.");
    }

    public void mouseClicked(MouseEvent event) {
        System.out.println("Mouse clicked at (" + event.getX() + "," +
event.getY() + ").");
    }

    public void mousePressed(MouseEvent event) {
        if(event.getModifiers() == InputEvent.BUTTON1_MASK)
            System.out.println("Left mouse button is now down.");
```

```
        else if(event.getModifiers() == InputEvent.BUTTON2_MASK)
            System.out.println("Middle mouse button is down.");
        else if(event.getModifiers() == InputEvent.BUTTON3_MASK)
            System.out.println("Right mouse button is now down.");

    }

    public void mouseReleased(MouseEvent event) {
        if(event.getModifiers() == InputEvent.BUTTON1_MASK)
            System.out.println("Left mouse button is now up.");
        else if(event.getModifiers() == InputEvent.BUTTON2_MASK)
            System.out.println("Middle mouse button is up.");
        else if(event.getModifiers() == InputEvent.BUTTON3_MASK)
            System.out.println("Right mouse button is now up. ");

    }


    public static void main(String args[]) {
        new MyMouseEvent();
    }
}
```

Figures 6-19, 6-20, and 6-21 show the preceding example in action.

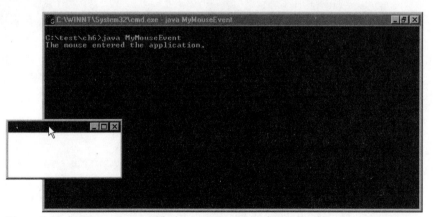

Figure 6-19: MyMouseEvent with the mouse entering the application.

Figure 6-20: MyMouseEvent with the left mouse button clicked inside the application.

Figure 6-21: MyMouseEvent with the mouse leaving the application.

Mouse Motion Events

To handle events from a mouse motion, you need to have an object that has implemented the MouseMotionListener interface. In this interface, methods mouseDragged() and mouseMoved() must be implemented, passing them a MouseEvent reference to each method.

Note: Dragged is defined as the action when a mouse button is pressed and kept depressed while the mouse is moved. It is important to recognize the difference between mouse movements and dragging if you wish to add drag-and-drop functionality to your programs.

Alternatively, you can subclass the empty MouseMotionAdapter class. As mentioned earlier, doing so allows you to concern yourself only with the methods that you are interested in using.

Example   The following shows an example of handling mouse motion events for an empty Frame object:

```
import java.awt.*;
import java.awt.event.*;

public class MyMouseMotionEvent extends Frame implements MouseMotionListener
{

    //The constructor
    public MyMouseMotionEvent() {

        addMouseMotionListener(this);
        setSize(200, 100);
        setVisible(true);
    }

    public void mouseDragged(MouseEvent event) {
        System.out.println("The mouse is being dragged.");
        System.out.println("Currently at: (" + event.getX() + "," +
event.getY() + ")");
    }

    public void mouseMoved(MouseEvent event) {
        System.out.println("The mouse is being moved.");
        System.out.println("Currently at: (" + event.getX() + "," +
event.getY() + ")");

    }

    public static void main(String args[]) {
        new MyMouseMotionEvent();
    }
}
```

Figures 6-22 and 6-23 show the preceding code in action.

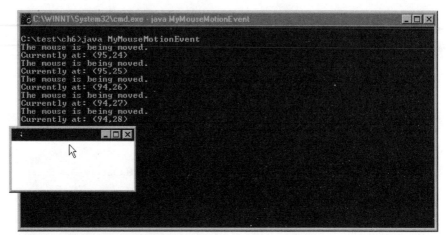

Figure 6-22: MyMouseMotionEvent with the mouse being moved.

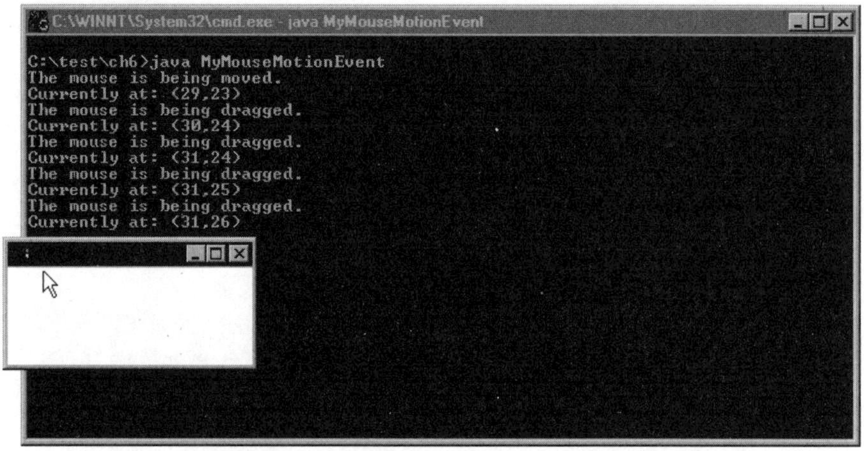

Figure 6-23: MyMouseMotionEvent with the mouse being dragged.

Low-level Event Handling

All of the preceding is useful for handling the events of preexisting components. However, there is an alternative way to handle events from events of
components that have been subclassed. When you subclass an existing component or create a new component that subclasses Component, you have the ability
to override the default event handling to handle events at a lower level, elimi-
nating the need for you to add a listener.

For all components, the default event handling is as follows: For each event precipitated, there is a processEvent() method that passes the event to an appropriate processXXXEvent() method (where *XXX* is the event type—e.g., Action, Item, Focus, etc.). This processXXXEvent() method is then responsible for calling the appropriate methods in the registered listeners.

Note: Java 1.0 programmers will see that processEvent() resembles the handleEvent() method.

To call the appropriate methods, you need to activate the types of events you want your component to listen for (otherwise, all events will be ignored by default). You activate the types of events to be listened for through the Component.enableEvents() method, passing it an AWTEvent mask constant. The following is an example of how to activate action events:

```
enableEvents(AWTEvent.ACTION_EVENT_MASK);
```

Note: This activation process takes place automatically when you add a listener.

There is an event mask for every event listener type. The following is a complete listing:

- ACTION_EVENT_MASK

- ADJUSTMENT_EVENT_MASK

- COMPONENT_EVENT_MASK

- CONTAINER_EVENT_MASK

- FOCUS_EVENT_MASK

- ITEM_EVENT_MASK

- KEY_EVENT_MASK

- MOUSE_EVENT_MASK

- MOUSE_MOTION_EVENT_MASK

- TEXT_EVENT_MASK

- WINDOW_EVENT_MASK

To process the event, you would use the appropriate processXXXEvent() method. For example, with action events you would use processActionEvent().

Example   The following shows a simple example of using low-level event handling to process action events for a Button subclass:

```
import java.awt.*;
import java.awt.event.*;
```

```
public class MyButton extends Button {

    MyButton(String label) {
        //Explicitly call the super constructor to set the
        //label
        enableEvents(AWTEvent.ACTION_EVENT_MASK);
    }

    public void processActionEvent(ActionEvent event) {
        System.out.println("Ouch!");
    }
}
```

Now MyButton contains the added event-handling functionality to print the statement "Ouch!" every time it is clicked.

Customizable Desktop Colors

Most environments (Windows, Solaris, etc.) supported by Java provide a user-definable color scheme for the desktop environment. This means that any entity (a program, icon, trash can, etc.) on the desktop conforms to the specified user-definable color scheme.

Note: Do not confuse the ability to conform to the desktop's colors with being able to change the desktop color scheme. Java does not let you change system colors during program execution (for example, most Windows programs process the WM_SYSCOLORCHANGE message).

The AWT provides support for Java programs to use colors other than a default gray, as well as the ability both to query the current desktop to determine the color scheme and to use and match it as closely as possible.

The class java.awt.SystemColor makes this functionality possible. SystemColor contains a set of static variables that you use in conjunction with the methods setBackground() and setColor() to have the environment specify a color. You will learn more about these methods in the next chapter.

The following shows an example of setting system colors for any text contained in a frame; this line of code would reside in the paint() method:

g.setColor(SystemColor.windowText);

Another example would be to use setBackground() with the user's system color:

setBackground(SystemColor.window);

TRAP

Not all environments supported by Java have complete support for this custom desktop color functionality. Those that do provide support for custom desktop colors may facilitate support for more colors than others. In this case, a default color will be substituted (if possible). Also, components written in the earlier version of Java may not display colors properly under the current version of Java.

Example: Customizable Desktop Colors

In this example, you will create a basic frame with some text in it to be color-coordinated with the user's environment. For this example, Windows NT 4.0 and its various schemes are used to test the application.

In a text editor, create a new file called SystemColorTest.java. Enter the following code or copy and paste it from this book's Companion CD-ROM:

```java
import java.awt.*;

public class SystemColorTest extends Frame
{
    public SystemColorTest()
    {
        super("This Frame uses SystemColor");
        setBackground(SystemColor.window);
        setSize(350, 100);
        setVisible(true);
    }

    public void paint(Graphics g)
    {
        g.setColor(SystemColor.windowText);
        Font f = new Font("TimesRoman",
            Font.PLAIN, 20);
        g.setFont(f);
        g.drawString("This is a test message!!",
            40, 40);
    }

    public static void main(String argv[]) {
        new
            SystemColorTest();

    }

}
```

SystemColorTest is a basic Java application that contains three short methods. Let's look at the first method, which happens to be its constructor:

```
public SystemColorTest()
{
    super("This Frame uses SystemColor");
    setBackground(SystemColor.window);
    setSize(350, 100);
    setVisible(true);
}
```

The constructor does three things. First, the constructor makes a call to the parent class's constructor (using a super reference), which is the Frame class, specifying a frame title of "This Frame uses SystemColor." Then, the constructor uses the SystemColor.window variable to specify the background color for the application. And finally, the constructor calls the setSize() method to specify a frame size of dimensions (350, 100).

The second method specifies the paint() method for the application:

```
public void paint(Graphics g)
{
    g.setColor(SystemColor.windowText);
    Font f = new Font("TimesRoman",
        Font.PLAIN, 20);
    g.setFont(f);
    g.drawString("This is a test message!!",
        20, 20);
}
```

The first thing paint() does is to use the SystemColor.windowText variable to specify the default color for all text that will be printed in the frame of this application. Then, Font f is constructed and set as the default font for the Graphics object in paint(), using the setFont() method. Finally, the arbitrary string "This is a test Message!!" is displayed.

The last method is main(), whose primary function is to instantiate SystemColorTest and display it, using the setVisible() method:

```
public static void main(String argv[]) {
    new
        SystemColorTest();
}
```

Save, build, and execute SystemColorTest.java. You should see something similar to Figure 6-24.

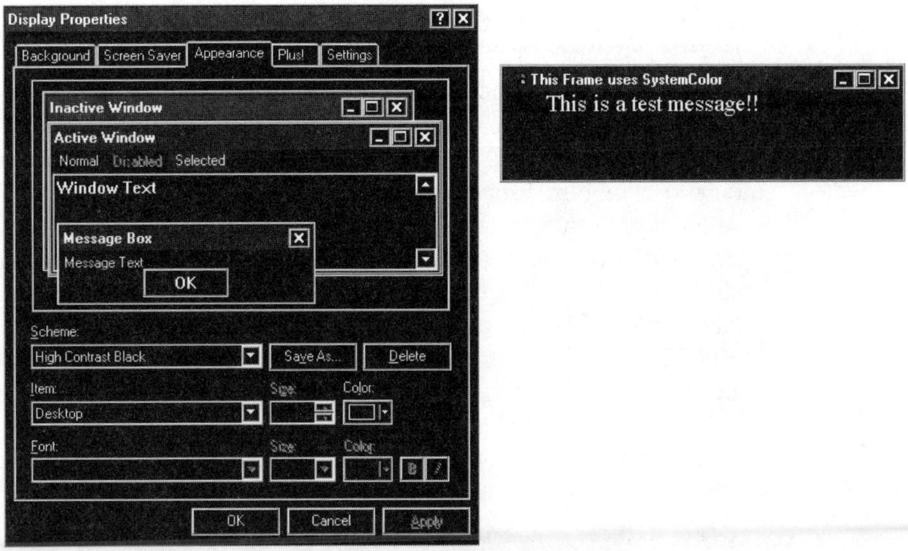

Figure 6-24: SystemColor using the High Contrast Black scheme.

In Figure 6-24, notice that the environment is Windows NT 4.0 with the High Contrast Black desktop scheme chosen. Then take a look at Figure 6-25.

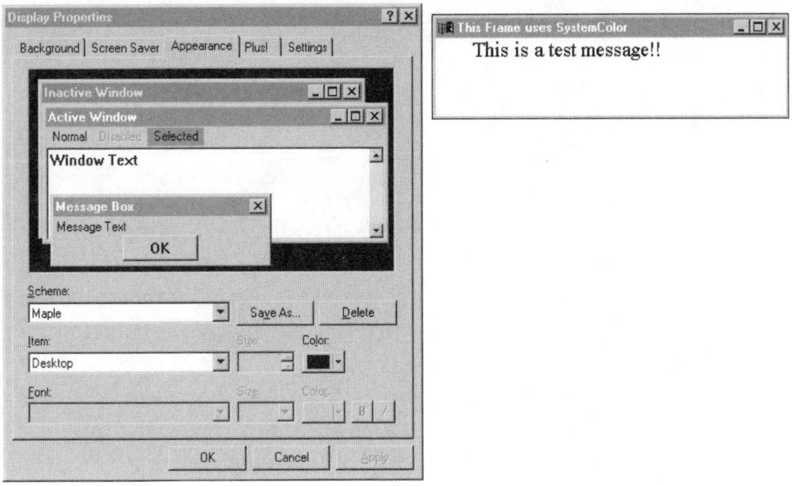

Figure 6-25: SystemColor using the Maple scheme.

Here, the Maple scheme has been set and the SystemColorTest application reloaded. Notice how the background and text colors have changed to follow the colors specified in the environment.

Tabbing Between Components

Current Windows and Motif environments allow you to move focus between components in your user interface (UI) by pressing Tab (Shift+Tab for reverse movement). This lets users navigate between components without using a mouse. The tabbing functionality is available by default to any AWT-based UI, so there is not much to say about it from a programming perspective.

Internally, just about everything is handled through the FocusManager object, including keeping track of which component currently has focus, and whether focus will be sent forward or backward based on the user's input of Tab or Shift+Tab. However, it is important to understand the order in which your components will receive focus as Tab (or Shift+Tab) is pressed. By default, components receive focus in the order that they were added to the container. However, you can override this default functionality by using an add() method of the java.awt.Container class:

```
TextArea txtName = new TextArea(40);
add(txtName, 5);  // add to the 5-th position
```

Here you declare a TextArea called txtName and then add it to the current container, specifying it to be in the fifth position in the list of components.

Another new method added to the java.awt.Component (and the java.awt.peer.Component) class is called isFocusTraversable(). This method returns true if the given component is capable of accepting focus:

```
Button btn10 = new Button("Sample Button");
if (btn5.isFocusTraversable())
    add(btn10, 10);  // add to the 10-th pos.
else
    add(btn10, -1);  // add to the end of list
```

After declaring the button btn10, you have an if conditional using the isFocusTraversable() method. If it is capable of receiving focus (from Tab, that is), isFocusTraversable() returns true, and btn10 will be added to the current container in the 10th position. Otherwise, isFocusTraversable() returns false, and btn10 will be added to the current container and placed at the end of the tab-ordering list.

Note: The method isFocusTraversable() also has been added to the java.awt.peer.Component class. It was added to provide compatibility between any tabbing inconsistencies among different environments supported by Java.

Example: Tabbing Between Components

In this example, you create a Java applet with four buttons. This simple example is meant to give you a chance to play with the Tab key to navigate between the four buttons.

In a text editor, create a new file called TabTest.java, and enter the following code:

```java
import java.awt.*;
import java.applet.*;

public class TabTest extends Frame
{

    public TabTest()
    {
        setLayout(null);

        Button btn1 = new Button("1 (tab to 3)");
        btn1.setBounds(10, 25, 80, 20);
        add(btn1, 0);

        Button btn2 = new Button("2 (tab to 4)");
        btn2.setBounds(100, 25, 80, 20);
        add(btn2, -1);

        Button btn3 = new Button("3 (tab to 2)");
        btn3.setBounds(190, 25, 80, 20);
        add(btn3, 1);

        Button btn4 = new Button("4 (tab to 1)");
        btn4.setBounds(280, 25, 80, 20);
        add(btn4, -1);

        btn1.requestFocus();

        setSize(400, 200);
        setVisible(true);
    }

    public static void main(String args[]) {
    new TabTest();
    }

}
```

TabTest is comprised of one large constructor. The first thing that the constructor does is to set the layout manager to be null so you can size and position the component to your exact specifications:

```
setLayout(null);
```

The next part of the applet declares four buttons, each one with a specific tab-ordering position:

```
Button btn1 = new Button("1 (tab to 3)");
btn1.setBounds(10, 10, 80, 20);
add(btn1, 0);

Button btn2 = new Button("2 (tab to 4)");
btn2.setBounds(100, 10, 80, 20);
add(btn2, -1);

Button btn3 = new Button("3 (tab to 2)");
btn3.setBounds(190, 10, 80, 20);
add(btn3, 1);

Button btn4 = new Button("4 (tab to 1)");
btn4.setBounds(280, 10, 80, 20);
add(btn4, -1);
```

The last part of the constructor calls requestFocus(), used to draw focus to the first button in the applet when it loads and uses the setBounds() and setVisible() methods to specify the size and visibility of the frame:

```
btn1.requestFocus();

setSize(400, 200);
setVisible(true);
```

Java *will not* work properly if you add() a component with an index value exceeding the current size of the component's list. Usually, you should use add(Component, -1) to add your component to the end of the list, or you can explicitly specify an index. Just make sure that it is inside the current list's size.

Save, build, and execute TabTest.java. You should see something similar to Figure 6-26.

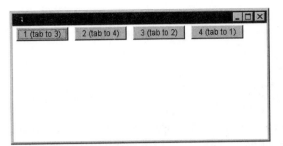

Figure 6-26: TabTest in action.

With `TabTest` loaded, try tabbing from button to button. Focus (i.e., the hash marks) will jump from one button to the next based on the inherent tab-ordering list. Then, try using your mouse to give a button focus. Finally, use a combination of mouse focus and Tab focus to appreciate `TabTest`'s tabbing functionality.

TIP

You can press the spacebar to push any of the buttons in `TabTest`. *This is another alternative to using the mouse for clicking on a button.*

Printing in Java

The AWT provides access to an environment's default print dialog(s), letting you print text, AWT components/containers, and even graphics based on a user's default print dialogs. In the next version of Java (after 1.1), you probably will have the added versatility of being able to create your own custom print dialogs to use instead of the default printing dialogs.

Printing in Java is fairly simple. Consider the following:

```
PrintJob prnJob =
getToolkit().getPrintJob(testFrame,
    "Printing Test", null);
```

You construct the instance of `PrintJob prnJob` based on three input parameters. The first parameter specifies the frame that will be printed. The second parameter gives this print job a name. Finally, the third takes a `Properties` object that you can use to send any platform-specific information to the printer—for example, how you want the pages printed, or which printer you wish to use.

Once you have created a `PrintJob` instance, you need to get the actual graphics that you wish to print, using the `getGraphics()` method from the `PrintJob` class:

```
Graphics pg = prnJob.getGraphics();
```

Here, you create an instance of the `Graphics` class called pg. Then, you use the `getGraphics()` method to retrieve the `Graphics` object you are going to print so that it may be translated to the appropriate environment-specific printer. It is possible to use this `Graphics` object to print exactly what would be displayed in `paint()`. At this point, you are ready to actually send your data to the printer:

```
if (pg != null) {

    testFrame.paintAll(pg);
    // print Frame
    pg.dispose(); // flush and send
}
prnJob.end();// end print job
```

Next, you call the `paintAll()` method that invokes the `paint()` method for the specified frame to be printed. You then call the `dispose()` method from the `Graphics` class; this flushes the page and releases any resources held for the pg instance of `Graphics`, sending everything to be printed to the printer. Finally, you end this print job by calling the `end()` method.

Note: You have not yet been introduced to Java applets. However, it is important to note that, for security reasons and by default, printing is not available inside of Java applets unless the applet is digitally signed. For more information on applets, please refer to the next chapter. For more information on using digital signature to create trusted applets, please refer to Chapter 9.

Printing in Java has been designed around a very customizable theme. The scope of this book does not permit us to cover all of the printing options and information available in Java. We won't cover topics that deal with environment-specific printing issues nor with the ability to pass environment-specific options to the printer through a `Properties` object.

Nevertheless, this section and the following example should give you a good idea of how printing in Java works.

Example: Printing in Java

In this example, you create a Java application that contains two frames. One will be a sample frame containing some text of various fonts, and the other frame will contain the button to print the sample frame. Once they are executed, you should be able to print the sample frame on a printer of your choice on any Java-supported environment using Java.

In a text editor, create a new file called PrintTest.java, and enter the following code, which also is available on the Companion CD-ROM:

```java
import java.awt.*;
import java.awt.event.*;
import java.applet.*;

public class PrintTest extends Frame
{
    // Command ID for printing
    static final int cmdPrintID = 1;

    // Frame to be printed.
    // Frame must be sub-classed to use
    // paint() method!
    TestFrame testFrame;

    public PrintTest()
    {
        super("PrintTest");

        // Create test Frame
        testFrame = new TestFrame();
        testFrame.addWindowListener(new
            WndAdapter());
        testFrame.setVisible(true);

        // Create button
        setLayout(new FlowLayout());
        Button btn = new Button(
            "Print sample Frame");
        btn.addActionListener(new
            ButtonAdapter(cmdPrintID));
        add(btn);
    }


    // Make action
    protected void makeAction(int commandID)
    {
        switch (commandID)
        {
        case cmdPrintID:
            // Get print job for test Frame
            PrintJob prnJob;
            try
            {
```

```java
                prnJob = getToolkit().
                    getPrintJob(testFrame,
                    "Printing Test", null);
            }
            catch(Exception e)
            {
            // User canceled or error occurred
            return;
            }
            if (prnJob != null)
            {
                Graphics pg;
                try {
                pg = prnJob.getGraphics();
                }
                catch(Exception e)
                {
                // User canceled or an error
                // occurred
                return;
                }
                if (pg != null)
                {
                testFrame.paintAll(pg);
                // print Frame
                pg.dispose();
                // Send to Printer
                }
            prnJob.end();// end print job
            }
            break;
        }
    }


// Action adapter
class ButtonAdapter implements
    ActionListener
{
    // Holds command's ID
    private int m_commandID;

    ButtonAdapter(int commandID)
    {
        m_commandID = commandID;
    }
```

```java
        public void actionPerformed(
            ActionEvent e)
        {
            makeAction(m_commandID);
        }

    }


    // Adapter for window events
    class WndAdapter
        extends WindowAdapter
    {
        public void windowClosing(WindowEvent e)
        {
            e.getWindow().dispose();
        }
    }


    // Test Frame
    class TestFrame extends Frame
    {
        public TestFrame()
        {
            super("Sample Frame to Print");
            setSize(500, 300);
            setBackground(Color.white);
        }

        // Paint some text using different fonts
        public void paint(Graphics g)
        {
            String sText[] = {
"Now you have a full set of methods to perform",
"graphical printing in your Java applications.",
"In particular, you can print your Frames",
"using their paint() methods." };

            // Paint title
            Font fTitle = new Font("TimesRoman",Font.PLAIN,24);
            g.setFont(fTitle);
            String sTitle = "Graphical Printing in Java";
            // Draw shadow
            g.setColor(Color.lightGray);
            g.drawString(sTitle, 20, 50);
            // Draw text
```

```
        g.setColor(Color.black);
        g.drawString(sTitle, 21, 51);

        // Paint rectangle
        g.drawRect(20, 80, 250, 80);

        // Paint body text in rectangle
        Font fText = new
        Font("TimesRoman",Font.ITALIC,12);
        g.setFont(fText);
        FontMetrics fm = g.getFontMetrics();
        int x = 25, y = 95;
        for (int k=0; k<sText.length; k++)
        {
            g.drawString(sText[k], x, y);
            y += fm.getHeight();
        }


    }
}


public static void main(String args[]) {
        PrintTest pt = new PrintTest();
        pt.setSize(300,200);
    pt.show();


}
 }
```

Because of the large size of PrintTest, let's analyze only the code relating specifically to printing. The first serious code that relates to printing is the makeAction() method:

```
protected void makeAction(int commandID)
{
    switch (commandID)
    {
    case cmdPrintID:
        // Get print job for test Frame
        PrintJob prnJob;
        try
        {
        prnJob = getToolkit().
            getPrintJob(testFrame,
            "Printing Test", null);
        }
        catch(Exception e)
```

```
{
// User canceled or error occurred
return;
}
```

Inside the switch statement is the declaration of the variable prnJob. In the following try/catch block, you call the method getPrintJob(), passing it three parameters: the frame to be printed, a name for this print job, and null.

Once you call getPrintJob() and it returns a PrintJob instance, you use an if condition to check to see if prnJob is not null (i.e., something was returned). If true, then you declare the Graphics variable pg. After that, you have another try/catch block. Inside this block, you call the getGraphics() method to retrieve what is to be printed and pass it to pg:

```
if (prnJob != null)
{
    Graphics pg;
    try {
    pg = prnJob.getGraphics();
    }
    catch(Exception e)
    {
    // User canceled or an error
    // occurred
    return;
    }
```

Now you have come to the last part of the makeAction() method. In this part, you first check to make sure that something was returned to pg. If true, then you use the paintAll() method to print pg. After that, you call dispose(), which sends everything to the printer (or the print manager) and reallocates resources. Finally, you call end() to clean things up:

```
    if (pg != null)
    {
    testFrame.paintAll(pg);
    // print Frame
    pg.dispose();
    // Send to Printer
    }
prnJob.end();// end print job
}
break;
}
}
```

Save, build, and execute PrintTest.java. You should see something similar to Figure 6-27.

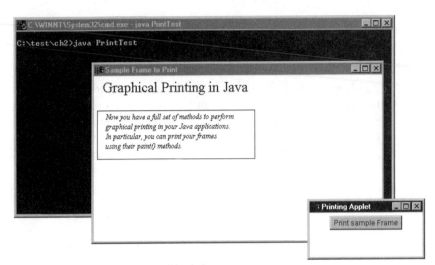

Figure 6-27: PrintTest application loaded.

Go to the PrintTest frame and click the Print Sample Frame button. A system-based print dialog appears. In this case, PrintTest is running on Windows NT, so a Windows-based print dialog appears (see Figure 6-28).

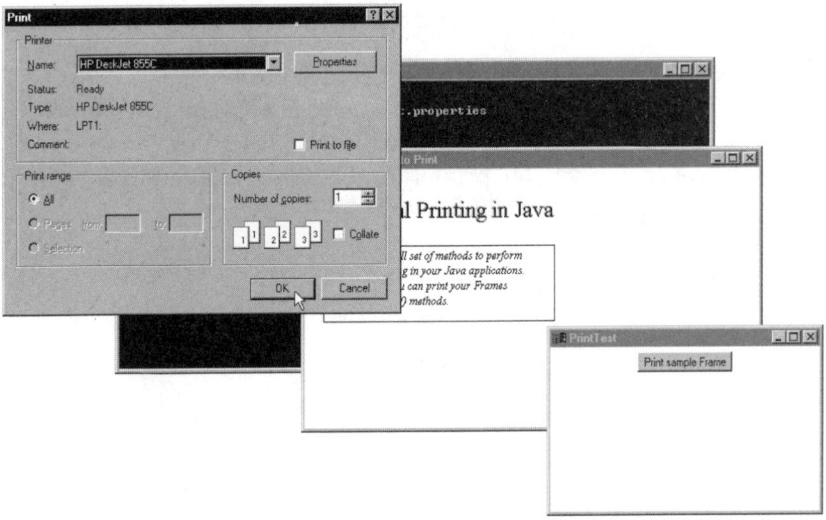

Figure 6-28: PrintTest preparing to print the sample frame.

If you click OK in the figure above, PrintTest prints the contents of the Sample Frame to Print frame.

Cutting, Copying & Pasting With Java

Data transfer between unrelated programs was pioneered quite some time ago. Clipboard operations give you the ability to transfer information between Java applications and between Java applications and non-Java applications.

This section introduces the classes contained in the new package java.awt.datatransfer. This section also explains how to use the classes to give your Java applications clipboard functionality.

Clipboard operations represent a very helpful way for users to send and retrieve data between programs (regardless of their relation to each other). This is possible because the user's operating system acts as an intermediary holding tank for the material to be transferred. Figure 6-29 shows a generic scheme for a typical clipboard operation.

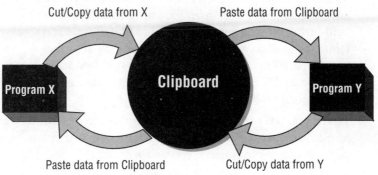

Figure 6-29: Generic clipboard operation.

A typical clipboard operation is a two-step process involving three entities (two programs and the system clipboard). The first step is to either cut or copy information from program X and send this snippet of information to the clipboard. The second step is to paste this information from the operating system to program Y and vice versa. Let's take a closer look at how Java does this.

The java.awt.datatransfer Package

The java.awt.datatransfer package is small compared to other packages in the Java Class Library. However, it can (and will) house all the functionality needed to perform a variety of data-transfer-based operations besides clipboard operations. Basically, it contains two interfaces and three classes. Let's introduce each of them here:

- **`java.awt.datatransfer.ClipboardOwner`.** This interface needs to be implemented by any Java program that needs to use clipboard operations.

- **`java.awt.datatransfer.Clipboard`.** This is the class used to implement clipboard functionality in your Java programs. In order to instantiate the Clipboard class, you need to get a link to the native clipboard on the user's operating system. This is done by calling the `getToolkit().getSystemClipboard()` methods from the `java.awt.Toolkit` class.

- **`java.awt.datatransfer.StringSelection`.** This class facilitates the ability to transfer a Java string in a plain text format. It also implements the Transferable interface, thus making it a vital key in the implementation of clipboard operations.

- **`java.awt.datatransfer.Transferable`.** This interface is the key component for any type of data transfer that takes place in Java. Only objects that have implemented this interface can be transferred by any of the current (and future) means being provided in the `java.awt.datatransfer` package. However, you do not need to implement this interface direct for clipboard operations. Instead, you will use the class `StringSelection` that has implemented this interface, simplifying the entire task of adding clipboard functionality to a Java program.

- **`java.awt.datatransfer.DataFlavor`.** This class represents the actual data format for any kind of data transfer. For clipboard operations, you usually do not need to concern yourself with `DataFlavor`.

Note: The functionality described here represents the foundation for technologies like drag-and-drop and the communication of Java Beans (see Chapter 10 for more information). Only topics specifically related to clipboard functionality are discussed in this section.

Implementing Clipboard Operations

This section shows you how to add clipboard functionality and implement actual clipboard operations in your Java programs.

To start, you need to implement the interface `ClipboardOwner` in your Java program. Then, you need to get a reference to the `Clipboard` object, as follows:

```
Clipboard theBoard =
getToolkit().getSystemClipboard();
```

The first thing you need to do (in the constructor of your application) is to use the `java.awt.Toolkit` class's `getSystemClipboard()` method from the current toolkit, using the `getToolkit()` method. You now have access to the native clipboard environment that resides on the operating system. Now, all you need to do is to program the functionality for the cut, copy, and paste operations.

Note: Prior versions of Java implemented cut, copy, and paste operations for TextArea and TextField components only. However, with 1.1, you are free to implement any clipboard operations for any Java components.

Setting Up the Copy & First Part of the Cut

This section shows a sample snippet of code that you can use to implement the copy operation in your Java program. This example assumes that you implemented the ClipboardOwner interface and called the getSystemClipboard() method to instantiate Clipboard. These are discussed in the last section:

```
String sCopy = myTextArea.getSelectedText();
if (sCopy != null)
    {
    StringSelection sSelection = new
        StringSelection(sCopy);
    theBoard.setContents(sSelection, this);
    }
```

First, you use the method getSelectedText() from the class java.awt.TextComponent. This method retrieves the selected text from the TextArea (or any other text-based component).

Then, using an if condition, you check to make sure that something was returned from getSelectedText(). If this if condition is true, then you instantiate the StringSelection class, passing the selected text from the string sCopy.

Finally, you call the method setContents(), which takes two parameters. The first parameter takes any object that has implemented Transferable. Since StringSelection has implemented Transferable, you pass its instance, sSelection. The second parameter takes a reference to the owner of the Clipboard instance. In most cases, a this reference will suffice.

Note: The operation just described is the same for cut. The only difference between cut and copy is that cut deletes the selected text before it finishes. The actual transfer to the clipboard is the same for both operations.

The Second Part of the Cut

You are not done if you are cutting. You have sent the selected data to the operating system's clipboard. However, you now need to remove the selected text. The following code does this:

```
int nStart = myTextArea.
    getSelectionStart();
int nEnd = m_txtEdit.getSelectionEnd();
myTextArea.replaceText("", nStart, nEnd);
```

Here you do three things. First, you find the starting point for the selected text by using the getSelectionStart() method from the java.awt.TextComponent class. Second, you find the ending point for the selected text, using the getSelectionEnd() method from the TextComponent class. Finally, you use the method replaceText() from the java.awt.TextArea class, passing what you wish to replace the text with (in this case, ""), the starting point, and the ending point.

Setting Up the Paste Operation

Let's take a closer look at how you would implement pasting in your Java program:

```
Transferable transferObj =
    theBoard.getContents(this);
```

The first thing you do (as shown above) is to instantiate the Transferable interface, using the getContents() method. Once you have retrieved the contents of the system clipboard, you need to make sure that there is something to paste. This is done using an if conditional:

```
if (transferObj!= null)
{
    try
    {
    String sPaste = (String)
        transferObj.getTransferData(
        DataFlavor.stringFlavor);
    int nStart = myTextArea.
        getSelectionStart();
    int nEnd = myTextArea.getSelectionEnd();
    myTextArea.replaceText(sPaste, nStart,
        nEnd);
    }
    catch (Exception e)
    {
    }
```

Inside the try/catch block, you use the getTransferData() method, passing it the DataFlavor.stringFlavor field. This method returns and is cast to the string sPaste. So, at this point sPaste holds the contents of whatever was contained in the operating system's clipboard on the user's environment.

In the next two lines of code, you use the methods getSelectionStart() and getSelectionEnd() to find the starting and ending points of the selected text in the given TextArea. (If no text is selected, then both nStart and nEnd will point to the current cursor's location.) Finally, the last line of code inside the block uses replaceText() to paste the code to the TextArea.

Example: Cutting, Copying & Pasting in Java

In this example, you create a Java application that will have clipboard functionality. Then you transfer text back and forth between the example Java application and a native program—in this case, Notepad.

In a text editor, create a new file called ClipTest.java. Enter the following code, or copy and paste it from the Companion CD-ROM:

```java
import java.awt.*;
import java.awt.event.*;
import java.awt.datatransfer.*;

public class ClipTest extends Frame implements
    ClipboardOwner
{
// Commands Ids for menu
    static final int cmdCutID = 10;
    static final int cmdCopyID = 11;
    static final int cmdPasteID = 12;
    static final int cmdAllID = 13;

    private Clipboard m_clBoard = null;

// Embedded TextArea
    TextArea m_txtEdit;

// Menu items
    MenuItem m_Cut;
    MenuItem m_Copy;
    MenuItem m_Paste;
    MenuItem m_SelAll;

// Constructor
    public ClipTest()
    {
        super("Sample Text Editor");
        addWindowListener(new WndAdapter());

// Get reference to system's clipboard
        m_clBoard =
        getToolkit().getSystemClipboard();

// Construct Edit menu
        Menu mEdit = new Menu("Edit");
```

```java
// Note usage Ctrl-Shift shortcuts
// to reconcile our clipboard functions
// from those embedded into TextArea class
        m_Cut = new MenuItem("Cut",
            new MenuShortcut('x', true));
        m_Cut.addActionListener(new
            MenuAdapter(cmdCutID));
        mEdit.add(m_Cut);

        m_Copy = new MenuItem(
            "Copy",
            new MenuShortcut('c', true));
        m_Copy.addActionListener(new
            MenuAdapter(cmdCopyID));
        mEdit.add(m_Copy);

        m_Paste = new MenuItem(
            "Paste",
            new MenuShortcut('v', true));
        m_Paste.addActionListener(new
            MenuAdapter(cmdPasteID));
        mEdit.add(m_Paste);

        m_SelAll = new MenuItem(
            "Select All",
            new MenuShortcut('a', true));
        m_SelAll.addActionListener(new
            MenuAdapter(cmdAllID));
        mEdit.add(m_SelAll);

        MenuBar mBar = new MenuBar();
        mBar.add(mEdit);
        setMenuBar(mBar);

        m_txtEdit = new TextArea(15, 40);
        add(m_txtEdit);
// Pack Frame. TextArea will be resized
// together with Frame.
        pack();
        m_txtEdit.requestFocus();
    }

// Process menu's actions
    protected void makeAction(int commandID)
    {
        String sCopy;
```

```
        switch (commandID)
        {
// Cut command
        case cmdCutID:
            sCopy = m_txtEdit.getSelectedText();
            if (sCopy != null)
            {
                StringSelection sSelection =
                new StringSelection(sCopy);
                m_clBoard.setContents(
                sSelection, this);
                // Remove selected area
                int nStart = m_txtEdit.
                    getSelectionStart();
                int nEnd = m_txtEdit.
                    getSelectionEnd();
                m_txtEdit.replaceRange("",
                    nStart, nEnd);
            }
            break;

// Copy command
        case cmdCopyID:
            sCopy = m_txtEdit.getSelectedText();
            if (sCopy != null)
            {
                StringSelection sSelection =
                new StringSelection(sCopy);
                m_clBoard.setContents(
                sSelection, this);
            }
            break;

// Paste command
        case cmdPasteID:
            Transferable sTransf =
                m_clBoard.getContents(this);
            if (sTransf != null)
            {
                try
                {
                String sPaste = (String)
                sTransf.getTransferData(
                DataFlavor.stringFlavor);
                int nStart = m_txtEdit.
                getSelectionStart();
```

```java
                int nEnd = m_txtEdit.
                getSelectionEnd();
                m_txtEdit.replaceRange(
                sPaste, nStart, nEnd);
                }
                catch (Exception e)
                {
                }
            }
            break;

// Select all command
        case cmdAllID:
            m_txtEdit.selectAll();
            break;


        }
    }


// not used, but must be implemented
    public void lostOwnership(
        Clipboard clipboard,
        Transferable contents)
    {
    }


// Menu's adapter
    class MenuAdapter implements ActionListener
    {
        private int m_commandID;

        public MenuAdapter(int commandID)
        {
            m_commandID = commandID;
        }

        public void actionPerformed(
            ActionEvent e)
        {
            makeAction(m_commandID);
        }

        }
```

```
// Window's adapter
   class WndAdapter
       extends WindowAdapter
   {
       public void windowClosing(WindowEvent e)
       {
           e.getWindow().dispose();
           System.exit(0);
       }
   }

   public static void main(String args[]) {
       ClipTest ct = new ClipTest();
       ct.setVisible(true);
   }
}
```

Due to ClipTest's large size, we will analyze only the code specifically relating to clipboard operations.

Starting from the top, you declare the Clipboard object m_clBoard:

```
private Clipboard m_clBoard = null;
```

Then, in the ClipTest's constructor, you use the getSystemClipBoard() method, retrieving the native clipboard environment for the operating system:

```
// Get reference to system's clipboard
       m_clBoard =
       getToolkit().getSystemClipboard();
```

The method makeAction() is the next code specific to clipboard operations. Looking closely at makeAction(), you see it is practically comprised of one large switch statement.

The first case cmdCutID represents the code to cut the selected text (if any). It is based on two distinct sections: The first sends the data to the operating system's clipboard, and the second deletes the selected text:

```
       case cmdCutID:
           sCopy = m_txtEdit.getSelectedText();
           if (sCopy != null)
           {
               StringSelection sSelection =
               new StringSelection(sCopy);
               m_clBoard.setContents(
               sSelection, this);
               // Remove selected area
               int nStart = m_txtEdit.
                   getSelectionStart();
```

```
        int nEnd = m_txtEdit.
            getSelectionEnd();
        m_txtEdit.replaceText("",
            nStart, nEnd);
    }
    break;
```

The second case, cmdCopyID, is really the same as the first half of the first (cut) case. All you are effectively doing is sending the selected text (if any) to the operating system's clipboard:

```
// Copy comment
    case cmdCopyID:
        sCopy = m_txtEdit.getSelectedText();
        if (sCopy != null)
        {
            StringSelection sSelection =
            new StringSelection(sCopy);
            m_clBoard.setContents(
            sSelection, this);
        }
        break;
```

The third case, cmdPasteID, represents the paste clipboard action. It retrieves data (if any) from the operating system clipboard and replaces any currently selected text with it. If no text has been selected, then it will paste the data at the current location of the cursor in the m_txtEdit:

```
// Paste comment
    case cmdPasteID:
        Transferable sTransf =
            m_clBoard.getContents(this);
        if (sTransf != null)
        {
            try
            {
            String sPaste = (String)
            sTransf.getTransferData(
            DataFlavor.stringFlavor);
            int nStart = m_txtEdit.
            getSelectionStart();
            int nEnd = m_txtEdit.
            getSelectionEnd();
            m_txtEdit.replaceText(
            sPaste, nStart, nEnd);
            }
```

```
        catch (Exception e)
        {
        }
    }
    break;
```

Note: With this release of Java, the `TextComponent.getSelectionStart()` and `TextComponent.getSelectionEnd()` methods are not able to handle multiple lines of text.

The last case, `cmdAllID`, represents the user's choice of Select All, in which case all text will be selected. While this is not an inherent clipboard operation involving data transfer, it is commonly added functionality that goes with clipboard operations:

```
// Select all comment
    case cmdAllID:
        m_txtEdit.selectAll();
        break;
    }
  }
```

Save, build, and execute `ClipTest.java`. Remember that this is a Java application, so you don't use the applet viewer; instead, you use the java.exe interpreter. Once you have started both `ClipTest` and Notepad, you should see something similar to Figure 6-30.

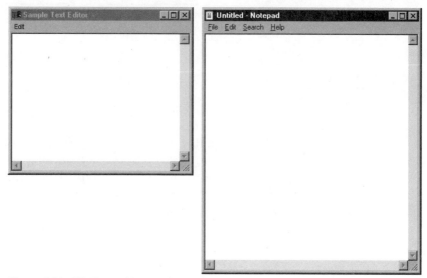

Figure 6-30: ClipTest and Notepad started.

Now enter the text **This is a test message** in Notepad. From the Edit menu, select Select All, then Copy.

At this point, you have copied the selected text to the operating system's clipboard and are ready to paste it into your Java application. To do this, select Paste from the Edit menu in your Java application. The text message drops into your Java application (see Figure 6-31).

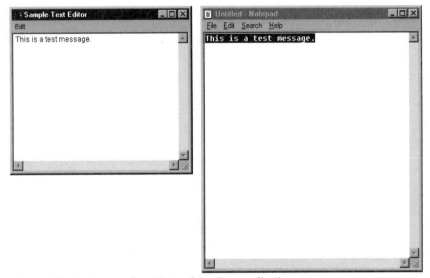

Figure 6-31: Pasting text from Notepad to a Java application.

Moving On

In this chapter you had a chance to use numerous examples to learn about Java's delegation event-handling model. You also learned about miscellaneous topics relating to the AWT, including adding custom tabbing functionality between components, customizing desktop colors, and printing in Java.

In the next chapter, you will learn about another type of Java application, known as a Java applet. Probably the single most powerful feature of a Java applet is its ability to be executed from any Java-compliant browser. You will learn to create applets and understand their life cycle. You will also be introduced to the security restrictions imposed on applets.

## PART II

Java on the Internet

Introduction to Java Applets

In this chapter you will learn about Java applets, what they are, how they work, and how they are different from applications. You also will learn how to embed an applet in a HyperText Markup Language (HTML) page. And you will have a chance to create a sample applet, which will be expanded in the next chapter to show how applets communicate via the Net.

What Are Java Applets?

A Java applet is a Java program that is specially organized to be embedded into an HTML Web page. Unlike JavaScript, only a reference to the actual compiled Java class file (discussed later on) is actually included in the HTML file (as opposed to including facilitating the actual source code in the Web page). This section describes the location of the applet's Java code and environmental parameters.

As soon as a browser finds the <APPLET> tag in any given HTML file, the following occurs:

1. The browser reserves the specified space in the document's window for the applet's panel.

2. The browser locates and runs the applet's Java code (i.e., the browser's Java interpreter executes the "class" file).

3. The Java interpreter for this browser automatically creates one instance of the applet's class.

4. The Java interpreter automatically invokes init(), start(), stop(), and destroy() methods based on what stage of the applet life cycle this applet is in.

All this functionality serves to make applets useful tools in the Internet development environment. It also distinguishes applets from Java applications. As you know from previous chapters, the main() method serves as an entry point for Java applications. However, applets do not even need a main() method. A little later on, we'll show you how to write Java programs that will work as both Java applets and Java applications (called *appletcations*).

The Life Cycle Methods

All Java applets must extend the java.applet.Applet class to be considered applets. This class declares four methods—init(), start(), stop(), and destroy()— each of which has a special role. They will be invoked by the Java interpreter in turn to encircle the applet's life cycle (see Figure 7-1).

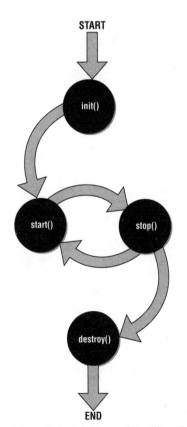

Figure 7-1: A diagram of the life cycle methods for the Java applet.

The default implementation for these methods is to have no inherent functionality. These methods are supposed to be overridden in concrete applet classes of your own design. By overriding some (or all) of these methods, you actually create the functionality of your Java applet. Let's take a closer look at the applet life cycle and what happens when an applet is born, lives, and dies.

init()

This method will be called when an applet is loaded into the system. Normally this method is responsible for the initializing of variables, creating and placing of components in the applet's panel, creating of listeners for them, and so on.

You almost always will implement this method in your applets. It will be called only once during an applet's life cycle.

TIP

Technically speaking, as with any Java class, an applet has a constructor. If you do not explicitly specify one, the Java compiler will generate a default constructor for you. The applet's constructor will be invoked automatically to create an instance of the class specified in the <APPLET> tag in the HTML code. You may use the applet's constructor to initialize members, variables, and so on. Remember that the constructor will be called before the applet is loaded into the system (hence before the init() *call), so you cannot create and place* Component *objects there (normally that is the job of the* init() *method) as you normally would do in a Java application.*

start()

This method will be called when an applet starts execution. It may be called more then once during an applet's life cycle. For example, if the user leaves the Web page that contains the applet and then comes back to it again, start() will be called on each return. You can place some initialization code here that should be executed every time the applet starts (or restarts) execution. If you are using threads in your applet (as an animation solution, for instance), you would use this method to resume the thread(s).

Where's the run() method?

Notice that the applet's life cycle is similar to the thread's life cycle that you learned about in Chapter 4, except for the absence of the run( ) method. This method holds the most functionality of a given thread; however, it is not present in the applet life cycle. Note, though, that the java.applet.Applet class extends the java.applet.Panel class and can hold any components added to that panel. The interface between the user and those components is supported by the standard Abstract WindowToolkit (AWT) event handling procedures that you learned about in the last chapter, so the result is that there is no need for a special run( ) method in the applet life cycle.

stop()

This method will be called when an applet stops execution. It may be called more than once during an applet, any time the user permanently or temporarily leaves the Web page that contains the applet. You can place some cleanup code here that should be executed every time the applet stops execution. If you use threads in your applet, you would use this method to block the thread(s) for this applet.

destroy()

This method is called only once during the applet's life cycle, just before the applet is unloaded from memory. In this method, you can place cleanup code that should be executed only once, when we know for certain that the applet is finished executing.

TIP

You do not have to use every life cycle method in a Java applet. You implement only those methods that you need (the others will revert back to the do-nothing methods of the superclass). Usually you will override at least the init( ) *method in order to provide some functionality to your applet.*

Example: Demonstration of the Applet Life Cycle

The following code demonstrates the life cycle of a Java applet. In your text editor, create a file called AppletTest.java (you can find this code on this book's Companion CD-ROM):

```java
import java.applet.*;

//  AppletTest : demonstrates applet's life
//  cycle
public class AppletTest extends Applet
{
    // Constructor
    public AppletTest()
    {
        System.out.println("AppletTest created.");
    }

    // Initialization
    public void init()
    {
        System.out.println(
            "AppletTest initialized.");
    }

    // Start
    public void start()
    {
        System.out.println("AppletTest started.");
    }

    // Stop
    public void stop()
    {
        System.out.println("AppletTest stopped.");
    }

    // Destroy
    public void destroy()
    {
        System.out.println(
            "AppletTest destroyed.");
    }

    static boolean bIsApplet = true;

    // main() method allows the applet to work
    // as an application
    public static void main(String args[])
```

```
    {
        System.out.println(
            "main() method involved");
        bIsApplet = false;
        AppletTest applet = new AppletTest();
        applet.init();
        applet.stop();
    }

}
```

Let's take a closer look at the preceding code:

```
import java.applet.*;
```

The first clause of our program imports all classes from the java.applet package and allows us to use them in this source file.

Note: Technically speaking, you do not always need to use import classes. You can explicitly specify full names for all Java classes used in your program, including package name. But that wouldn't be wise, especially in a large program. Normally, you will import the most common packages, like java.awt, java.applet, and java.awt.event. The more rarely used packages and classes, like java.util.Random, could be specified by full name rather than by importing the whole package.

```
// AppletTest : demonstrates applet's life
// cycle
public class AppletTest extends Applet
{
    static boolean bIsApplet = true;
```

This code declares class AppletTest, which extends the Applet class. Note that the AppletTest class is public; that is, it can be used outside its own (currently default) package. Please recall that a public class in Java must be located in the program file with the same (case-sensitive) name and have the extension "java," which is why we told you earlier to put this code in a file named AppletTest.java.

```
    // Constructor
    public AppletTest()
    {
        System.out.println("Create AppletTest");
    }
```

The constructor of the AppletTest class simply prints a message on the Java console window to trace the applet's life cycle. In the real Java program, you can initialize your variables and arrays here.

```java
// Initialization
public void init()
{
    System.out.println(
        "AppletTest initialized.");
}
```

The init() method of class AppletTest simply prints a message on the Java console window to trace the applet's life cycle. In the real Java program, you will create the applet's components and make other initialization here.

```java
// Start
public void start()
{
    System.out.println("AppletTest started.");
}
```

The start() method of class AppletTest simply prints a message on the Java console window to trace the applet's life cycle. In the real Java program, you will perform the applet's initialization here, which must be done every time the applet is started or restarted.

```java
// Stop
public void stop()
{
    System.out.println("AppletTest stopped.");
}
```

The stop() method of class AppletTest simply prints a message on the Java console window to trace the applet's life cycle. In the real Java program, you will perform the applet's clean-up here, which must be done every time the applet is stopped.

```java
// Destroy
public void destroy()
{
    System.out.println(
        "AppletTest destroyed.");
}
```

The destroy() method of class AppletTest simply prints a message on the Java console window to trace the applet's life cycle. In the real Java program, you will perform the applet's clean-up here, which must be done every time the applet is destroyed.

```java
static boolean bIsApplet = true;

// main() method allows the applet to work
// as an application
public static void main(String args[])
```

```
    {
        System.out.println(
            "main() method involved");
        bIsApplet = false;
        AppletTest applet = new AppletTest();
        applet.init();
        applet.start();
    }
```

This code is included to demonstrate that a Java applet also may work as a Java application. The static boolean bIsApplet field is used to reconcile between applet and application regimes; this field is set to true by default. Method main() declared here will simply be ignored in the applet regime; but the method will serve as a program's entry point for an application. It will print a message on the Java console window to trace the program's life cycle and explicitly create an instance of class AppletTest. Then it invokes the init() and start() methods to execute the program (which would have been done automatically if this program had been executed from a browser).

TIP

In actuality, we created what is commonly known as a Java appletcation, meaning that the Java program can be executed as either an applet or an application, depending on where it originates.

At this point, save, build, and execute the preceding program as you have done for applications throughout this book. Figure 7-2 shows an example of what you will see:

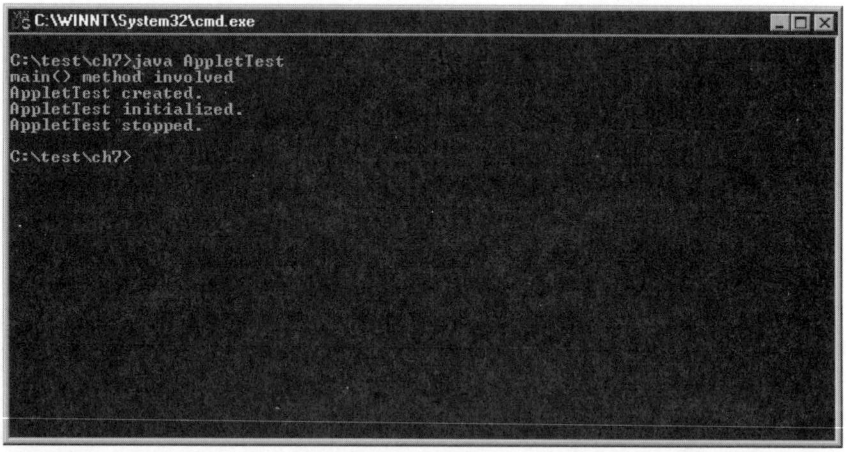

```
C:\WINNT\System32\cmd.exe

C:\test\ch7>java AppletTest
main() method involved
AppletTest created.
AppletTest initialized.
AppletTest stopped.

C:\test\ch7>
```

Figure 7-2: Executing AppletTest as an application.

Technically speaking, you executed `AppletTest` as an application. The only reason the applet worked is because we explicitly added the versatility to execute in this way (i.e., because we added the `main()` method, which is not used by an applet). To actually execute this program as an applet from an Internet browser, we need to have HTML code that calls the applet through an `<APPLET>` tag reference. The next section introduces exactly how this is done.

`<APPLET>` Tag of HTML Files

To include an applet in your Web page, you need to use the HTML tag `<APPLET>` and specify information necessary to run the applet. The minimum set of such information required by `<APPLET>` is the class name of the applet and the width and height of the applet's panel. Here's an example:

```
<APPLET
        CODE  = MyApplet
        WIDTH = 450  HEIGHT = 220
>

</APPLET>
```

This simple example specifies the class name `MyApplet` and the applet's panel to be 450 X 220 pixels. Additionally, you can specify the applet's parameters. (You will learn how to actually read parameters in Java a little later on in this chapter, which allows you to customize an applet without modifying the program's source code.) Here's an example:

```
<APPLET
        CODE  = MyApplet
        WIDTH = 450  HEIGHT = 220
>
<PARAM NAME = Background VALUE = "Red">

    Sorry, but you do not have Java applet viewing capabilities. <p>

</APPLET>
```

This example declares parameter `Background` and sets its value to the string "Red." It's up to your program to interpret this parameter and its value.

Note: Parameters are case sensitive, and unless the applet is designed to look for some specific parameter (`Background`, for instance), the parameter will simply be ignored.

This example also includes plain text ended by `<p>` inside the `<APPLET>` tag. This text will appear in place of the applet's panel if the given browser does not support Java. Currently, such browsers are obsolete, but it makes sense to place such a warning message into the `<APPLET>` tag just in case.

The general form of the <APPLET> tag is:

```
<APPLET
     CODE  = AppletClassName
     WIDTH = NumPixels  HEIGHT = NumPixels
...  place other attributes here
>
<PARAM NAME = ParamName1 VALUE = "Value1">
<PARAM NAME = ParamName2 VALUE = "Value2">
...  place optional parameters here

...  place alternative text here

</APPLET>
```

There are a number of other optional attributes for the <APPLET> tag. Most of them either will be discussed later on in the book or are common options to the HTML syntax and will not be discussed any further. Table 7-1 lists other parameters available.

Syntax	Description
CODEBASE = codebaseURL	Specifies the Uniform Resource Locator (URL) directory of the applet code. If not specified, the HTML document's directory is used.
ARCHIVE = archiveList	Contains the list of Java Archives (JARs) containing classes of this applet (see Chapter 9 for details about JAR archives).
OBJECT = serializedApplet	Specifies the name of the file that holds the serialized applet.
ALT = alternateText	Contains the text that will be displayed if the browser understands the <APPLET> tag but for some other reason cannot run this applet.
NAME = appletInstanceName	Specifies the name of this applet. This name is used for applets in the same HTML page to reconcile and communicate.
ALIGN = alignment	Specifies the alignment of the applet: left, right, top, texttop, middle, absmiddle, baseline, bottom, and absbottom.
VSPACE = pixels HSPACE = pixels	Specifies an extra margin space (in pixels) around the applet's panel.

Table 7-1: Optional attributes in an <APPLET> tag.

To put our `AppletTest` to work as an applet, enter the following in the text file `test.htm`:

```
<APPLET
        CODE  = AppletTest
        WIDTH = 100   HEIGHT = 100
>

</APPLET>
```

If you have experience writing HTML files, you know that this is not the proper HTML syntax, but it works and will provide an effective demonstration of embedding an applet in an HTML file. At this point, load `test.htm` in your browser (in our case, Netscape Navigator). See Figure 7-3.

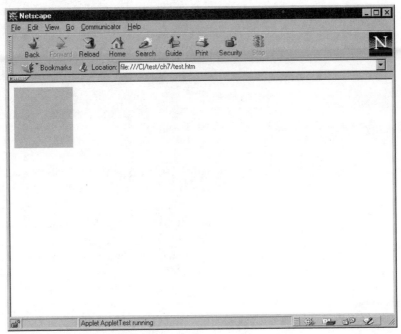

Figure 7-3: Loading test.htm.

Now go to the `Communicator` menu and choose the `Java Console` menu item. This will open up the console that you can use to see text printed from the `println()` method (see Figure 7-4).

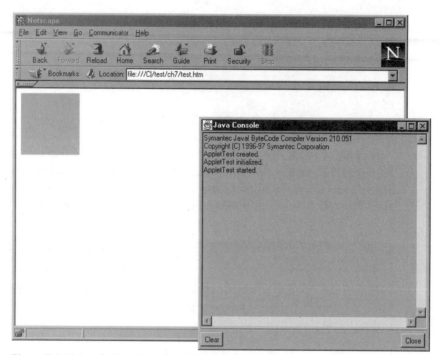

Figure 7-4: Using the Java Console in Netscape Navigator.

In this console window, you will see the trace of the applet's life cycle. The first two messages from the constructor, the init( ) and start( ) methods (respectively), appear almost immediately after you open the HTML file. Then the program waits, because we didn't add any actual functionality to that sample applet. Experiment with the applet. For instance, load another page and then use the Back button to return. Or try File | Close to unload the page, and watch what happens.

TIP

In Netscape Navigator, you can watch messages output from System.out *and* System.err *in the Java Console window, which can be brought up by selecting Java Console from the Communicator menu.*

Understanding an Applet's Relationship to Panel

Take a look at the Java documentation, and you will find out that the class `java.applet.Applet` is derived from `java.awt.Panel`, which, in turn, is derived from `java.awt.Container`. What does this mean? It means that applets are in actuality AWT containers that occupy a part of some HTML document's window and may hold AWT components, such as buttons, labels, or other containers.

Note: Java also provides `Frame` and `Dialog` classes, which appear as separate windows. Unlike them, the applet's panel is embedded into the document and is in many ways considered to be embedded in the browser.

Example: A More Complex Applet

In the last section, you created a very simple Java applet. However, at this point we are ready for a more complex demonstration that includes AWT controls and passing parameters. This applet will be expanded in Chapter 8 to show how Java networking works.

In your text editor, create a file called `FirstApplet.java` (you can find this code on the book's Companion CD-ROM):

```java
import java.awt.*;
import java.awt.event.*;
import java.applet.*;

// Sample Java applet, demonstrates usage of
// AWT components
public class FirstApplet extends Applet implements ActionListener
{
    // Background color
    Color m_Background = Color.lightGray;
    final String PARAM = "Background";

    // AWT components in applet's panel
    TextField m_txtName;
    TextField m_txtAddress;
    Button    m_btnProceed;
    TextArea  m_txtMessages;

    // Init applet
    public synchronized void init()
```

```
    {
        String param;
        param = getParameter(PARAM);
        if (param != null)
        {
            if (param.equalsIgnoreCase("black"))
                m_Background = Color.black;
            else if (param.equalsIgnoreCase("blue"))
                m_Background = Color.blue;
            else if (param.equalsIgnoreCase("cyan"))
                m_Background = Color.cyan;
            else if (param.equalsIgnoreCase("darkGray"))
                m_Background = Color.darkGray;
            else if (param.equalsIgnoreCase("green"))
                m_Background = Color.green;
            else if (param.equalsIgnoreCase("gray"))
                m_Background = Color.gray;
            else if (param.equalsIgnoreCase("magenta"))
                m_Background = Color.magenta;
            else if (param.equalsIgnoreCase("orange"))
                m_Background = Color.orange;
            else if (param.equalsIgnoreCase("pink"))
                m_Background = Color.pink;
            else if (param.equalsIgnoreCase("red"))
                m_Background = Color.red;
            else if (param.equalsIgnoreCase("white"))
                m_Background = Color.white;
            else if (param.equalsIgnoreCase("yellow"))
                m_Background = Color.yellow;
        }

        Label lblWelcom = new Label(
        "Welcome To My Web Site", Label.CENTER);
        lblWelcom.setFont(new Font("TimesRoman",
            Font.PLAIN, 24));
        lblWelcom.setBackground(m_Background);
        add(lblWelcom);

        Panel pn = new Panel();
        pn.setLayout(
            new GridLayout(2, 2, 10, 3));
        pn.setBackground(m_Background);
```

```java
        Label lbl1 = new Label(
        "Please Enter Your Name:", Label.RIGHT);
        pn.add(lbl1);
        lbl1.setBackground(m_Background);
        m_txtName = new TextField(20);
        pn.add(m_txtName);

        Label lbl2 = new Label(
        "Your E-Mail Address:", Label.RIGHT);
        pn.add(lbl2);
        lbl2.setBackground(m_Background);
        m_txtAddress = new TextField(20);
        pn.add(m_txtAddress);

        add(pn);

        m_btnProceed = new Button("Proceed");
        m_btnProceed.addActionListener(this);
        add(m_btnProceed);

        m_txtMessages = new TextArea(5, 40);
        m_txtMessages.setEditable(false);
        add(m_txtMessages);

        setBackground(m_Background);
    }

    // Start applet
    public synchronized void start()
    {
        m_txtName.setText("");
        m_txtAddress.setText("");
    }

    // Make action according to ID
    public void actionPerformed(ActionEvent e)
    {
        if (e.getSource() == m_btnProceed) {
            // Put Event Handling Code here...
        }
    }

}
```

Let's consider this code in detail:

```
import java.awt.*;
import java.awt.event.*;
import java.applet.*;

// Sample Java applet, demonstrates usage of
// AWT components
public class FirstApplet extends Applet
{
```

The code starts by importing the required classes. Moving to the class declaration, we see that FirstApplet is declared public, extends the java.applet.Applet class, and implements the ActionListener interface.

```
// Background color
Color m_Background = Color.lightGray;
final String PARAM = "Background";

// AWT components in applet's panel
TextField m_txtName;
TextField m_txtAddress;
Button    m_btnProceed;
TextArea m_txtMessages;
```

The code then declares the variables used by this applet:

- **Color m_Background**. The background color for the applet.

- **final String PARAM**. A string used to read parameters for this applet. Note that it is final, meaning the value of this variable cannot be changed later in the program.

- **TextField m_txtName**. A reference to the text field, which will be used for the user's name.

- **TextField m_ txtAddress**. A reference to another text field, which will be used for the user's Internet address.

- **Button m_btnProceed**. A reference to the button that will start data processing.

- **TextArea m_txtMessages**. A reference to the text area used to display the response from the host machine.

Let's now move to the init() method:

```
// Init applet
public synchronized void init()
```

```
{
    String param;
    param = getParameter(PARAM);
    if (param != null)
    {
        if (param.equalsIgnoreCase("black"))
            m_Background = Color.black;
        else if (param.equalsIgnoreCase("blue"))
            m_Background = Color.blue;
        else if (param.equalsIgnoreCase("cyan"))
            m_Background = Color.cyan;
        else if (param.equalsIgnoreCase("darkGray"))
            m_Background = Color.darkGray;
        else if (param.equalsIgnoreCase("green"))
            m_Background = Color.green;
        else if (param.equalsIgnoreCase("gray"))
            m_Background = Color.gray;
        else if (param.equalsIgnoreCase("magenta"))
            m_Background = Color.magenta;
        else if (param.equalsIgnoreCase("orange"))
            m_Background = Color.orange;
        else if (param.equalsIgnoreCase("pink"))
            m_Background = Color.pink;
        else if (param.equalsIgnoreCase("red"))
            m_Background = Color.red;
        else if (param.equalsIgnoreCase("white"))
            m_Background = Color.white;
        else if (param.equalsIgnoreCase("yellow"))
            m_Background = Color.yellow;
    }
}
```

Method `init()` is usually large because it creates the AWT components and performs other necessary initialization(s). We start by reading the applet parameter from the HTML file, using the `getParameter()` method (from the `Applet` class).

TIP

No matter what type you are interested in retrieving from a given applet parameter —a text string, an integer, or a reference type—the `getParameter()` *method always returns a string representing the parameter value. It is then up to you to provide the necessary code (as we did to find the appropriate* `Color` *in the previous code) to match it to the type you need to use in your applet.*

If the result is not null (i.e., the parameter is present in this <APPLET> tag and was read successfully by the applet), the program processes the parameter and matches it to the color specified. If the parameter has not been read or does not fit to any valid choices, the background variable remains unchanged, using its default value: Color.lightGray.

TIP

Always provide a default value for parameters from HTML files because you (as the Java programmer) cannot assume that users of your applet will always define a correct value or even remember to use this parameter.

```
Label lblWelcom = new Label(
"Welcome To My Web Site", Label.CENTER);
lblWelcom.setFont(new Font("TimesRoman",
    Font.PLAIN, 24));
lblWelcom.setBackground(m_Background);
add(lblWelcom);
```

This code creates the Label used as the title for this applet. Then it sets a large font (Times New Roman, size 24) and common background for this component. Finally, the Label is added to the applet's panel:

```
Panel pn = Panel();
pn.setLayout(new GridLayout(2, 2, 10, 3));
pn.setBackground(m_Background);
```

Now we create a new Panel object to be added to the applet's panel. We do this because each panel can have its own characteristics, such as a layout manager. If your applet is large, it makes perfect sense to build its working space from several panels. In this case, we create this panel to better organize some of its components using GridLayout. You learned about layout managers in Java in Chapter 5.

```
Label lbl1 = new Label(
"Please Enter Your Name:", Label.RIGHT);
pn.add(lbl1);
lbl1.setBackground(m_Background);
m_txtName = new TextField(20);
pn.add(m_txtName);

Label lbl2 = new Label(
"Your E-Mail Address:", Label.RIGHT);
pn.add(lbl2);
```

```
lbl2.setBackground(m_Background);
m_txtAddress = new TextField(20);
pn.add(m_txtAddress);

add(pn);
```

This code creates two labels and two text boxes and places them into `Panel` pn created earlier. These components will be handled automatically by `GridLayout`. Finally, we add the panel itself to the applet's panel.

Should I Always Use Layout Managers?

Although you can resize components explicitly and place them on an applet's panel, it's recommended that you use layout managers instead: Different browsers on different platforms (and sometimes even on the same platform!) place components in different ways.

It is important to note that the Java world is not perfect, and the result of using layout managers may not always fit your expectations. Use your Java experience to decide whether to use and how to use layout managers. And be sure to test to make sure that the job gets done right.

```
m_btnProceed = new Button("Proceed");
m_btnProceed.addActionListener(this);
add(m_btnProceed);

m_txtMessages = new TextArea(5, 40);
m_txtMessages.setEditable(false);
add(m_txtMessages);

setBackground(m_Background);
}
```

This code creates the last two components of our applet: a button labeled "Proceed" and the text area. Notice that the `FirstApplet` will "listen" for any actions from this button and perform appropriate actions if the button is pressed (we'll discuss that later).

The `TextArea` m_txtMessages will be used to display messages from the host machine. That's why we prevent the user from editing its contents by calling `setEditable(false)` method. Finally, the `init()` method sets the applet's background to m_Background's value.

```
// Start applet
public synchronized void start()
{
    m_txtName.setText("");
    m_txtAddress.setText("");
}
```

The start() method will be called every time the applet starts execution. Here we clear the contents of our text fields by calling the setText("") method.

```
public void actionPerformed(ActionEvent e)
{
    if (e.getSource() == m_btnProceed) {
        // Put Event Handling Code here...
    }
}
```

Thus, any time an action event occurs, the actionPerformed() method will be invoked. This method, in turn, will check to see whether our button (m_btnProceed) was pressed; if so, then the code (at this point there is only a comment) will be processed.

Putting FirstApplet to Work

Now compile FirstApplet.java and create an HTML file containing the <APPLET> tag (or you can copy test2.htm from the Companion CD-ROM):

```
<APPLET
        CODE      = FirstApplet
        WIDTH = 450   HEIGHT = 220
        NAME = "Java Applet"
        ALIGN = top
    >
    <PARAM NAME = Background VALUE = "lightGray">

</APPLET>
```

At this point, open the HTML file in your browser, and you should see something similar to Figure 7-5.

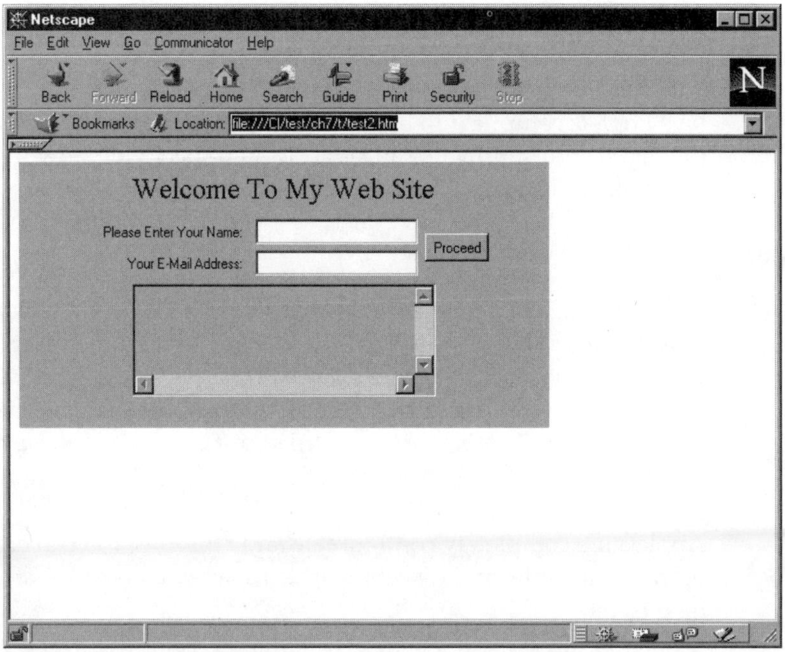

Figure 7-5: FirstApplet in action.

At this point, we have not added any real event-handling functionality (we will do so in the next chapter). However, this should give you an opportunity to see what an applet looks like in an HTML page. Experiment with the components, and notice that they behave in exactly the same manner as if they were executed as a Java application. Also, try loading this applet on other browsers in other platforms to see if you can notice any differences.

Understanding Applets

So far, you have been introduced to the concept of applets, and you have had a chance to get your feet wet by creating an applet. Since you now have some exposure to applets, the rest of this chapter will focus on some of the generic advantages and disadvantages of the Java applet.

Also, since applets are exposed to the Net, security is an extremely important topic for both users and programmers. This chapter will end with a look at how applets have been safeguarded for users and the implications such safeguarding has for programmers.

The Advantages of Applets

The advantages of applets include:

- Java applets compile into binary class files, so there is no source code on the server. You simply use an <APPLET> tag, specifying how the browser should load the applet.

> **TIP**
>
> *Java is a compiled and interpreted language. It is compiled to an "intermediate machine language" known as bytecodes, and then a Java interpreter on the target platform (known as the Java Virtual Machine) interprets these bytecodes to the appropriate native-machine code for that environment. In this way, Java is platform independent but still retains the basic attributes of a compiled language.*

- Applets are completely configurable and reusable. You can create a useful Java applet and distribute it as a shareware (or freeware) program on the Net.

- Anyone using Netscape Navigator (version 2.0 or later) or Internet Explorer (version 3.0 or later) and/or a 32-bit operating system (Windows95, PowerPC, UNIX, etc.) can view Java applets. Remember that Java applets contain all of the inherent functionality behind Java, which means that Java applets are 100 percent portable (from the ground up).

- Java applets follow a very secure programming model, so users do not have to worry about having their networks or computers hacked into by malignant applets. In some extreme cases, these safeguards can be bypassed; but for all practical purposes, Java applets do not create a security risk for their users.

The Disadvantages of Applets

While applets can be very useful, there are certain limitations that you should be aware of before continuing. Still, these limiting factors have not put a damper on the applet industry. The disadvantages include:

- Java applets are said to be too secure and are therefore limiting (see the overview of security issues in the next section). Interestingly enough, security is a double-edged topic, seen both as an advantage and a disadvantage.

■ Applets are said to be too slow. There are two reasons for this. First, it may be more of a bandwidth issue than a Java issue. If a user has a low-bandwidth connection to the Internet, everything—not just the applet—will be slow. Second, Java applets are bytecode verified (to ensure their integrity) and interpreted when they are downloaded to the user's system. This causes the applet to be slower than a typical C/C++ compiled program. There is a solution to this: using a Just In Time (JIT) compiler that speeds up execution by as much as 1,000 percent. Currently, several development environments have JIT compilers.

TIP

Netscape Navigator 4.0 uses a speedy JIT compiler for viewing applets.

Java Applets & the Security Manager

Java imposes strong security restrictions on untrusted applets that come from the Net. Generally speaking, any action that involves direct access to a resource on the user's environment (including other Java programs currently running) is prohibited. This security is enforced by Java's security manager (`java.lang.SecurityManager`). Before granting access to a system resource, the Java interpreter will check in with the security manager to make sure this operation is allowed.

For applications, this is not a concern because the program is executed locally by the user. However, in the case of applets, the security manager has a much more important role. Applets are restricted from:

■ Opening any files, for reading or writing (unless they reside at the location from which this applet originated).

■ Creating arbitrary connections (unless the connection goes back to the location from which this applet originated).

■ Accessing the system clipboard.

■ Accessing the system event queue.

■ Accessing the system printing resources.

TIP

You may have noticed the term "untrusted" or "unsigned" used in conjunction with applets. These terms arose from Java's ability (as of 1.1) to grant applets a trusted status, which will be discussed in Chapter 9. In brief, the user can verify the origin of a digitally signed applet. Trusted applets are free from the preceding security restrictions.

Moving On

In this chapter, you had an introduction to Java applets, what they are and how they work. You also had a chance both to create a Java applet and to understand some of the implications of applets, particularly the implications of security.

In the next chapter, you will learn about creating interactive Web sites with applets. The FirstApplet created in this chapter will be enlarged and used for real Java networking.

Creating Interactive Web Sites With Applets

This chapter will give you a high-level understanding of how communication takes place in Java and on the Net. You will learn what you need to know to design a Java program effectively to connect to the Internet, a server, or even another applet. A complete discussion of networking and Java could easily be the topic for an entire book. So, this chapter will introduce you to only a few of the key concepts and programming techniques used in Java, with several examples to give you a chance to have some "hands-on" learning experience.

Network Programming in Java

Network programming in Java deals with the implementation of communication over a network (particularly the Internet), all of it relating to the java.net package. There are classes and levels at which you can make your Java programs network-aware. In this section (and those that follow), you will have a chance to learn more about these classes and levels.

To start, Java has the java.net.URL class that represents a URL (Uniform Resource Locator). You can use this class to connect to URLs on the Internet. Remember that a URL can use the HyperText Transfer Protocol (HTTP) for hypertext documents, File Transfer Protocol (FTP) for transferring files, or other Internet-supported protocols—Gopher, for example. In your Java programs you can use the URL class to connect to a specific resource on the Net.

In effect, instances of the URL class represent pointers to a given resource on the Net. For example, the following shows an example of creating a new URL that points to the Web site http://www.netscape.com.

```
try
{
    URL myURL = new URL(
        "http://www.netscape.com");
    URLConnection MyConnection =
        myURL.openConnection();
}
catch(MalformedURLException e) {}
```

Notice that the constructor of the URL class throws the MalformedURLException if the URL address string has incorrect format and cannot be parsed. There are a total of four constructors available to create a new URL object; see Table 8-1.

Syntax	Parameters passed to create URL
URL(String)	URL.
URL(String, String, int, String)	Protocol, host, port number, and filename.
URL(String, String, String)	Protocol, host, and filename.
URL(URL, String)	URL context object, and string specification.

Table 8-1: Constructors of class URL.

As soon as you've created a URL object, you can connect to that URL by using the openConnection() method. This will create an instance of the java.net.URLConnection class. In turn, URLConnection allows you both to get an InputStream instance by using the getInputStream() method and to get access to data of the specified URL. At this point, let's take a closer look at URLConnection.

URLConnection

The URLConnection class represents the actual network connection to a specified URL on the Net. You use some of its many available methods to retrieve and set various data, options, and other miscellaneous items relating to the connection. The following example demonstrates a few of these methods. However, for a complete listing, please refer to either JavaSoft's online application programming interface (API) specification or Chapter 12 of *The Java 1.1 Programmer's Reference* [ISBN: 1-56604-687-4] published by Ventana.

Example: Networking in Java

The following example demonstrates how to open a specified URL and read data from it. In a clean text file labeled TestURL.java, enter the following code (or you can copy it from this book's Companion CD-ROM):

Note: Opening a network connection is considered potentially dangerous and, as you learned in the last chapter, is restricted for untrusted applets. Because of that, this example runs both as an applet and as an application. It will be used as an application in this chapter. But you will see how it can be used as an applet in Chapter 9.

```java
import java.awt.*;
import java.awt.event.*;
import java.applet.*;
import java.util.*;
import java.net.*;
import java.io.*;


public class TestURL extends Applet
{
    static final int cmdReadID = 1;
    static String m_sURL = "http://www.netscape.com";

    TextArea   m_Display;
    Button     m_Connect;

    // Applet initialization
    public void init()
    {
        setLayout(new FlowLayout());

        m_Display = new TextArea(15, 60);
        add(m_Display);

        m_Connect = new Button("Connect to "+m_sURL);
        m_Connect.addActionListener(new ActAdapter(cmdReadID));
        add(m_Connect);
    }

    // Read specified URL
    protected void ReadURL()
    {
        LineNumberReader lr;
```

```java
    try
    {
        URL myURL = new URL(m_sURL);
        URLConnection MyConnection = myURL.openConnection();
        InputStream in = MyConnection.getInputStream();
        InputStreamReader r = new InputStreamReader(in);
        lr = new LineNumberReader(r);
    }
    catch (MalformedURLException ee)
    {
        System.err.println("Malformed URL: "
            +m_sURL);
        return;
    }
    catch (Exception e)
    {
        System.err.println("Error: "+e.getMessage());
        return;
    }

    // Read up to 50 lines of text
    for (int k=0; k<50; k++)
    {
        try
        {
            String str = lr.readLine();
            if (str == null)
                break;
            m_Display.append(str + "\n");
        }
        catch (Exception e)
        { break; }
    }

    try
    { lr.close(); }
    catch (Exception e) {}
}


// Make action
protected void makeAction(int commandID)
{
    switch (commandID)
```

```java
        {
        case cmdReadID:
            ReadURL();
            break;
        }
    }


    public static void main(String args[])
    {
        Frame frame = new Frame("URL Test");
        frame.setSize(450, 380);

        TestURL appl = new TestURL();
        frame.add("Center", appl);
        appl.init();
        appl.start();

        frame.addWindowListener(appl. new WndAdapter());
        frame.setVisible(true);
    }


// Action adapter
class ActAdapter implements ActionListener
{
    private int m_commandID;

    ActAdapter(int commandID)
    {
        m_commandID = commandID;
    }

    public void actionPerformed(ActionEvent e)
    {
        makeAction(m_commandID);
    }
}


// Window adapter
class WndAdapter extends WindowAdapter
{
    public void windowClosing(WindowEvent e)
```

```
        {
            e.getWindow().dispose();
            destroy();
            System.exit(0);
        }
    }

}
```

Let's pause to consider this code in detail:

```
import java.awt.*;
import java.awt.event.*;
import java.applet.*;
import java.util.*;
import java.net.*;
import java.io.*;



public class TestURL extends Applet
{
    static String m_sURL = "http://www.netscape.com";

    TextArea   m_Display;
    Button     m_Connect;
```

As always, the Java program starts by importing the necessary packages. Then we declare the `public` class `TestURL`, a string variable to be used as the address of the URL to be read, and references for two graphical user interface (GUI) components.

```
    // Applet initialization
    public void init()
    {
        setLayout(new FlowLayout());

        m_Display = new TextArea(15, 60);
        add(m_Display);

        m_Connect = new Button("Connect to "+m_sURL);
        m_Connect.addActionListener(this);
        add(m_Connect);
    }
```

Method `init()` creates the two GUI components (`TextArea` and `Button`) and places them on the applet's panel.

```
// Read specified URL
protected void readURL()
{
    LineNumberReader lr;

    try
    {
        URL myURL = new URL(m_sURL);
        URLConnection MyConnection = myURL.openConnection();
        InputStream in = MyConnection.getInputStream();
        InputStreamReader r = new InputStreamReader(in);
        lr = new LineNumberReader(r);
    }
    catch (MalformedURLException ee)
    {
        System.err.println("Malformed URL: "
            +m_sURL);
        return;
    }
    catch (Exception e)
    {
        System.err.println("Error: "+e.getMessage());
        return;
    }
```

This method will be called to read textual data from the specified URL. First, it creates URL and URLConnection instances as discussed earlier. This allows us to get an InputStream instance (if the operation is successful), using the getInputStream() method.

Java provides many classes for input/output operations in the java.io package. To read text lines from InputStream, you need to create an InputStreamReader instance based on the given stream and a LineNumberReader instance based on the given reader. This class provides a readLine() method to actually do the job. Note that MalformedURLException as well as other exceptions have to be caught here.

```
        // Read up to 50 lines of text
        for (int k=0; k<50; k++)
        {
            try
            {
                String str = lr.readLine();
                if (str == null)
                    break;
                m_Display.append(str + "\n");
            }
```

```
            catch (Exception e)
            { break; }
    }

    try
    { lr.close(); }
    catch (Exception e) {}
}
```

This part of readURL() reads up to 50 lines of text from the open stream and appends them to the text area of this applet. Finally, it closes the reader. Note that neither the URL nor the URLConnection class provides any special methods to close the connection, so you have to do it directly.

```
public static void main(String args[])
{
    Frame frame = new Frame("URL Test");
    frame.setSize(450, 380);

    TestURL appl = new TestURL();
    frame.add("Center", appl);
    appl.init();
    appl.start();

    frame.addWindowListener(appl. new WndAdapter());
    frame.setVisible(true);
}
```

As you know, the main() method represents the entry point for Java applications. Since we want this program to work both as an applet and as an application, we do the following actions here:

- Create a Frame instance that will hold our application (instead of the browser's window).

- Create an instance of TestURL class (which eventually extends the Panel class) and add it to the frame.

- Explicitly call init() and start() methods (recall that in the case of an applet they will be called automatically).

- Create and add a WindowListener instance for the given Frame (that will be discussed later).

- Call the setVisible(true) method to make our applet's frame visible.

```
    public void actionPerformed(ActionEvent e)
    {
        if (e.getSource() == m_Connect) {
            readURL();
        }
    }
}
```

If the button of our GUI component is clicked, then the readURL() method (defined in this program) will be called.

```
// Window adapter
class WndAdapter extends WindowAdapter
{
    public void windowClosing(WindowEvent e)
    {
        e.getWindow().dispose();
        destroy();
        System.exit(0);
    }
}
}
```

Implementations of the WindowListener interface are used to listen to window-related events, such as window activated, closed, and minimized. We need the WindowListener interface here to close our Frame object when the user attempts to close the window (remember that for most platforms this behavior, which is usually a default, is not present in Java). To do this, the listener disposes of the frame, destroys the application, and calls the System.exit(0) method.

Save, build, and execute TestURL as an application. Figure 8-1 demonstrates the TestURL application in action.

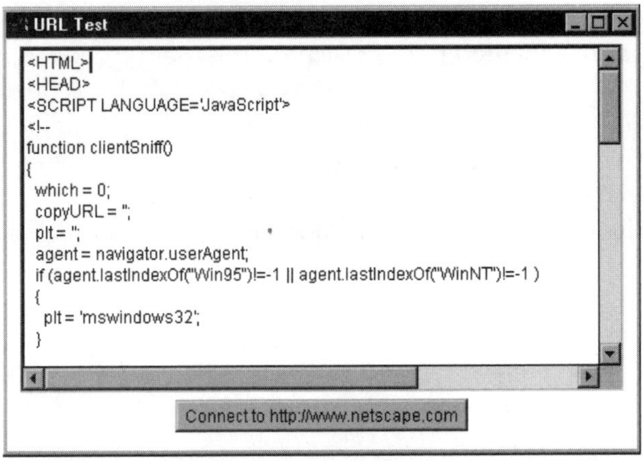

Figure 8-1: TestURL *application in action.*

You can see the first lines of the Netscape Web page in Figure 8-1. Obviously, in more professional solutions, you might want add some parsing functionality to interpret what is actually being read, rather than just displaying the HTML source in a TextArea object.

Interapplet Communications

As mentioned in Chapter 7, the HyperText Markup Language (HTML) provides a special naming mechanism allowing applets located on the same Web page to be reconciled. We also mentioned that this was facilitated so applets could communicate with each other. The following snippet of code shows the basic idea for using this mechanism from HTML.

Suppose that you have an applet named "MyApplet1" (specified in the NAME attribute of the <APPLET> tag) that belongs to class MyApplet (see Chapter 7 for details). Any other applet located at the same Web page can request a reference to that applet using its name:

```
Applet Partner = getAppletContext().
        getApplet("MyApplet1");
if (Partner != null &&
    Partner instanceof MyApplet)
{
    MyApplet appPartner = (MyApplet)Partner;
    // Access any public method in MyApplet
    // using the available reference
}
```

This example uses the getApplet() method from the java.applet.AppletContext class to obtain a reference corresponding to the given name. If this reference is not null and belongs to the MyApplet class (using the instanceof operator), the program casts the obtained reference to a MyApplet class type. After that, you can access any public method in the MyApplet class.

Note: If the Partner reference is null, the right part of the && operator in an if condition will not be evaluated owing to properties of the logical AND operator. Otherwise, we would get an error because we would be using a null reference. Please refer to Chapter 2 for more information.

Let's take a look at the real example of interapplet communication.

Example: Interapplet Communication

In a text file entitled `MailApplet.java`, enter the following code (or you can copy it from the Companion CD-ROM):

```java
import java.awt.*;
import java.applet.*;
import java.util.Enumeration;


public class MailApplet extends Applet
    implements Runnable
{
    String m_sPar1 = "undefined";
    String m_sPar2 = "undefined";
    String m_sName = "";
    final String PARAM1 = "Partner1";
    final String PARAM2 = "Partner2";
    final String PARAM3 = "MyName";

    Label    m_lblName;
    TextArea m_txtMessages;

    // Init applet
    public synchronized void init()
    {
        String param;

        param = getParameter(PARAM1);
        if (param != null)
            m_sPar1 = param;

        param = getParameter(PARAM2);
        if (param != null)
            m_sPar2 = param;

        param = getParameter(PARAM3);
        if (param != null)
            m_sName = param;
        System.out.println("Init Applet: "
            +m_sName+", "+m_sPar1+", "+m_sPar2);

        m_lblName = new Label(m_sName,
            Label.CENTER);
        m_lblName.setFont(new Font(
            "TimesRoman",Font.PLAIN,24));
        add(m_lblName);
```

```java
        m_txtMessages = new TextArea(5, 25);
        m_txtMessages.setEditable(false);
        add(m_txtMessages);

        new Thread(this).start();
        System.out.println(m_sName+
            " is started");
    }


    public void addMessage(String str)
    {
        m_txtMessages.append(str + "\n");
    }

    public void run()
    {
        while (true)
        {
            try
            {
                String name = Math.random() >=
                    0.5 ? m_sPar2 : m_sPar1;
                Applet Partner =
                    getAppletContext().
                    getApplet(name);
                if (Partner != null &&
                Partner instanceof MailApplet)
                {
                    MailApplet appPartner =
                    (MailApplet)Partner;
                    appPartner.addMessage(
                    "Hi, this is "+m_sName);
                }
                Thread.sleep(5000);
            }
            catch (InterruptedException e)
            {
                stop();
            }
        }
    }

}
```

Let's pause to consider this code in detail:

```java
import java.awt.*;
import java.applet.*;
import java.util.Enumeration;


public class MailApplet extends Applet
    implements Runnable
{
    String m_sPar1 = "undefined";
    String m_sPar2 = "undefined";
    String m_sName = "";
    final String PARAM1 = "Partner1";
    final String PARAM2 = "Partner2";
    final String PARAM3 = "MyName";

    Label    m_lblName;
    TextArea m_txtMessages;
```

This code imports the necessary packages and declares the `MailApplet` class, extending `Applet` and implementing the `java.lang.Runnable` interface. Three `String` variables are prepared for the applet's parameters, along with corresponding key words: "Partner1," "Partner2," and "MyName." Two GUI components—`Label m_lblName` and `TextArea m_txtMessages`—also are declared for this applet.

TIP

The Runnable interface provides a way to use threads without subclassing the `java.lang.Thread` class. If your class implements the `Runnable` interface, it must override the `run()` method, which can use a `Thread` instance assigned to that object. Please refer to Chapter 4 for more information.

```java
// Init applet
public synchronized void init()
{
    String param;

    param = getParameter(PARAM1);
    if (param != null)
        m_sPar1 = param;
```

```
param = getParameter(PARAM2);
if (param != null)
    m_sPar2 = param;

param = getParameter(PARAM3);
if (param != null)
    m_sName = param;
System.out.println("Init Applet: "
    +m_sName+", "+m_sPar1+", "+m_sPar2);

m_lblName = new Label(m_sName,
    Label.CENTER);
m_lblName.setFont(new Font(
    "TimesRoman",Font.PLAIN,24));
add(m_lblName);

m_txtMessages = new TextArea(5, 25);
m_txtMessages.setEditable(false);
add(m_txtMessages);
```

This part of the init() method should not be new to you. It reads three parameters from the HTML file and creates and places the GUI components declared earlier. Note that the Label object displays the results of the parameter named "MyName." The TextArea m_txtMessages is reserved to display information only.

```
new Thread(this).start();
System.out.println(m_sName+
    " is started");
}
```

This part of the init() method first creates a Thread object for this Runnable instance and then starts it. It then prints a confirmation control message to the Java console.

```
public void addMessage(String str)
{
    m_txtMessages.append(str + "\n");
}
```

This method merely adds a line of text to the display text area.

```
public void run()
{
    while (true)
    {
        try
```

```
        {
            String name = Math.random( ) >=
                0.5 ? m_sPar2 : m_sPar1;
            Applet Partner =
                getAppletContext( ).
                getApplet(name);
            if (Partner != null &&
            Partner instanceof MailApplet)
            {
                MailApplet appPartner =
                (MailApplet)Partner;
                appPartner.addMessage(
                "Hi, this is "+m_sName);
            }
            Thread.sleep(5000);
        }
        catch (InterruptedException e)
        {
            stop( );
        }
    }
}

}
```

As you already know, the run( ) method actually implements what the Runnable instance will do. Like most run( ) implementations, it contains an endless while loop and catches InterruptedException, which may be thrown in this loop (if Thread had been interrupted).

The most interesting parts of this applet are inside the while loop and try block. The applet randomly chooses from one of its two partners by using a random number generated by the static Math.random( ) method. Then, using the AppletContext.getApplet( ) method, the applet gets a reference to the applet with a randomly chosen name. If this process is successful, the current applet sends a greeting message to its partnering applet and sleeps for five seconds.

Now let's look at the HTML file for this example:

```
<APPLET
        CODE  = MailApplet
        WIDTH = 250   HEIGHT = 150
        NAME  = "John"
        ALIGN = left
```

```
        >
        <PARAM NAME = MyName VALUE = "John">
        <PARAM NAME = Partner1 VALUE = "Bill">
        <PARAM NAME = Partner2 VALUE = "Ann">

</APPLET>

<APPLET
        CODE  = MailApplet
        WIDTH = 250  HEIGHT = 150
        NAME  = "Bill"
        ALIGN = center
        >
        <PARAM NAME = MyName VALUE = "Bill">
        <PARAM NAME = Partner1 VALUE = "John">
        <PARAM NAME = Partner2 VALUE = "Ann">

</APPLET>

<APPLET
        CODE  = MailApplet
        WIDTH = 250  HEIGHT = 150
        NAME  = "Ann"
        ALIGN = right
        >
        <PARAM NAME = MyName VALUE = "Ann">
        <PARAM NAME = Partner1 VALUE = "John">
        <PARAM NAME = Partner2 VALUE = "Bill">

</APPLET>
```

As you can see, this HTML file contains three <APPLET> tags. All of them refer to the MailApplet code and have the same size but different sets of parameters. In effect, we are going to have three MailApplet applets loaded on a single page. Load the HTML file that contains the above HTML source in your browser, and you should see something similar to Figure 8-2.

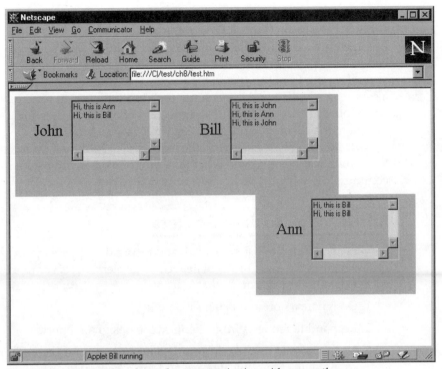

Figure 8-2: Three MailApplet applets communicating with one another.

Java Sockets

Sockets offer the most efficient and comprehensive approach to communication in Java. Technically speaking, in the first part of this chapter you used sockets; however, you used them at what is considered a much higher level. This section will delve into more of the nitty-gritty of how to perform the low-level communications directly.

Note: Sockets are where the actual communication takes place between the client and server. A socket includes a source Internet Protocol (IP) address and port and a destination IP address and port. Sockets are responsible for the physical transmission between the client and the server. Note that it is possible to have more than one socket connect to a single port, allowing multiple clients to access the same port; you'll see that in the example for this section.

Unfortunately, a comprehensive discussion of sockets must be left for books about Transmission Control Protocol/Internet Protocol (TCP/IP). At this point, we are assuming that you are familiar with TCP/IP and how communication takes place on the Net. Programming in sockets will require you to use several classes from the java.net package. Specifically, you need to implement a server and a client and insert some code for these two to communicate with one another. The following subsections show how you can create a server Java program or a client Java program. Let's take a closer look.

Note: As you saw earlier with the higher-level solutions, Java is not limited to communicating only with other Java programs. You can use sockets to communicate with just about any entity on the Net.

Introduction to Java Sockets

Servers are defined to listen to, read, and respond to queries from a client. The following lists the exact protocol needed to implement server functionality for sockets in a Java program:

1. Designate a port and listen for activity.

2. Respond to requests from clients at the designated port.

3. Use streams to read the incoming data and respond accordingly. Then continue to communicate back and forth as needed.

The key class in Java that deals with the server implementation of sockets is java.net.ServerSocket. ServerSocket is responsible for retrieving a port, which is done when creating an instance of the ServerSocket class. The following shows an example using port 2345:

```
try
{
    theServerSocket = new ServerSocket( 2345 );
}
catch(IOException e) {}
```

TIP

If the specified port is already in use, then an IOException exception will be thrown. If this happens, try using another port. Usually, the higher the port number you choose, the less likely it is to be in use.

Once you successfully get a port for a server (and a ServerSocket instance), you need to have it continually listen for any activity by using the accept() method from the ServerSocket class:

```
try
{
    Socket s = theServerSocket.accept();
}
catch(IOException e) {}
```

This method cycles continually (holding program execution), listening to the designated port until a client contacts this port with a request for communication. If a request comes through and the security manager does not throw a security exception, the method accept() returns an instance of the java.net.Socket class that contains a connection to the client that requested communication. At this point, you can begin communication with the client using the getOutputStream() and the getInputStream() methods from the Socket class to send and retrieve data from the connection.

On the client side, Java uses the Socket class to connect to a server through a specified port. Creating a client is a fairly simple process:

1. The client requests a connection with the server.

2. The client uses streams to send data and wait for a response from the server. They continue to communicate back and forth as needed.

The following code snippet shows an example of creating an instance of the Socket class, which will request a socket connection to the remote host (i.e., the server); the first parameter specifies the IP address (alternatively, you can use a host name), and the second parameter specifies the port where the server is listening:

```
try
{
    Socket s = new Socket(
        "205.12.1.123", 2345);
}
catch(IOException e) {}
```

When a connection has been successfully established, you can use the getOutputStream() and the getInputStream() methods from the Socket class to send and retrieve data from the connection.

Example: Creating a Client/Server Java Solution

The following shows the code to create an example server. In a text editor, create a file labeled MyServer.java and enter the following code (which is also available on the Companion CD-ROM of this book):

```java
import java.awt.*;
import java.awt.event.*;
import java.io.*;
import java.net.*;

public class MyServer extends Frame implements
    Runnable
{

    TextArea      m_txtPane;
    ServerSocket m_SocketServer = null;

    // Constructor
    MyServer()
    {
        //Create the user interface
        super("The Server v 1.1");
        m_txtPane = new TextArea(
            "Status Window:\n", 10, 30);
        add("Center", m_txtPane);
        pack();
        setSize(400, 300);
        addWindowListener(new WndAdapter());
        setVisible(true);

        try
        {
            m_txtPane.append(
                "Initializing the port... \n");
            // Create socket for the port 1055
            m_SocketServer = new
                ServerSocket( 1055 );
        }
        catch( IOException e )
        {
            m_txtPane.append(
            "IO Error has been raised. Error " +
            e + "\n");
        }
```

```java
        if (m_SocketServer != null)
            new Thread(this).start();
}

public void run()
{
    while (true)
    {
        try
        {
            //Listen at the port 1055 until
            //connection is established
            m_txtPane.append(
                "Listening...\n");
            Socket socketReturn =
                m_SocketServer.accept();

            //Connection has been achieved
            m_txtPane.append(
            "Connected to a Client \n");

            //Get data from the Socket
            InputStream rawDataIn =
            socketReturn.getInputStream();
            InputStreamReader r = new
            InputStreamReader(rawDataIn);
            LineNumberReader lr = new
            LineNumberReader(r);

            //Get data and print them in
            //the display window
            String sName = lr.readLine();
            String sAddr = lr.readLine();

            String sGreeting = "";
            if (sName != null &&
                sAddr != null)
                sGreeting = "Hello " +
                sName + " at " + sAddr +
                " !";
            m_txtPane.append(
                sGreeting + "\n");
```

```java
                //Send response to the Socket
                OutputStream rawDataOut =
                socketReturn.getOutputStream();
                rawDataOut.write(
                    sGreeting.getBytes());

                // Close all
                lr.close();
                r.close();
                rawDataIn.close();
                rawDataOut.close();

                socketReturn.close();
            }
        catch( UnknownHostException e)
        {
            m_txtPane.append(
            "Unable to find Server. Error"
            + e + "\n");
        }
        catch( IOException e )
        {
            m_txtPane.append(
            "IO Error has been raised. Error "
            + e + "\n");
        }
        }
    }

    public static void main(String argv[])
    {
        new MyServer();
    }


    //  Window Adapter
    class WndAdapter extends WindowAdapter
    {
        public void windowClosing(WindowEvent e)
        {
            e.getWindow().dispose();
            System.exit(0);
        }
    }
}
```

Let's pause to consider the code in detail:

```
import java.awt.*;
import java.awt.event.*;
import java.io.*;
import java.net.*;

public class MyServer extends Frame implements
    Runnable
{

    TextArea     m_txtPane;
    ServerSocket m_SocketServer = null;
```

This code imports the necessary packages for the `MyServer` class that extends the `java.awt.Frame` class and implements the `java.lang.Runnable` interface.

Note: We did not extend `java.applet.Applet` since we have no intention of ever having this program run as an applet.

Since `MyServer` inherits the functionality present from `Frame`, it automatically will have a frame in which to place all necessary components. The `Runnable` interface has been implemented so that this application can use threads. Following the class declaration are the two references: `TextArea` and `ServerSocket`.

```
    // Constructor
    MyServer()
    {
        //Create the user interface
        super("The Server v 1.1");
        m_txtPane = new TextArea(
            "Status Window:\n", 10, 30);
        add("Center", m_txtPane);
        pack();
        setSize(400, 300);
        addWindowListener(new WndAdapter());
        setVisible(true);
```

Moving to the constructor, it first creates a parent object—a frame entitled "The Server v 1.1." Then it creates a user interface containing only one GUI component, `TextArea m_txtPane`. The following call to the `pack()` method ensures that the component will occupy all of the frame's area and will be resized accordingly if and when the parent frame is resized.

```
try
{
    m_txtPane.append(
        "Initializing the port... \n");
    // Create socket for the port 1055
    m_SocketServer = new
        ServerSocket( 1055 );
}
catch( IOException e )
{
    m_txtPane.append(
    "IO Error has been raised. Error " +
    e + "\n");
}

if (m_SocketServer != null)
    new Thread(this).start();
}
```

This code creates a ServerSocket instance for port 1055. Note that IOException has to be caught. If the port is bound successfully (i.e., SocketServer is not null), the program starts a thread for this Runnable object.

```
public void run()
{
    while (true)
    {
        try
        {
            //Listen at the port 1055 until
            //connection is established
            m_txtPane.append(
                "Listening...\n");
            Socket socketReturn =
                m_SocketServer.accept();

            //Connection has been achieved
            m_txtPane.append(
            "Connected to a Client \n");
```

Going back to our discussion on threads (see Chapter 4), the run( ) method actually implements what the Runnable instance will do. In this case, the instance contains an endless while loop and catches an InterruptedException exception, which is thrown if the given thread has been interrupted. Inside the while loop and try block, the program listens to port 1055 until the connection to the client has been achieved. Specifically, this code uses the `SocketServer.accept()` method, which returns an instance of the `java.net.Socket` class if successful. After that, the program sends a message to the text area letting the user know that this operation was successful.

```
//Get data from the Socket
InputStream rawDataIn =
socketReturn.getInputStream();
InputStreamReader r = new
InputStreamReader(rawDataIn);
LineNumberReader lr = new
LineNumberReader(r);
```

In short, after the connection is established, the program prepares to receive textual data from the client socket. First, it gets an `InputStream` instance using the `Socket.getInputStream()` method. To read text lines from `InputStream`, this code takes an `InputStreamReader` instance based on the given stream and a `LineNumberReader` instance based on the given reader.

```
//Get data and print them in
//the display window
String sName = lr.readLine();
String sAddr = lr.readLine();

String sGreeting = "";
if (sName != null &&
    sAddr != null)
    sGreeting = "Hello " +
    sName + " at " + sAddr +
    " !";
m_txtPane.append(
    sGreeting + "\n");

//Send response to the Socket
OutputStream rawDataOut =
socketReturn.getOutputStream();
rawDataOut.write(
    sGreeting.getBytes());
```

This code assumes that the client will send two lines of text containing a name and an e-mail address. The program reads those two lines, creates a greeting, and displays it in the text area. Then the program uses the `getOutputStream` method to open an `OutputStream` instance to send a response back to the client. It then writes the greeting text to that stream.

```
            // Close all
            lr.close();
            r.close();
            rawDataIn.close();
            rawDataOut.close();

            socketReturn.close();
        }
        catch( UnknownHostException e)
        {
            m_txtPane.append(
            "Unable to find Server. Error"
            + e + "\n");
        }
        catch( IOException e )
        {
            m_txtPane.append(
            "IO Error has been raised. Error "
            + e + "\n");
        }
    }
}
```

This code closes all streams that are opened for the connection, as well as for the socket. Note that UnknownHostException and IOException have to be caught in the body of the run() method. The program will display an error message if these exceptions occur.

```
public static void main(String argv[])
{
    new MyServer();
}
```

The main() method simply creates an instance of the MyServer class.

```
// Window Adapter
class WndAdapter extends WindowAdapter
{
    public void windowClosing(WindowEvent e)
    {
        e.getWindow().dispose();
        System.exit(0);
    }
}
}
```

The WndAdapter class is responsible for closing the application when the user attempts to close the frame.

At this point, save and compile the program. However, before you run it, we need to look at how to implement the client example. This Java application will use the user interface described earlier in the last chapter, so you can see how to get a real use from the Java program.

Create a text file labeled MyClient.java, and enter the following code (which is also available on the Companion CD-ROM for this book):

```java
import java.awt.*;
import java.awt.event.*;
import java.net.*;
import java.io.*;


public class MyClient extends Frame implements ActionListener
{

    TextField m_txtName;
    TextField m_txtAddress;
    Button    m_btnProceed;
    TextArea  m_txtMessages;

    // Constructor
    MyClient()
    {
        super("The Client");
        setLayout(new FlowLayout());
        setSize(450, 250);

        Label lblWelcom = new Label("Welcome To My Web Site", Label.CENTER);
        lblWelcom.setFont(new Font("TimesRoman",Font.PLAIN,24));
        add(lblWelcom);

        Panel pn = new Panel();
        pn.setLayout(new GridLayout(2, 2, 10, 3));

        Label lbl1 = new Label("Please Enter Your Name:", Label.RIGHT);
        pn.add(lbl1);
        m_txtName = new TextField(20);
        pn.add(m_txtName);

        Label lbl2 = new Label("Your E-Mail Address:", Label.RIGHT);
        pn.add(lbl2);
        m_txtAddress = new TextField(20);
        pn.add(m_txtAddress);
```

```java
        add(pn);

        m_btnProceed = new Button("Connect");
        m_btnProceed.addActionListener(this);
        add(m_btnProceed);

        m_txtMessages = new TextArea(5, 40);
        m_txtMessages.setEditable(false);
        add(m_txtMessages);

        addWindowListener(new WndAdapter());
        setVisible(true);
    }

    public void actionPerformed(ActionEvent e)
    {
        if (e.getSource() == m_btnProceed)
            connectToServer();
    }

    // Connect to the server
    public void connectToServer()
    {
        //Initialize Socket
        Socket theClientSocket = null;

        try
        {
            InetAddress iaddr = InetAddress.getLocalHost();
            System.out.println("Server: "+iaddr.getHostAddress());
            //Instantiate a new Socket
            theClientSocket = new Socket(iaddr, 1055);
            theClientSocket.setSoTimeout(5000);
        }
        catch ( IOException e )
        {
            m_txtMessages.append("An IO error has been raised. Error " +
e.getMessage()+"\n");
            return;
        }

        // Send Data to Server and get response
        try
        {
            OutputStream DataOut = theClientSocket.getOutputStream();
            String str1 = m_txtName.getText()+"\n";
```

```
                    DataOut.write(str1.getBytes());
                    String str2 = m_txtAddress.getText()+"\n";
                    DataOut.write(str2.getBytes());

                    InputStream DataIn = theClientSocket.getInputStream();
                    InputStreamReader r = new InputStreamReader(DataIn);
                    LineNumberReader lr = new LineNumberReader(r);
                    String str = lr.readLine();
                    if (str != null)
                        m_txtMessages.append(str + "\n");

                    // Close all
                    DataOut.close();
                    lr.close();
                    r.close();
                    DataIn.close();

                    theClientSocket.close();
                }
            catch(Exception e)
            {
                System.err.println("Error: "+ e.getMessage());
            }

        }


    public static void main(String argv[])
    {
        new MyClient();
    }

    //  Window Adapter
    class WndAdapter extends WindowAdapter
    {
        public void windowClosing(WindowEvent e)
        {
            e.getWindow().dispose();
            System.exit(0);
        }
    }
}
```

Let's pause to consider the code in detail:

```java
import java.awt.*;
import java.awt.event.*;
import java.net.*;
import java.io.*;

public class MyClient extends Frame implements ActionListener
{

    TextField m_txtName;
    TextField m_txtAddress;
    Button    m_btnProceed;
    TextArea  m_txtMessages;
```

This code imports some necessary packages and declares the MyClient class to extend the java.awt.Frame class and implement the ActionListener interface. Finally, four GUI components are declared as class-wide variables.

```java
// Constructor
MyClient()
{
    super("The Client");
    setLayout(new FlowLayout());
    setSize(450, 250);
```

The constructor for this application first creates a parent object—a frame entitled "The Client." Then it creates a user interface, which contains two TextFields with corresponding Labels—a Button, and a TextArea.

Note: This user interface should not be new to you; it was discussed in Chapter 7.

```java
public void actionPerformed(ActionEvent e)
{
    if(e.getSource() == m_btnProceed)
        connectToServer();
    }
}
```

If the button for this program is clicked, the method will be invoked and, in turn, will call the connectToServer() method.

```java
// Connect to the server
public void connectToServer()
{
    //Initialize Socket
    Socket theClientSocket = null;
```

```
try
{
    InetAddress iaddr = InetAddress.getLocalHost();
    System.out.println("Server: "+iaddr.getHostAddress());
    //Instantiate a new Socket
    theClientSocket = new Socket(iaddr, 1055);
    theClientSocket.setSoTimeout(5000);
}
catch ( IOException e )
{
    m_txtMessages.append("An IO error has been raised. Error " +
e.getMessage()+"\n");
    return;
}
```

The connectToServer() method, which performs the connection to the server, is the most interesting part of this application. First, it declares a Socket reference: theClientSocket. Then, in a try/catch block, it does the following:

- Takes and prints the InetAddress for this machine.

- Creates an instance of Socket for this InetAddress using port 1055.

- Sets timeout value of that Socket to 5,000 milliseconds (5 seconds).

Note that IOException has to be caught. The program will display an error message if this exception occurs.

```
// Send Data to Server and get response
try
{
    OutputStream DataOut = theClientSocket.getOutputStream();
    String str1 = m_txtName.getText()+"\n";
    DataOut.write(str1.getBytes());
    String str2 = m_txtAddress.getText()+"\n";
    DataOut.write(str2.getBytes());

    InputStream DataIn = theClientSocket.getInputStream();
    InputStreamReader r = new InputStreamReader(DataIn);
    LineNumberReader lr = new LineNumberReader(r);
    String str = lr.readLine();
    if (str != null)
        m_txtMessages.append(str + "\n");
```

At this point, we have established a connection to the server. Now we are ready to use streams. The program takes an OutputStream instance by using the Socket.getOutputStream() method and writes two text strings (with the end-of-line symbol "\n") to that stream.

Now we're ready for a response from the server. For that, we get an InputStream using the Socket.getInputStream() method. To read text lines from InputStream, this code takes an InputStreamReader instance based on the given stream and a LineNumberReader instance based on the given reader. Then the program reads a single line of text from the InputStream and displays it.

```
        // Close all
        DataOut.close();
        lr.close();
        r.close();
        DataIn.close();

        theClientSocket.close();
    }
    catch(Exception e)
    {
        System.err.println("Error: "+ e.getMessage());
    }

}
```

This part of the connectToServer() method closes all streams and the socket. Note that all exceptions thrown in the code described previously will be caught here.

```
public static void main(String argv[])
{
    new MyClient();
}
```

The main() method simply creates an instance of the MyServer class.

```
// Window Adapter
class WndAdapter extends WindowAdapter
{
    public void windowClosing(WindowEvent e)
    {
        e.getWindow().dispose();
        System.exit(0);
    }
}
```

The WndAdapter class is responsible for closing the application when the user clicks the Close system button. An identical adapter was described earlier in this chapter.

At this point, save and compile `MyClient.java`, but do not execute it just yet. The next section will show you what to do in order to execute both the client and the server applications you have just created.

Putting the Server & Client to Work

In order for this example to work, you must have established an Internet connection using CompuServe 3.0 or some other Internet service provider (ISP). For the sake of simplicity, both the client and the server will reside on the same system. Naturally, in more complex solutions, it is quite possible for the server and the client to reside on different systems.

Once you have your connection, run the server application by typing **javaw MyServer** in the command window. Then run the client application on the same machine by typing **javaw MyClient** in the command window. Enter some data and click on the Connect button. Notice how client-server communication works. Finally, run another instance of the client application on the same machine by typing **javaw MyClient** in the command window. Enter some data, and click the Connect button on that client. Figure 8-3 shows an example.

Figure 8-3: A server and two client applications at work.

What Is javaw.exe?

The javaw.exe is a utility supplied by the Java Development Kit (JDK) 1.1 that works like java.exe; however javaw.exe disconnects the Java program from the command window as soon as the process is started, thereby freeing up the command window so you can type another command.

Please note that these applications are simple examples and have been designed to run on the same machine. Nonetheless, communications among multiple machines can be established in the same way, although a comprehensive description of these items lies beyond the scope of this book. We'll limit ourselves to outlining the main features to be implemented in such a program:

- You need to know the URL address of the server and use it on the client side when creating a socket connection.

- On the server's side, you must create a Thread instance for every client to perform real data reading and writing functions to the communication streams between the server and client.

- On the client's side, create an interface allowing real communication. Try to check user's mistakes as much as possible.

Moving On

In this chapter, you had an introduction to network programming in Java. You learned about some of the higher-level solutions as well as the lower-level ones by using various classes from the java.net package. This chapter is by no means comprehensive; but with the text and examples, you should have had a good introduction.

In the next chapter, you will learn about Java archives and trusted applets. Specifically, you will learn how to enable a Java applet (through digital signatures), how to have its origin verified, and how to free the applet from so many security restrictions.

Java Archives &
Trusted Applets

This chapter is going to give you a hands-on look at two complementary concepts that are somewhat new to Java (they were added as of Java 1.1): Java ARchives (JAR) files and trusted applets.

JAR files can be used to house everything you need for your Java applets. This includes sound, image, compiled class files, and so on. You can also specify to add entire directories recursively to a JAR file. You then can use these JAR files to more efficiently download Java applets and any of their supporting files in a single and optionally secure format. You will learn how to use jar.exe from the Java Development Kit (JDK) to create your own JAR files.

The concept of JAR files in Java is closely related to the idea of trusted applets. You will learn how to create trusted applets by using digital signatures that allow an applet to leave the sandbox on the client computer and perform actions once reserved only for applications. As a demonstration, we will use one of the examples you worked with previously.

Note: The concepts of compression and security on the Net are advanced topics. This chapter assumes that you have at least a high-level understanding of these concepts as well as an understanding of the vocabulary so that we may focus specifically on how to use these two technologies in Java. If you are in need of a more detailed overview, please refer to Chapters 5 and 6 of Ventana's *Migrating From Java 1.0 to Java 1.1* [ISBN: 1-56604-686-6].

Introduction to JAR Files

The realistic advantage of using JAR technology is that it takes designated files (and/or directories) and compresses them (using ZIP compression technology from PKWARE) into one file. In fact, a JAR file is nothing more than a ZIP archive that contains a Java program.

When users download an applet, only one HyperText Transfer Protocol (HTTP) transaction will need to take place to download the entire applet and all its supporting files if you have archived all your files in a JAR file. Furthermore, each of the entries in a JAR file is compressed (unless otherwise instructed), reducing each file's size and the size of the JAR file as a whole. This compression reduces the download time as well.

Understanding JAR File Formats & Concepts

A JAR file is, in essence, a ZIP file. You can open any JAR file using a ZIP tool (for instance, WinZip) either to see the file's contents or to manipulate files compressed into the Java archive. The only difference between a JAR file and a ZIP file is that a Java archive automatically adds one system file. This file—the *manifest file*—contains information about the archive to which it belongs. Furthermore, the file is an integral part of security and trusted applets, which we'll discuss later in this chapter. The attractive features of Java archives include:

- JAR files are cross-platform archives.

- JAR files are backward compatible with existing Java applications and applets.

- JAR files can handle any kind of files, including class files, images, audio clips, and anything else that may be used by the applet. Typically, in the context of Web pages, the HTML documents and associated multimedia components are combined into a JAR file.

- JAR files are part of a standard for compression in software development, because they're based on the ZIP format.

Using the jar.exe Tool

One of the new tools added to the JDK is jar.exe. This tool is actually a compiled Java application that uses the java.util.zip package. This tool lets you archive a specified list of files (or directories) into one compressed file, making it quick, efficient, and effective for download from the Net. In this section, you will receive a demonstration of jar's functionality and usefulness in the Windows environment. For information on using jar with other environments, consult the Java 1.1 JAR site at http://java.sun.com/products/JDK/1.1/docs/guide/jar/index.html.

Using java.util.zip Directly

The ZIP functionality for Java belongs to the java.util.zip package. It is the key package used by the jar tool and can also be used directly in your Java programs. Since most solutions will find the jar tool more than sufficient, we will not discuss how to use java.util.zip directly. However, if you are interested in such a discussion, please refer to the second half of Chapter 5 in Ventana's *Migrating From Java 1.0 to Java 1.1* [ISBN: 1-56604-686-6].

Syntax

The jar command line tool is very simple to use. For example, consider the following:

```
jar -cf test *.*
```

Entering this code in a command line with the JDK properly installed will generate the file test.jar, which represents the JAR file. Looking at it from left to right, starting with the parameter options, -c means that you are specifying to create a new archive. The -f specifies that you are giving the archive a name test. The *.* means that you wish to have every file in the current directory. If the directory contains any subdirectories, they (and the files contained within them) are also included. Table 9-1 shows a listing of the various options (and their descriptions) used by the jar utility.

Option	Definition
c	Creates a new archive.
f	Specifies the JAR file. If used with c, then this option specifies the JAR file to be created. If used with t, then this option specifies the JAR file to be listed. If used with x, then this option specifies the JAR file to be extracted.
m	Specifies an existing manifest file to use.
M	Creates an archive without creating a manifest file.
v	Generates verbose output during the execution of the jar tool.
t	Lists all the entries in a JAR file.
x	Extracts the files from a JAR file. If specific files are named, then only those files will be extracted.
0	Creates the archive without using any compression.

Table 9-1: Options for jar utility.

TIP

The jar tool in the JDK is very similar to the TAR command used in UNIX-based environments.

The following subsections show you a standard jar session in which you will see, first, how to create a JAR file, second, how to read information in an existing JAR file, and third, how to extract the file's contents.

Creating a JAR File

At this point, let's take a closer look at using the jar tool. Figure 9-1 shows a directory containing some files (and other directories).

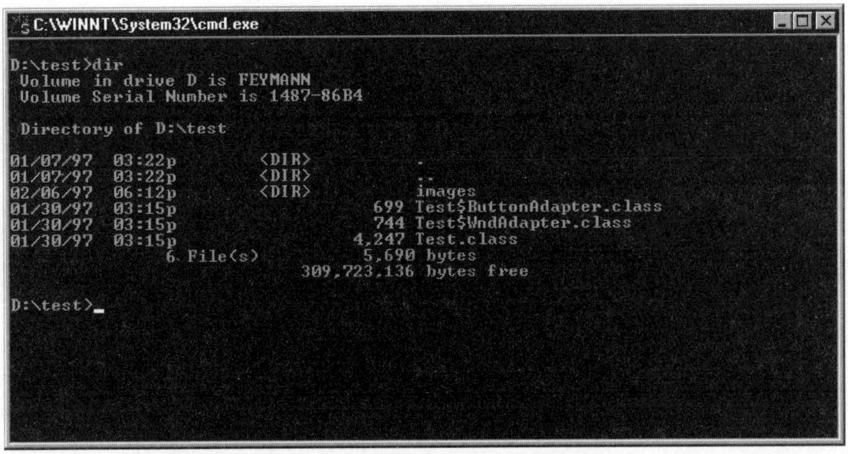

Figure 9-1: List of files and one directory in the D:\test directory.

Notice in Figure 9-1 that there are a few compiled class files and a directory called images. Inside this directory is a list of images in a Graphics Interchange Format (GIF) or Joint Photographic Experts Group (JPEG) format. At this point, the following is entered at the command line:

```
jar cvf test.jar *
```

Above, c specifies that you are creating a new archive. Second, v will display the verbose output for each entry. Finally, f lets you specify a filename for your JAR file, which in this case will be test.jar.

Figure 9-2 shows what the previous line would look like.

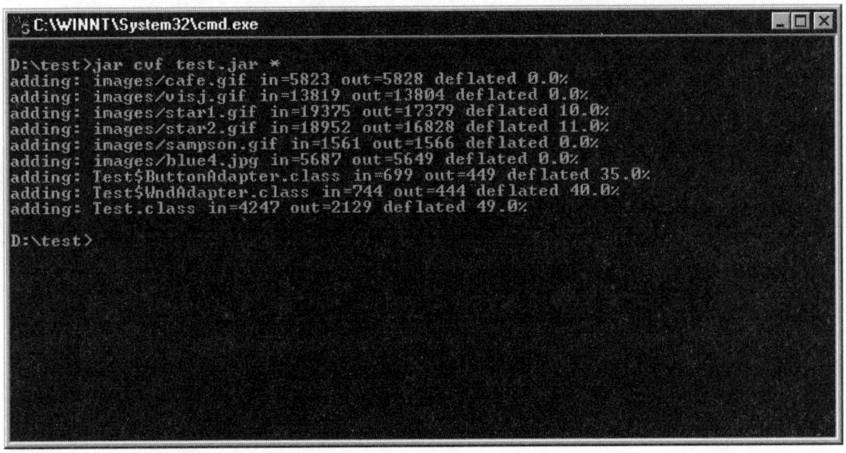

Figure 9-2: Creating the test.jar file.

TIP

Alternatively, you can specify specific files (and/or directories) to be included, leaving any unspecified entries out. For instance, using our example with the D:\test directory:

```
jar cvf test2.jar Test.class images
```

This would create the test2.jar *file containing only the* Test.class *file and the contents of the* \images\ *directory.*

Notice in Figure 9-2 that verbose information for each file (including those contained in the \images\ directory) is displayed. Table 9-2 explains each of the options described in the verbose using the last entry in the figure.

Filename	File Size (bytes)	Compressed File Size (bytes)	Deflated (percent)
Test.class	in = 4247	out = 2129	49.0%

Table 9-2: Understanding the verbose for an entry.

The JAR file test.jar now has been created and can be used in Java.

Looking at a JAR File

There may come a time when you will come across a JAR file that you created some time ago, but you can't remember what's inside. In such a case, it will be useful to have a way to look at the file's contents. You can do this by using the t option in jar.

Figure 9-3 shows a new directory, D:\test2. It is empty except for the test.jar file that was just created in the last section.

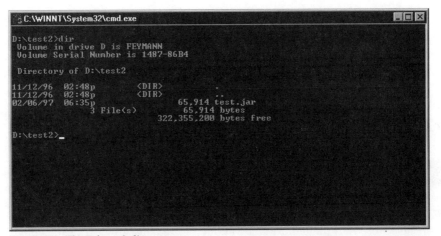

Figure 9-3: The D:\test2 directory.

The following command uses the t option:

```
jar tf test.jar
```

Using the t option, a complete list of all entries contained in the specified JAR file will be printed.

Figure 9-4 shows the result of executing the previous command.

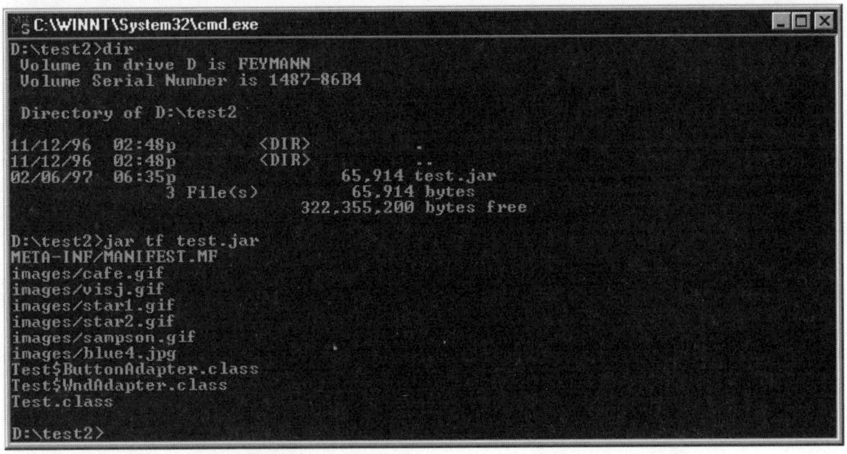

Figure 9-4: Listing the contents of test.jar.

TIP

You can also specify the v option when looking at the contents of a JAR file to get detailed information on each entry, including the uncompressed size and date the file was last modified. The following shows a basic example of how you would use the v option with the t for the test.jar file:

```
jar tvf test.jar
```

A Note on the META-INF/MANIFEST.MF Entry

If you look at the list of entries in test.jar, you will notice that the entry META-INF/MANIFEST.MF entry has been created by the jar utility.

This file stores any metainformation about the created JAR file. This includes information on each file and its MD5 and SHA hashes. Also, the file itself is stored in a readable ASCII format.

Alternatively, you can specify an existing manifest file using the m option. For example, the following creates the JAR file test2.jar and writes its manifest information to testManifest:

```
jar cmf testManifest test2.jar *
```

You will learn more about manifest files a little later on in this chapter.

Extracting a JAR file

At this point in the D:\test2 directory, you have looked at the contents of the test.jar file, but you may want to extract the files. Using the x option, the jar utility lets you do just that. The following command shows how you would extract all of the files in the test.jar archive:

```
jar xf test.jar
```

When you execute this command, nothing shows up on the screen. However, if you look at the directory, you will see that all of the files and subdirectories have been extracted (see Figure 9-5).

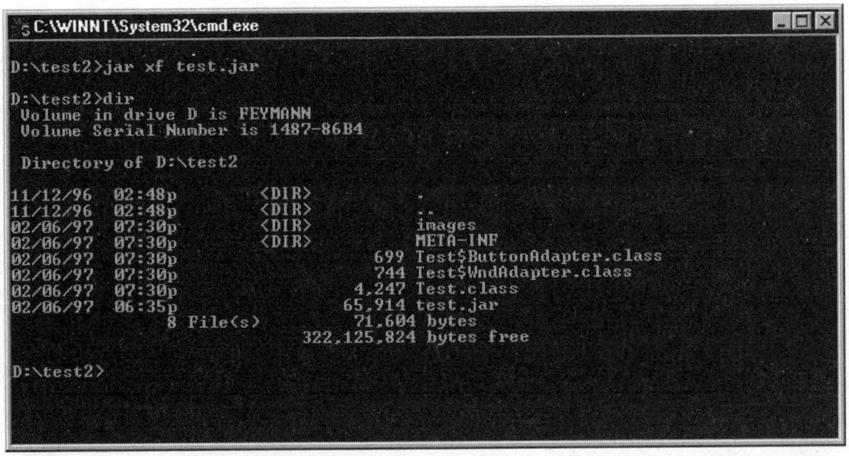

Figure 9-5: Extracting test.jar in D:\test2.

TIP

Alternatively, you can specify which files (or directories) you wish to extract. This is done by appending the names of the files or directories that you wish to extract to the command shown in the text. Consider the following:

```
jar xf test.jar Test.class images
```

If this command were executed, only the `Test.class` *file and* `\images\` *directory would be extracted from* `test.jar`.

Notice the new directory \META-INF\ in Figure 9-5. This directory contains the file `MANIFEST.MF` that contains all the metainformation about the `test.jar` file. This directory is where you would specify any digital signature files to authenticate any specific files in the `test.jar` archive. The following subsection takes a closer look at the manifest file.

Looking at the Manifest File

The manifest file is a header text file added by `jar.exe` to the JAR archives. By default, it is located in the META-INF/ directory at the top level of the path tree, with a filename META-INF/MANIFEST.MF. The manifest file starts with the version information and, optionally, may contain the required version:

```
Manifest-Version: 1.0
Required-Version: 1.0
```

Next, it contains the set of specifications for each file in the archive. Each specification contains the filename, list of hash algorithms, and base-64 representation of each hash:

```
Name: sample1.txt
Hash-Algorithms: MD5 SHA
MD5-Hash: O6dmBIP+qxMefZeevbZQuA==
SHA-Hash: kVAmg9zD7xJVzg4ArfPOutfmpDA=
```

The manifest file also contains information about any digital signature files included in the JAR archive. This section starts from the signature version and lists signature files: name, list of hash algorithms, and base-64 representation of each hash. You will learn more about how this file is useful when we discuss trusted applets in the second half of this chapter.

Specifying JARs in the <APPLET> Tag

Once you have created your applet's JAR file, the only other thing that you need to do is to specify the file in the <APPLET> tag of your HyperText Markup Language (HTML) code. You do this by specifying which JAR file(s) needs to be downloaded, using the special ARCHIVES parameter that specifies the location of a JAR file (or files) for the corresponding applet. For example:

```
<APPLET CODE="Test.class" WIDTH=300 HEIGHT=200
    <param=ARCHIVES value="Test.jar">
</APPLET>
```

TIP

The ARCHIVES *entry for the parameter specification is case sensitive.*

In the preceding snippet of code, you have the applet class Test.class and the JAR file Test.jar. If you have more than one JAR file, you can specify them in the same ARCHIVES parameter by separating the entries with plus signs (+):

```
<APPLET CODE="Test.class" WIDTH=300 HEIGHT=200
    <param=ARCHIVES value="Test.jar + Test2.jar">
</APPLET>
```

How Java Applets Look for Files

Java applets look for files in distinct order. First, any archive that has been identified will be downloaded and extracted automatically. Then, as the applet comes along and looks for a file (e.g., sound or image file), the applet looks first to the archive(s) present. If it cannot find the file there, the applet then looks to see if the file exists on the server where the applet came from or wherever the CODEBASE attribute is pointing.

JAR files make applets and applications more efficient, adding better organization and version control to programs that require several files (perhaps originating from more than one directory). Furthermore, these archives can be digitally signed and verified, thereby proving the origin of the given applet (or application) and its supporting files.

Trusted Applets

The Java security manager considers an applet trusted when the applet is digitally signed and verified (i.e., no longer under the sandbox restrictions discussed in Chapter 7). Security on the Net is a huge topic (covering many books in and of itself), so we will only touch upon a few of the theoretical topics here. In the rest of this chapter, the following topics will introduce you to the Java Security application programming interface (API):

- **Security and Java**. An introduction to the Java Security API, who it benefits, and how.

- **How security for Net software works in general**. This introduction is a quick whistle-stop tour, defining some of the buzzwords and key topics that relate to this field.

- **Using the javakey.exe JDK tool**. You will have a chance to learn about the javakey tool, used to create your own public/private key pairs as well as digital certificates.

- **Trusted applets, a demonstration**. You'll revisit TestURL (created in the last chapter and available on this book's Companion CD-ROM), to digitally sign and verify the file.

By the end of this chapter you should have a good understanding of how to create your own trusted applets. Let's get started.

Java, Security & the Security API

Security on the Internet is a big topic. And when Java introduced the concept of a Java applet, security was a very big concern. In the end, rather than having potentially dangerous applets running around on the Net, JavaSoft designed applets to have a very stringent security model. In effect, when an applet is downloaded off the Net to a user's system, a sort of firewall (commonly referred to as a *sandbox*) is set up in the user's environment, separating the applet from various resources on the user's system.

While this practically solved any potential security issues with Java, it turned into a big functionality compromise. When working with applets, what was gained in safety from a user's perspective was lost in functionality and versatility from a programmer's perspective. However, Java also has what is known as the Java Security API to help resolve this security/functionality compromise.

The purpose of the Java Security API is to give Java programs the ability to be signed when placed on a Web site and verified each time they are downloaded so one can be sure that a Java applet or application originates from where it says it does. This assures the user that an applet can be verified, that it has not been tampered with in any way, and that it is not misrepresenting its origin. The usefulness for the programmer is that a signed applet is considered "trusted" by the Java security manager for a user's Java Virtual Machine (JVM). *Trusted* means that the applet is no longer held in the sandbox model and—unless the user specifies otherwise—the applet has the freedom to access a variety of resources on the user's system. For example, a normal Java applet is not allowed to have direct access to the user's file system. However, if the applet is digitally signed and considered trusted by the user's JVM, it can have this access.

The Java Security API is not just for applets. Applications can also benefit from it. Having an application signed using the Java Security API provides an extra guarantee that it has not been tainted with any hidden agendas. For instance, many virus-type programs could append themselves to a program and piggyback their way to a specific resource on a user's system. However, if an application were digitally signed, an anomaly would be detected during the actual verification process that would alert the user that something has changed.

Introduction to Security on the Net

The security features and tools implemented in Java are based on the same standard security model used on the Net for a wide variety of entities. Specifically, an *entity* can be an individual, organization, or corporation that wants to transmit information securely from one point to another. Information transmission can refer to sending e-mail, transferring software via a File Transfer Protocol (FTP) site, or loading a Web site.

Security stems from the need for both privacy and safety. The available security technologies give users privacy from being "listened to" on the Net. This makes everyone more comfortable when relaying any kind of personal or otherwise confidential information. Security technologies also enhance safety, preventing viruses or other entities with malicious intent from tainting or intercepting information without being detected and/or blocked.

Security is attained by using one form or another of *encryption*. Encryption is a process that makes data indecipherable except to those who have the *key*. If an entity has the key to a piece of data, the entity can view the otherwise-scrambled data. Encryption is very useful when data are in transit (e.g., over the Net) or in storage (e.g., on a server). It is very safe because it does not permit any portion of the data to be read, tampered with, or deleted without detection.

Public key encryption is the type of encryption most commonly used on the Net. This is based on a public/private key pair. The public key contains only the functionality to encrypt the data, and the private key contains only the functionality to decrypt the data. Further, if someone steals one of the keys (for example, the public key), it is usually impossible to decipher the corresponding key. In a typical session, the sender encrypts the data using the public key, then sends the data along with the private key to the receiver. The receiver then unscrambles the encrypted data with the private key.

The idea behind this type of encryption is very simple. You have a piece of data and the public/private key pair that has been created specifically for the data. Using the public key, you can encrypt and send the data along with the corresponding private key. The receiver then takes the private key and decrypts the data. In this way, only the sender and receiver will be able to read the data. This thwarts anyone else from trying to listen to, append, or mutilate the data in transit or steal the data afterward. Unless someone has the unique private key created for that particular piece of data, he or she would not be able to decode the message. Figure 9-6 shows a model of a typical encrypted session.

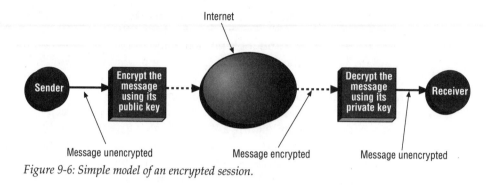

Figure 9-6: Simple model of an encrypted session.

Using the javakey Tool

To manage a database of entities (people, companies, etc.) and their public and private keys and certificates, the JDK provides a tool called javakey.exe. This tool can also generate and verify signatures for JAR files. The following shows the basic syntax to use this command:

`javakey [`*`options`*`]`

Options may be specified with or without a preceding minus sign (-), but only one option may be specified each time you issue the javakey command. This command-line tool uses the SUN security provider.

> **TIP**
>
> *Alternatively, you can use a third-party provider or one of your own design. It allows you to generate and verify digital signatures for JAR files. If such a file is signed, it confirms that a file came from the specified person, department, or organization (referred to as the* signer*). To generate a signature for a particular file, the signer first must have the public and private keys associated with that file and also one or more certificates authenticating its public key.*

Options to Support the Database of Entities

The javakey.exe tool is used to build and maintain a database of entities and their keys and certificates, including a flag that indicates whether each entity is considered trusted. Currently the JDK supports one database per installation.

The following subsections define options (and combinations of options) most commonly used to support a database of entities. Let's take a closer look:

-c option   This option creates a new identity specified by *UserName*. The optional flag (true or false) specifies whether or not the identity is to be considered trusted. The default is false.

```
-c UserName {true|false}
```

The following example creates a trusted identity John:

```
javakey -c John true
```

-cs option   This option creates a new signer specified by *SignerName*. The optional flag (true or false) specifies whether or not the identity is to be considered trusted. The default is false.

```
-cs SignerName {true|false}
```

The following example creates a trusted signer John:

```
javakey -cs John true
```

-t option   This option sets or resets the trust flag for the identity or signer specified by *UserName*.

```
-t UserName {true|false}
```

The following example sets a signer John to be untrusted:

```
javakey -t John false
```

-l option   This option displays a brief list of information about all entities (identities and signers) in the database currently managed by the javakey tool.

```
-l
```

The following example lists all registered signers:

```
javakey -l
```

-ld option   This option displays a list of detailed information about all entities (identities and signers) in the database managed by javakey.

```
-ld
```

The following example lists all registered signers:

```
javakey -ld
```

-li option   This option displays detailed information about the identity or signer specified by *UserName*.

`-li UserName`

The following example requests information about the signer John:

`javakey -li John`

-r option   This option removes the identity or signer specified by *UserName* from the database.

`-r UserName`

The following example removes signer John:

`javakey -r John`

Options to Manage Keys in the Database

This subsection introduces the various options using javakey to manage the actual key pairs.

-ik option   This option imports the public key from the file *PubKeyFile* for the identity or signer specified by *UserName*. The key must be in X509 format.

`-ik UserName PubKeyFile`

The following example imports the public key for the signer John from file pubJohn.key:

`javakey -ik John pubJohn.key`

> **TIP**
>
> *X509 is a digital certificate version that is used by the Java Security API. For our purposes, it is only important to know that Java specifically uses the X509 certificate.*

-ikp option   This option imports the public key from the file *PubKeyFile* and private from the file *PrivKeyFile* for the identity or signer specified by *UserName*. The keys must be in X.509 format.

`-ikp UserName PubKeyFile PrivKeyFile`

The following example imports the key pair for the signer John from files pubJohn.key and privJohn.key:

`javakey -ikp John pubJohn.key privJohn.key`

-ic option   This option imports the public key certificate from the file `CertKeyFile` for the identity or signer specified by `UserName`. If a public key for `UserName` was already defined in the database, javakey verifies that it is the same as the public key defined in `CertKeyFile`. Otherwise, javakey will report an error. If the `UserName` does not yet have a public key associated with it, javakey will create the association, using the public key in `CertKeyFile`.

`-ic UserName CertKeyFile`

The following example imports the public key certificate for the signer John from file `pubJohn.crt`:

`javakey -ic John pubJohn.crt`

-ii option   This option sets information for the identity or signer specified by `UserName`. For this option, javakey prompts "Please enter the info for this identity." To finish entering, type a period (.) on a single line. Entered text information will be reported by -ld and -li options.

`-ii UserName`

The following example enters information for the signer John:

`javakey -ii John`

-gk option   This option generates a public/private pair for the signer specified by `UserName` using the specified `Algorithm`. Keys generated will have the length `KeySize` bits (KeySize must be a number between 512 and 1024, inclusively). If a parameter `PubKeyFile` is specified, the public key will be written to that file. If a parameter `PrivKeyFile` also is specified, the private key will be written to that file.

`-gk UserName Algorithm KeySize {PubKeyFile} {PrivKeyFile}`

> **TIP**
>
> *The `javakey` tool always generates signatures using the Digital Signature Algorithm (DSA). Nevertheless, you must explicitly specify "DSA" as the parameter for the -gk option. This is because future versions will no doubt support other signature algorithms.*

The following example generates the key pair of 512 bits for the signer John and writes them into `pubJojn.key` and `privJojn.key` files:

`javakey -gk John DSA 512 pubJojn.key privJojn.key`

-g option   This option is the same as –gk option.

`-g UserName Algorithm KeySize {PubKeyFile} {PrivKeyFile}`

-gc option   This option generates a certificate according to information supplied in the `DirectiveFile`. The directive file is a text file that you supply using the following information:

- The signer signing the certificate (required).
- The subject—the entity whose public key is being authenticated (required).
- The certificate itself (required).
- The name of the file used to store a copy of the certificate (optional).

    `-gc DirectiveFile`

Note: All lines in the directive file that start with the equal and parallel symbol (#) are considered comment lines.

The directive file may contain the keywords described in Table 9-3.

Keyword	Meaning	Required?
`issuer.name`	Issuer's name	Yes
`issuer.cert`	1-based index of certificate stored in the database generated in previous steps	Yes
`subject.name`	Short name of subject (user that will use the public key)	Yes
`subject.real.name`	Full name of subject of certificate	Yes
`subject.org`	Name of the subject's organization	Yes
`subject.org.unit`	Name of the division of the subject	Yes
`subject.country`	Country of the subject	Yes
`start.date`	Beginning date of certificate	Yes
`end.date`	Expiration date of certificate	Yes
`serial.number`	Unique serial number of certificate	Yes
`out.file`	Name of output filename for certificate	No

Table 9-3: Keywords for certificate directive file.

The following generates a certificate file according to the *CertFile.dir*:

```
javakey -gc CertFile.dir
```

Here is a sample of how a typical directive file might look:

```
# Information about the issuer (required).
issuer.name=John

# The certificate to use (required).
issuer.cert=1

# Information about the subject (required).
subject.name=James
subject.real.name= James Birch
subject.org=RSAW
subject.org.unit= RSAW Systems
subject.country=USA

# Information about the certificate.
#(required)
start.date=1 Jan 1997
end.date=1 Jan 1998
serial.number=1033

# Filename for the copy of the certificate
#(optional).
out.file= CertFile.cer
```

-dc option   This option displays the certificate stored in the file *CertFile*.

```
-dc CertFile
```

The following example displays the certificate stored in the file CertFile.cer:

```
javakey -dc CertFile.cer
```

-gs option   This option signs the specified JAR file according to information supplied in the *DirectiveFile* (see Table 9-4).

```
-gs DirectiveFile JarFile
```

Keyword	Meaning	Required?
Signer	Name of the signer stored in the database	Yes
Cert	1-based index of certificate stored in the database generated in previous steps	Yes
Chain	Currently not supported	N/A
signature.file	Filename for generated signature and associated signature block (cannot exceed 8 characters)	No

Table 9-4: Keywords for JAR directive file.

The following signs a JAR file according to `CertJAR.dir`:

```
javakey -gs CertJAR.dir Sample.jar
```

Here's how a sample JAR directive might look:

```
# Which signer to use.
signer=John

# Certificate number to use for this signer.
cert=1

# Certificate chain depth.
chain=0

# The name to give to the generated signature.
signature.file=JOHNSIGN
```

Digital Signatures for Java Applets

Now let's put it all together and define all the steps necessary to sign a Java applet. In this demonstration, we are going to sign the applet `MyApplet.class`, assuming that `MyApplet` has been written, compiled, and executed locally to test that it works.

TIP

To make the task simpler, you should design your applets as appletcations, facilitating a `main()` method as described in Chapter 7, and giving the program the ability to be tested as an applet or an application.

Step 1: Create the Archive

Create a JAR file as described earlier in this chapter. Here's a sample command to compress all class files from the current directory to MyApplet.jar file:

```
jar cvf MyApplet.jar *.class
```

Step 2: Create the Signer in the javakey Database

Create your signer entity in the javakey database. Here's a sample command to create a new trusted signer entity:

```
javakey -cs MySigner true
```

No new files are created, but an entry in your javakey database has been generated. To verify that this operation has completed successfully, use the list command:

```
javakey -li MySigner
```

At this point, you have neither keys nor certificates registered for your signer, so let's go ahead and create them.

Step 3: Generate the Key Pair & the X509 Certificate

Now you need to generate a key pair for MyApplet and an X509 certificate. Start with the generation of the key pair:

```
javakey -gk MySigner DSA 512 MyKey.public MyKey.private
```

The Java documentation encourages you to create your own certificates by using the javakey utility; however, an alternative could involve obtaining an X509 certificate from some third party. If you do not wish to obtain a certificate, you will need to write a directive file for it by following the directions outlined earlier in the chapter. The following shows how you would generate a certificate specifying the directive file MySigner.cert:

```
javakey -gc MySigner.cert
```

> **TIP**
>
> *Naturally, the certificates you create will have more limited legitimacy than those obtained from a recognized third-party CA (Certificate Authority). So, in cases in which your users require a high degree of security, the preferred way is to obtain your certificate from a CA. There are a number of CAs available on the Net (e.g., http://www.verisgn.com).*

As soon as you've got the key pair and the certificate, you need to import them into your signer's database. Here's an example:

```
javakey -ic MySigner MySigner.x509
```

To verify that you are done, use the list command:

```
javakey -li MySigner
```

At this point, you should have both keys and certificates registered for your signer.

Step 4: Sign Your Applet

Now you're ready to actually sign your applet. Prepare your signing directive file MyApplet.sign as shown earlier in the chapter, and execute the following command:

```
javakey -gs MyApplet.sign MyApplet.jar
```

This will add two associated files to your JAR file—MISIGN.SF and MISIGN.DSA. More important, it also will create a signed copy of your MyApplet.jar file named MyApplet.jar.sig.

Step 5: Create the HTML File & Run the Signed Applet

Now you can actually run your signed applet and enjoy freedom from the sandbox imposed on untrusted applets. The following gives you a snippet of the <APPLET> tag for the HTML file that you would use for this example:

```
<applet
archive="MyApplet.jar.sig"
code= MyApplet
width=400
height=200>
</applet>
```

Example: Signing TestURL

In this example, you are going to go through the steps outlined in the last section and sign TestURL. As you learned in Chapter 8, TestURL is a Java program that demonstrates creating a network connection to a specified Uniform Resource Locator (URL) in Java. However, this network connection functionality is available only to trusted Java programs (i.e., Java applications and trusted applets). So, in this section, we are going to take TestURL (which requires trusted status to get data from the specified URL) and digitally sign it, thereby giving it the ability to run as a Java applet.

If you did not try the TestURL *example in Chapter 8, copy the file* TestURL.jar *from this book's Companion CD-ROM and proceed to "Trying the Applet Without Digitally Signing It," two subsections later.*

Create the TestURL.jar Archive

Using the jar JDK tool, take the TestURL class files (TestURL$ActAdapter.class, TestURL$WndAdapter.class, and TestURL.class) and generate a JAR archive called TestURL.jar:

```
jar cvf TestURL.jar *.class
```

Figure 9-7 shows the previous command line in action.

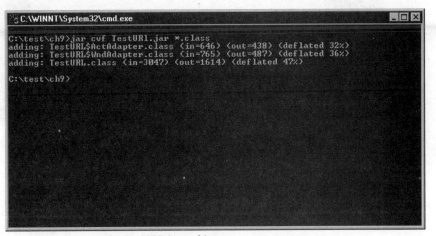

Figure 9-7: Creating the TestURL.jar archive.

Try the Applet Without Digitally Signing It

With the TestURL.jar archive created, let's go ahead and see what might happen if we were to execute the applet without signing it. First, we have to create an HTML file to run the applet. In your text editor, create a file called index.html, and enter the following:

```
<APPLET
        ARCHIVE = "TestURL.jar"
        CODE    = TestURL
        WIDTH   = 450  HEIGHT = 400
        ALIGN   = top
    >
```

```
<PARAM NAME = URL VALUE =
    "http://www.netscape.com">
```

```
</APPLET>
```

Save the file in the same directory as the `TestURL.jar` archive that you just created. Using the `appletviewer` in the JDK 1.1, execute `TestURL` using the `index.html` file (see Figure 9-8).

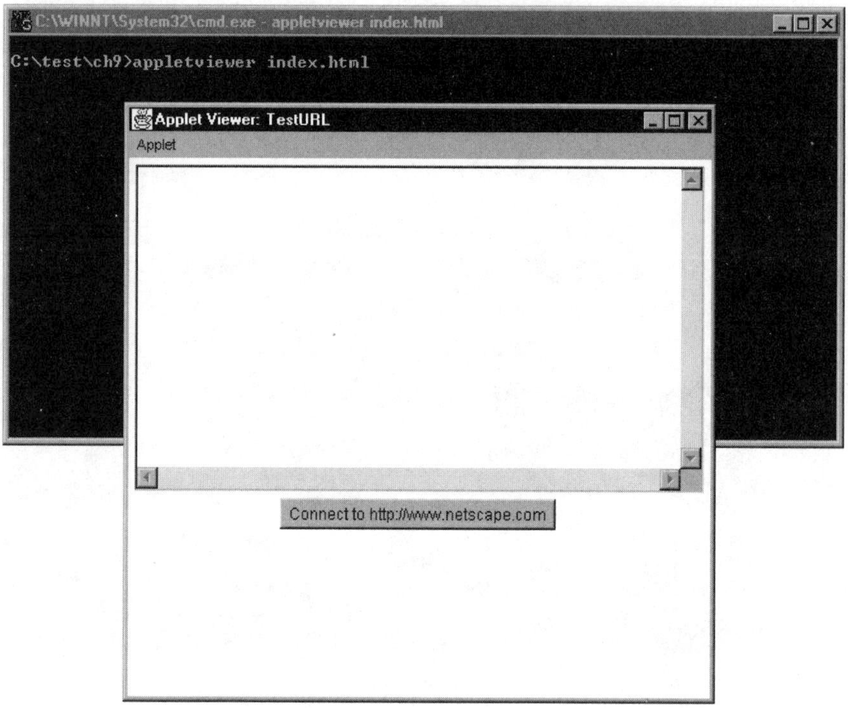

Figure 9-8: Executing TestURL without its being digitally signed.

When the `TestURL` applet loads, notice that a security exception is raised (see Figure 9-9). As you can see, running `TestURL` as an applet causes a security exception when it tries to make a connection to the URL. So, it is obvious that we need to digitally sign the applet to allow `TestURL` to do its job.

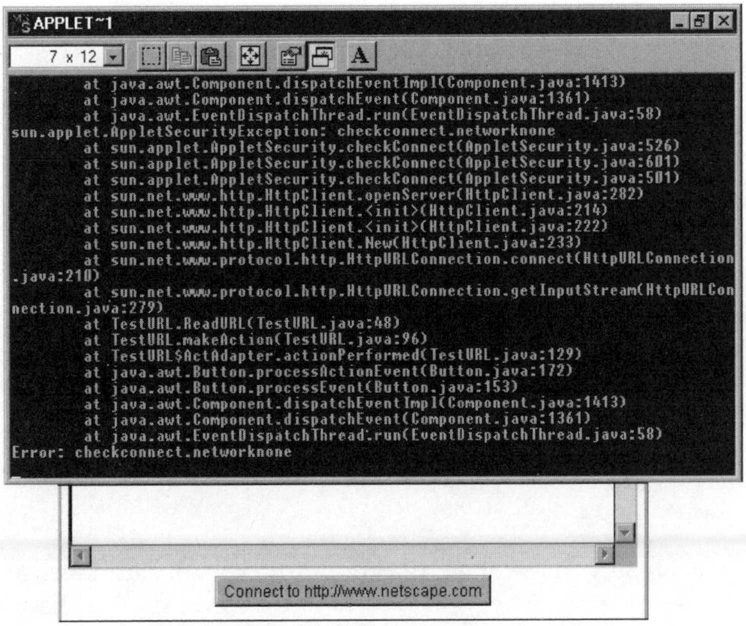

Figure 9-9: Unsigned TestURL with a security exception raised.

Note: When you create a newly signed copy of your TestURL.jar file, the suffix .sig will be appended to the JAR filename. So you will need to change the name of your archive (or rename your signed archive) attribute in index.html. Details on how and when to do this follow.

Create URLSigner in the javakey Database

To start, you need to create an identity signer for TestURL. In this case, enter the following command line to create the URLSigner signer for our TestURL example:

```
javakey cs URLSigner true
```

Enter the following to verify what you have done:

```
javakey li URLSigner
```

Figure 9-10 shows both of the prior commands executed.

Figure 9-10: Creating and viewing URLSigner.

As you can see in Figure 9-10, there are no keys or certificates present in URLSigner (at least not yet). So, now that we have a signer, we need to create a key pair and certificate from TestURL to add to URLSigner.

Generate the Key Pair & the X509 Certificate

Now you are ready to generate a key pair for our TestURL example. The following shows the command line to do this:

```
javakey gk URLSigner DSA 512 URLKey.public URLKey.private
```

This specifies the algorithm and number of bits in the certificate. Figure 9-11 shows this code in action.

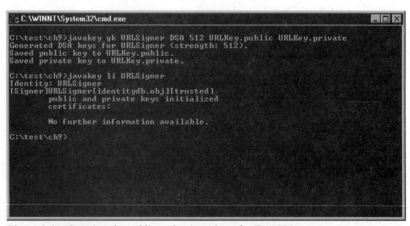

Figure 9-11: Creating the public and private keys for TestURL.

Generating the key pair may take a few moments. Even if there is no disk activity, be patient.

Next, you need to create a certificate for TestURL. However, before you run off and generate it, you need to create a directive file. In a new text file called URLKey.cert, enter the following:

```
# This is an example certificate directive file.
issuer.name=URLSigner

# The cert to use for the signing.
issuer.cert=1

# The id of the subject.
subject.name=URLSigner

# The components of the X500 name for the subject.
subject.real.name=URLSigner
subject.org.unit=MyOrg.unit
subject.org=MyOrg
subject.country=US

# Various parameters: start and end date for validity and expiration
# of the certificate. Serial number. File to which to output the
# certificate (optional).
start.date=17 Jan 1997
end.date=16 Jan 1998
serial.number=1001
out.file=URLKey.x509
```

With the directive file at hand, execute the following, specifying the directive file URLKey.cert to generate the certificate:

```
javakey gc URLKey.cert
```

Generating the certificate may take a few moments. Even if there is no disk activity, be patient.

Once this completes successfully, the certificate URLKey.x509 will be generated. You then will need to add URLKey.x509 to URLSigner using the following command:

```
javakey ic URLSigner URLKey.x509
```

To make sure everything is in order, execute the following command to list all the information about the URLSigner entry:

```
javakey li URLSigner
```

Figure 9-12 shows the previous three commands in action.

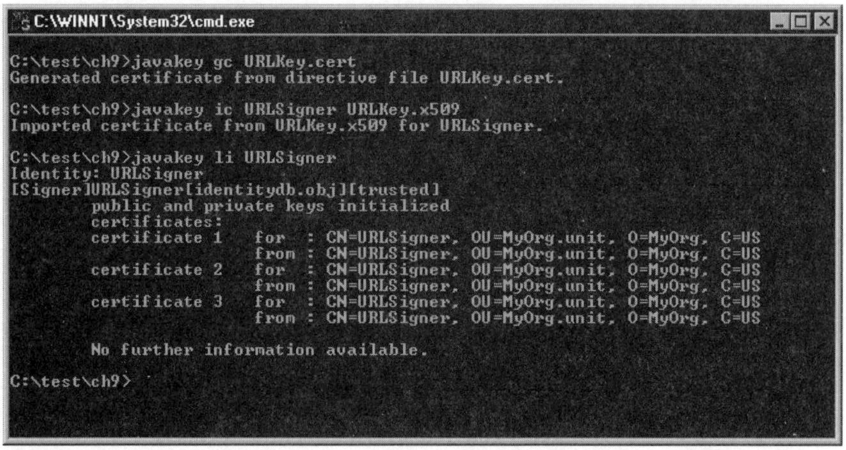

Figure 9-12: Generating and adding the URLKey.x509 certificate to URLSigner.

With the keys and certificate generated and added to URLSigner, all that is left is for you to sign the TestURL.jar archive, update index.html, and execute it again.

Sign & Execute TestURL as an Applet

The last step that you need to take is to sign the archive. However, before you can do this, you need to specify a directive file for the signing process. So, in your text editor, create a new file called URLKey.sign, and enter the following:

```
# This is an example signing directive file.

# The signer to use.
signer=URLSigner

# The cert to use for the signing.
cert=1

# The cert chain depth.
chain=0
```

```
# The name for the signature file and associated signature block
# (.SF and .DSA).
signature.file=URLKey
```

Save the file in the same directory as your archive, then execute the following command:

```
javakey gs URLKey.sign TestURL.jar
```

This will sign the TestURL.jar archive by creating the new file called TestURL.jar.sig (see Figure 9-13).

Figure 9-13: Signing the TestURL archive.

The last thing you need to do is update the index.html file so it looks like the following:

```
<APPLET
        ARCHIVE = "TestURL.jar.sig"
        CODE    = TestURL
        WIDTH   = 450  HEIGHT = 400
        ALIGN   = top
    >
    <PARAM NAME = URL VALUE =
        "http://www.netscape.com">

</APPLET>
```

Save this file and execute it with the appletviewer. This time you will be able to connect to the URL without a problem (see Figure 9-14).

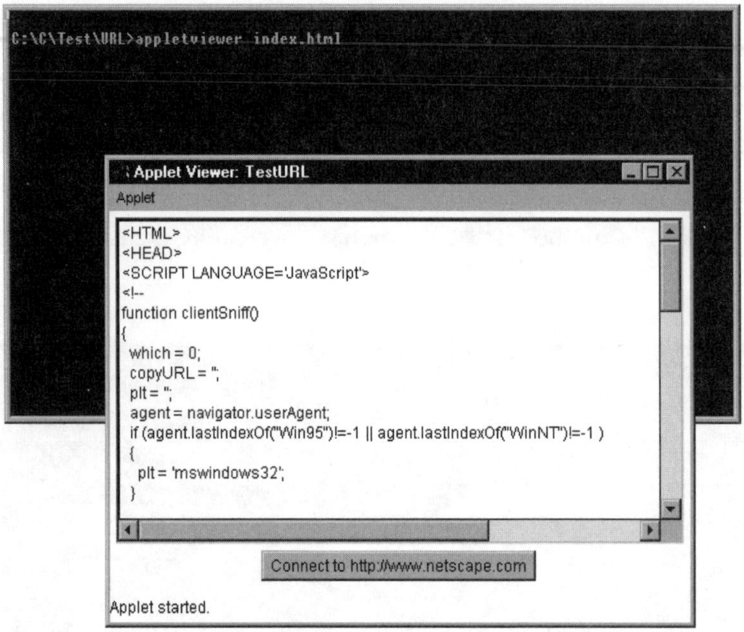

Figure 9-14: Signed TestURL example.

Moving On

In this chapter you had a chance to learn about JAR files—what they are and how they can improve the efficiency as well as the organization of your Java programs. You also received a hands-on introduction to digitally signing and verifying Java applets so they can execute as trusted Java programs.

In the next chapter, you will learn about Java Beans and why it is getting so much attention. You will have a chance to learn what it is, to study the classes that make up the Java Beans API, and to create a bean of your own.

Java Beans

In this chapter, you will be introduced to a variety of concepts about Java Beans, including how they are designed, how they interact, and how they run on various component platforms. You will also be introduced to a large body of the classes contained in the Java Beans application programming interface (API). Finally, you will have a chance to create a reusable component that uses Java Beans technology.

Introduction to Component Architecture

Components are reinventing objects in the same way that objects and object-oriented programming (OOP) reinvented functions and procedural programming. Designing programs into a collection of objects with OOP became a better way to organize parts of the program, to segregate tasks to different people (or departments), to promote reuse, and to provide a better way of doing business. Components are the next level in improving organization, design, and implementation, picking up where OOP left off.

A component is a piece of software that is completely reusable. In some cases, it can act like a stand-alone program, but more often the component combines with other components to become part of a larger, more sophisticated program. In other cases, it will be used as a building block in some rapid development environment. As you know, Java is inherently object-oriented. Java Beans is a component architecture designed by JavaSoft based on the Java platform.

Note: It is important to note that Java Beans is an integrated part of the Java platform (as of version 1.1). Therefore, no additional enhancements or adjustments are needed to create and use Beans components that can take full advantage of all Java capabilities. Furthermore, as a Java developer, once you have familiarized yourself with the Java Beans architecture and API, you can create Beans components in no time.

Overview of Java Beans

Java Beans is designed for the creation of reusable components that belong to a larger builder or Rapid Application Developer (RAD) development application. Java Beans components are very similar to OLE custom controls (OCXs) or their predecessor Visual Basic Extension (VBX), and are used in a variety of Windows development environments, such as Visual C++, Visual Basic, Delphi, and so on. In this case, you have a component that is a building block to be used again and again in each of your development environment's projects.

Java Beans also gives you the ability to create larger, more independent reusable components. These components could be programs in and of themselves, but an independent component design like this usually will be integrated as a major part of another program. Object Linking & Embedding (OLE) Automation used in Windows provides a very good example of this implementation. Through OLE, you can embed an Excel Spreadsheet in a Word document. It is quite possible to create a reusable Beans component that can stand on its own or be integrated into another program.

Creating reusable Beans components in Java is very useful, particularly because a Beans component is (like Java) not limited to any single platform. There is also platform independence (or at least bridging) between Microsoft's Component Object Model (COM) and ActiveX. So, for example, a Java Beans component can be used in any of the following three ways:

- In place of an ActiveX component.
- As a Live Object that uses OpenDoc architecture.
- Through LiveConnect in Netscape Navigator.

Defining ActiveX, OpenDoc & LiveConnect

The following are brief definitions of several component-related technologies:

ActiveX is a Microsoft technology that includes an implementation of a Windows-based software component model.

OpenDoc is a multiplatform architecture used for generating component-based software used on various Macintosh environments. Specifically geared toward compound document architecture using CORBA, OpenDoc enables programs to be embedded within other programs.

LiveConnect is a plug-in API, designed by Netscape specifically for Netscape Navigator, that allows third-party support in extending the native features of Navigator. These plug-ins are transparent with the rest of Netscape and therefore appear as if they are intimately part of Navigator. Usually, plug-ins via LiveConnect are controlled by Java and JavaScript.

The important point to bring up is that one Beans component can run on any of these environments as if it were a typical component for that technology. There is no rewriting, recompiling, or compromising in functionality.

> *Note*: In the event that one environment supports functionality that is not present in another, the Java Beans architecture compensates for this internally; it does not rely on the programmer to anticipate the inconsistencies that may arise when the Java Beans component is moved between environments.

The Java Beans Architecture

At this point, you probably have an understanding of what components are and how Java Beans fits into the component model. To summarize, a Beans component is a reusable piece of software that usually is included with other Beans components in some sort of component editor or graphical user interface (GUI) designer. Let's take a closer look at the five specific features of the Java Beans architecture:

- **Introspection**. At design time (by the builder tool) and/or during run time, *introspection* gives the ability to look in on a Beans component. It is crucial that your Beans component have an interface with which it can expose its attributes and other characteristics. This is accomplished by introspection. Using a specific design pattern (discussed in more detail later in this chapter) based on the Java Beans architecture, your beans can be introspected automatically. In more sophisticated situations, you can create separate classes (e.g., using `java.beans.BeanInfo`) that let you explicitly detail the characteristics of your Java bean.

TIP

The automatic introspection discussed here actually is done through reflection; therefore it is closely related to the Reflection API. It's not crucial that you understand this sophisticated API to create Beans components, but the API has been detailed in Chapter 3 of Ventana's Migrating From Java 1.0 to Java 1.1 [ISBN: 1-56604-686-6] if you are interested.

■ **Customization**. Customization is the ability to specify and/or retrieve properties in a given Beans component. For example, in a component editor or GUI builder, when users copy a Beans component to their project, they will need to add special attributes to the copied bean. Depending on the sophistication of your solution, you can use what are known as *property editors* for each type of property your Beans component uses. A typical GUI editor that uses this bean will use introspection to go through and collect all of these editors into a property sheet.

TIP

Sometimes, just editing properties may not be enough. In such cases, you can create a wizard (i.e., a Customizer *object) for your Beans component. For efficiency, this customizer is usually encapsulated in a separate class from the actual classes that make up the Beans component.*

■ **Events**. Events are one of the basic parts of a Beans component and are based on Java's standard delegation event-handling model that you learned about in Chapter 5. Through events (and event handling), you will be able to give your Beans component the ability to respond to input from the user (or other source). You will also be able to better interface it with other components, a component editor (or GUI builder), or a scripting environment.

■ **Properties and methods**. Properties and methods are a vital part of the Beans architecture. A *property* represents a changeable attribute that affects the behavior and/or appearance of the Beans component object to which it belongs. Simply stated, properties in component architecture really mean nothing more than the actual data that you encapsulate through methods inside a given object. This should not be new to you, as you learned about effective object-oriented design (OOD) in Chapter 3. Understanding OOD is important because Java Beans follows a very similar formula.

■ **Persistence**. In most Beans components, there is a need to save a Beans object and any customizations contained therein—not just temporarily in memory but *permanently*—so that when users shut down their systems and return the next day, properties and other customized characteristics will still be present. While persistence is not a requirement, you can use object serialization to store and retrieve Beans components.

TIP

A discussion of object serialization is beyond the scope of this book. For more information, please go to JavaSoft's site at www.javasoft.com.

Security & Java Beans

A bean receives no additional privileges or restrictions beyond the standard Java security model. So, if a bean is run in an untrusted Java applet, it has to conform to the security restrictions imposed on a typical Java applet. On the other hand, if a bean is part of a normal Java application (or a trusted applet, which you learned about in the last chapter), it has the same security rights as its hosting application.

The Java Beans API

In the last section, you were introduced to the Java Beans architecture and how it is integrated seamlessly into the Java platform. In this section, we are going to move forward to take a look at the API that makes up the Java Beans technology. This API is contained in the java.beans package. In the following subsections, you will have a chance to take a closer look at most of the package's classes and the job they do for Java Beans.

Note: The Beans Development Kit (BDK) is an extension to the JDK 1.1. Developed by JavaSoft, the BDK fully supports the Java Beans API and includes a test container (called a "bean box"), example Beans components, source code, and other documentation. For more information go to http://splash.javasoft.com/beans/index.html.

Introspection

As mentioned earlier, introspection (using the `Introspector` class) is used to learn about the features available in a Beans component. If your bean (and the methods contained in it) follows a specific design pattern, the bean automatically has the ability to be introspected. You do not have to follow the design pattern outlined by JavaSoft (or even use one at all, although that would be poor OOD). However, in order for your Beans components to take advantage of the automatic introspection capabilities available in the API, it is highly recommended that you do follow the pattern.

A design pattern is nothing more than a method-naming convention in which the type signatures and/or interfaces are standardized and printed in the method name. For instance, the name of the method is based on the property, event, or method contained in the Beans component.

Note: For a complete listing of the design pattern used by Java Beans, please go to the Java Beans white paper available at splash.javasoft.com/beans/spec.html.

For example, if you want to retrieve the value of a `boolean` property, you would use a corresponding `isXXX()` method (where *XXX* is the property name). Consider the following method declaration that retrieves the value of the `boolean` property `definable`:

```
public boolean isDefinable();
```

Alternatively, if a Beans component has implemented the `BeanInfo` interface, you can learn about the properties, methods, and events of that Beans component by calling methods from the interface. Effectively, you call a `BeanInfo` class (normally a separate class from the actual Beans component), which returns a descriptor object that contains specific information on the specified Beans component based on your request. This gives you the ability to gather information about a component implicitly (through normal introspection) and explicitly (through the `BeanInfo` interface).

Note: Using the `BeanInfo` interface allows you to be selective about what behavior you wish to expose about the Beans component. This is particularly useful for those Beans that require special/unique attention that must be conveyed to the Beans user.

Security & Introspection

Security, as it relates to introspection, follows the same model as that of the Reflection API. Effectively, a normal Java program (i.e., a component editor or GUI builder) will have access to all members of a specific Beans component. However, when dealing with untrusted applets, only the public members will be available.

Let's take a closer look at the classes that make up introspection in the java.beans package.

Class BeanDescriptor

The BeanDescriptor class returns global information about a specified bean and its customizer (if available). BeanDescriptor is one of the classes that can be returned by a BeanInfo object. See the BeanInfo class, later in this section, for more information.

The following example uses the BeanDescriptor class to retrieve a bean's class, using the getBeanClass() method. It also uses the getCustomizerClass() method from the BeanDescriptor class to retrieve information on the customizer for this bean (or null if one isn't specified). Note also that exceptions IntrospectionException and ClassNotFoundException are caught:

```
try
{
    Class source = Class.forName("myBean");
    BeanInfo beanInfo = Introspector.
        getBeanInfo(source);
    BeanDescriptor beanDescr = beanInfo.
        getBeanDescriptor();

    Class beanClass = beanDescr.getBeanClass();
    System.out.println("Bean class: "+
        beanClass.getName());
    Class custClass = beanDescr.
        getCustomizerClass();
    if (custClass != null)
        System.out.println("Customizer: "+
            custClass.getName());
}
catch(IntrospectionException e)
{
}
catch(ClassNotFoundException e)
{
}
```

Interface BeanInfo

The BeanInfo interface is implemented by the class that needs to provide explicit information about a specified Beans component. As mentioned earlier, BeanInfo allows you to retrieve information about a Beans component explicitly.

> ### TIP
> *If you must obtain a complete picture for a given bean, you should use the* Introspector *interface.*

For an example of BeanInfo in action, see the BeanDescriptor, MethodDescriptor, and PropertyDescriptor subsections, below.

Class EventSetDescriptor

The EventSetDescriptor class returns a group of method names for a specific listener interface that the specified bean fires. You then can use these methods to register (or deregister) a listener for a specific event in the given Beans component.

The following example uses the EventSetDescriptor class to retrieve information about registered events, their listeners, and the add*XXX*( ) and remove*XXX*( ) methods for a specified bean:

```
try
{
    Class source = Class.forName("myBean");
    BeanInfo beanInfo = Introspector.
        getBeanInfo(source);
    BeanDescriptor beanDescr = beanInfo.
        getBeanDescriptor();

    EventSetDescriptor[] events =
        beanInfo.getEventSetDescriptors();
    if (events != null)
        for (int k=0; k<events.length; k++)
        {
            Class listener = events[k].
                getListenerType();
            if (listener!=null)
                System.out.println(
                "Listener:\t"+listener.
                getName());
            Method add = events[k].
                getAddListenerMethod();
            if (add!=null)
                System.out.println(
                    "Add method:\t"+add.
                    toString());
            Method remove = events[k].
                getRemoveListenerMethod();
            if (remove!=null)
```

```
                    System.out.println(
                        "Remove method:\t"+
                        remove.toString());
            }
        }
catch(IntrospectionException e)
{
    System.err.println(
        "IntrospectionException:"+
        e.getMessage());
}
catch(ClassNotFoundException e)
{
    System.err.println(
        "ClassNotFoundException: "+
        e.getMessage());
}
```

Class FeatureDescriptor

The FeatureDescriptor class is the root class for the following descriptor classes also defined in the java.beans package:

- java.beans.BeanDescriptor
- java.beans.EventSetDescriptor
- java.beans.FeatureDescriptor
- java.beans.IndexedPropertyDescriptor
- java.beans.MethodDescriptor
- java.beans.ParameterDescriptor
- java.beans.PropertyDescriptor

This class defines the methods used by all introspection-based descriptor classes.

TIP

The FeatureDescriptor *class also provides the ability to associate various attribute/value pairs with a design pattern.*

For an example of usage, see the examples in the BeanDescriptor, MethodDescriptor, and PropertyDescriptor subsections, elsewhere in this chapter.

Class IndexedPropertyDescriptor

The IndexedPropertyDescriptor class is used to describe any array-like properties in a specified Beans component. The class also facilitates the ability to read or write to a specific element in this array-like property. Note that the property may also contain generic read/write methods that address the array-like property in its entirety.

The following example uses the IndexedPropertyDescriptor class to retrieve information about read and write methods of properties with indexes:

```
PropertyDescriptor prop;
if (prop instanceof IndexedPropertyDescriptor)
{
    IndexedPropertyDescriptor indProp =
        (IndexedPropertyDescriptor)prop;
    Method mRead = indProp.
        getIndexedReadMethod();
    if (mRead != null)
        System.out.println(
            "Read method:\t"+mRead.toString());
    Method mWrite = indProp.
        getIndexedWriteMethod();
    if (mWrite != null)
        System.out.println(
            "Write method:\t"+
            mWrite.toString());
}
```

See the example in the PropertyDescriptor class for another example of implementation for this class.

Class Introspector

The Introspector class is the standard way to gather a complete picture for a specified Beans component. It works by walking through the bean and its superclasses, looking for explicit and implicit information. The explicit process involves looking for an implemented BeanInfo instance. The implicit process involves using low-level reflection and design-pattern matching. The results of the search then are compiled into a single BeanInfo instance.

Note: Introspector can throw the IntrospectionException, also part of the java.beans package.

For an example of the Introspector class in action, look at the BeanDescriptor, MethodDescriptor, and PropertyDescriptor classes, elsewhere in this section.

Class MethodDescriptor

The MethodDescriptor class is used to describe a specified method contained in the specified Beans component. The following example uses the MethodDescriptor class to retrieve the methods in a specified bean, using the getMethodDescriptors() method from the BeanInfo class. The exceptions IntrospectionException and ClassNotFoundException must be caught:

```
try
{
    Class source = Class.forName("myBean");
    BeanInfo beanInfo = Introspector.
        getBeanInfo(source);

    MethodDescriptor[] beanMethods = beanInfo.
        getMethodDescriptors();
    if (beanMethods != null)
        for (int k=0; k<beanMethods.length; k++)
        {
            Method mthd =
                beanMethods[k].getMethod();
            if (mthd.getDeclaringClass()==
                beanClass)
            {
            System.out.println(
                "\t"+mthd.toString());
            ParameterDescriptor[] params =
                beanMethods[k].
                getParameterDescriptors();
            if (params != null)
                for (int i=0; i<params.length;
                    i++)
                {
                    String str = params[i].
                        getDisplayName();
                    if (str != null)
                        System.out.println(
                            "\t\t"+str);
                }
            }
        }
}
catch(IntrospectionException e)
{
```

```
    System.err.println(
        "IntrospectionException:"+
        e.getMessage());
}
catch(ClassNotFoundException e)
{
    System.err.println(
        "ClassNotFoundException: "+
        e.getMessage());
}
```

Note: The getMethodDescriptors() method returns the methods that are defined in the actual Beans component but *not* the inherited ones.

Class ParameterDescriptor

The ParameterDescriptor class is closely related to the MethodDescriptor class just discussed. It is used to describe parameters for a given Beans component method. See ParameterDescriptor in use in the example in the MethodDescriptor class in the previous section.

Class PropertyDescriptor

The PropertyDescriptor class is used to describe an exported property for the specified bean (via a selector/mutator method, i.e., get*XXX*() and set*XXX*()). The following example uses the PropertyDescriptor class to retrieve the get and set methods of the property that is arbitrarily named Ben:

```
try
{
    Class source = Class.forName("myBean");
    BeanInfo beanInfo = Introspector.
        getBeanInfo(source);

    PropertyDescriptor[] beanPropr =
        beanInfo.getPropertyDescriptors();
    if (beanPropr != null)
        for (int k=0; k<beanPropr.length; k++)
        {
            System.out.println("Property: "+
                beanPropr[k].getName());
            Method mthdGet = beanPropr[k].
                getReadMethod();
            if (mthdGet!=null)
                System.out.println(
                "\t"+mthdGet.toString());
            Method mthdSet = beanPropr[k].
                getWriteMethod();
```

```
            if (mthdSet!=null)
                System.out.println(
                "\t"+mthdSet.toString());
        }


    }
    catch(IntrospectionException e)
    {
        System.err.println(
            "IntrospectionException:"+
            e.getMessage());
    }
    catch(ClassNotFoundException e)
    {
        System.err.println(
            "ClassNotFoundException: "+
            e.getMessage());
    }
```

Class SimpleBeanInfo

The SimpleBeanInfo class is a supporting class to the BeanInfo class, facilitating an easier way to provide BeanInfo classes to give explicit information on a bean.

This class always defaults by denying that it has explicit information on a requested topic for the specified Beans component. The Introspector class uses this denial as a queue to invoke low-level reflective introspection and design patterns on the Beans component. For an example of usage, go to the BeanDescriptor, MethodDescriptor, and PropertyDescriptor subsections, elsewhere in this section.

Customization

The ability to customize on the user and developer level is a vital part of the Beans anatomy. After all, a Beans component is a reusable component of software that either plugs into a larger program or is used as a building block in a program development project. In all of these cases, there are specific properties that will need to be set for each use of the bean. For instance, imagine you that you create a Beans component that provides similar functionality to that of the GUI button object. Every time this bean is used, the user will probably want to change the label on it. Therefore, this button bean needs to be designed with a specific architecture to allow this property to be retrieved and set at design time. Furthermore, this same bean may have another property that lets us reconcile whether it currently has focus and allows such a property to be retrieved and set at run time.

The Java Beans API supports customization in two forms:

- The first form is used for most bean situations in which you define a property editor in which the user can change the property for the bean.
- The second form deals with what are known as customizers.

Property Editors

A property editor allows you to edit the property of a bean in some sort of visual format. This editor can be basic and can simply facilitate getting and setting functionality to a particular property. Or, a property editor can be more sophisticated and can actually be a Java component (extending java.awt.Component, which you learned about in Chapters 5 and 6) and be displayed any time its property is edited. In some situations, the editor may need to be designed to work in both a simple (i.e., programmatic) and a visual format. While this is possible, it is up to the programmer to actually implement the details in the associated property editor.

Building a GUI Property Sheet

For customization in your Java bean, you have a property editor. However, in a professional component editor or GUI builder, this can be extremely scattered. Therefore, most of these environments will put all the properties for a given Beans component into one property sheet.

During design time, the Java Beans API can facilitate property editors for some of the basic data types. Also, the component editor or GUI builder to which the bean belongs may provide several property editors of its own. The result is that you are going to have a heterogeneous set of property editors coming from a variety of sources. As a result, the Java Beans API has included the java.beans.PropertyEditorManager class. This class is used to locate the right property editors for a bean component. It also maintains a registry of property editors for a specified Java type.

TIP

Watch out for indirect property changes. For instance, changing the value of one property may precipitate a change of another property (or properties). To protect yourself from these situations, reread all the properties for that bean, verifying that they were not affected.

Customizers

A property editor works well for basic implementations. However, the more sophisticated beans—those that can almost stand alone as separate programs—may find a property editor too limiting. For these situations, the Java Beans API has defined the `Customizer` interface that lets its implementations behave like a wizard for the given Beans component.

Note: *Wizards* are like miniprograms that are specifically designed to step users through a complex or time-consuming process. In most cases, a normal wizard will wait until the very end to perform any action based on the user's input. However, in the case of using a customizer for your Beans component, it is entirely up to you to update the bean as you go along or wait until the end, giving the user a chance to confirm everything.

Any class that you design to be a customizer should inherit the `java.awt.Component` interface (directly or indirectly) and implement the `Customizer` interface. Usually, a customizer is in a completely separate window with no ties to the component editor that invoked it.

TIP

A customizer may also contain property editors, giving you an alternative to creating a property sheet. Instead, you can put all of your property editors into one spiffy customizer wizard.

Let's now take a closer look at the classes that make up customization in the `java.beans` package.

Interface Customizer

The `Customizer` interface is used to provide a customizer for a Java bean. A customizer is a wizard-like tool used to customize more sophisticated Java beans. Any class that needs to be a customizer must implement this interface and should extend the `java.awt.Component` class to have a stand-alone (or at least an embedded) visual presence in Java.

Note: Customizers also can include property editors for the bean in the editors' implementation.

This example demonstrates how to implement the `Customizer` interface in a typical Beans component. It extends a `TextField` object (thereby indirectly extending the `java.awt.Component` class) to enter integer values for a bean property. Implementation of the `Customizer` interface allows `myBean` to add and remove `PropertyChangeListeners` where the `PropertyChangeSupport` instance manages them.

The myBean class holds one property—integer X. This property can be modified, using the setX( ) method defined in the Beans component, which notifies all registered PropertyChangeListeners by firing a PropertyChangeEvent event. Correspondingly, the X property also can be retrieved using the getX( ) method defined in the Beans component:

```java
class myBean extends TextField
    implements Customizer, TextListener
{
    private Integer X;
    private PropertyChangeSupport m_ChSupp;

    public myBean()
    {
        m_ChSupp = new
            PropertyChangeSupport(this);
        addTextListener(this);
        X = new Integer(0);
    }

    public void setX(Integer value)
    {
        m_ChSupp.firePropertyChange("X",
            X, value);
        X = value;
        setText(String.valueOf(X));
    }

    public Integer getX()
    {
        return X;
    }

    public void textValueChanged(TextEvent evt)
    {
        try
        {
            int newX = Integer.parseInt(
                getText());
            if (newX != X.intValue())
                setX(new Integer(newX));
        }
        catch(NumberFormatException e)
        {
            setText(String.valueOf(X));
        }
    }
```

```
public void addPropertyChangeListener(
    PropertyChangeListener Listener)
{
    m_ChSupp.addPropertyChangeListener(
        Listener);
}

public void removePropertyChangeListener(
    PropertyChangeListener Listener)
{
    m_ChSupp.removePropertyChangeListener(
        Listener);
}

public void setObject(Object bean) {}

}
```

In this simple example, you use a TextField object to edit an integer value and implement the textValueChanged() method used as part of the event handling for this TextField (please see Chapter 6 for more information on event handling). This method verifies that the content of the field represents an integer value. If the number differs from the current property's value, it invokes the setX() method.

Note: Without some blocks in place, an endless loop is possible: textValueChanged() invokes the setX() method, which in turn displays the new property value, using the setText() method, resulting in a TextEvent that will precipitate a call to the textValueChanged() method again, and so on. To avoid this potential problem, you see in the previous example that we invoke the setX() method only if the value of X is different.

The following code shows the applet myApplet. This applet implements the PropertyChangeListener interface to hold the customizer component in the previous example. It starts by creating and adding a new instance of the myBean class. It then registers itself as a PropertyChangeListener for that bean's object. Finally, the method propertyChange() displays the new value for that property as its Label:

```
public class myApplet extends Applet
    implements PropertyChangeListener
{
    myBean m;
    Label l;

    public void init()
    {
```

```
        setLayout(null);
        l = new Label();
        l.setBounds(10, 50, 80, 25);
        add(l);

        m = new myBean();
        m.addPropertyChangeListener(this);
        m.setX(new Integer(50));
        m.setBounds(10, 10, 80, 25);
        add(m);
    }

    public void propertyChange(
        PropertyChangeEvent evt)
    {
        l.setText(evt.getNewValue().toString());
    }
}
```

Note: Notice how Label gets its initial value. When the setX() method is called, the myApplet instance already is registered as PropertyChangeListener. So it receives notification back, and the propertyChange() method sets value 50 to the Label.

Figure 10-1 shows the previous applet customizer being executed.

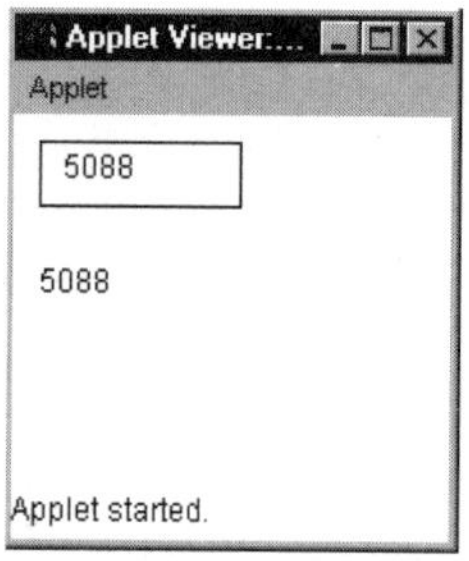

Figure 10-1: Customizer in action.

Interface PropertyEditor

Implementations of the PropertyEditor interface are used to let the user change a given type (either primitive or reference) of a property for the Beans component. Usually, this is done in some sort of visual format (directly or indirectly extending the java.awt.Component class). However, at the very least, you can simply define a set of get/set methods to access/change the property. For an example of the PropertyEditor in action, go to the PropertyEditorSupport class, later in this section.

Class PropertyEditorManager

The PropertyEditorManager class is used both to locate the appropriate property editors for a Beans component and to maintain a registry of property editors for each registered property Java type.

The PropertyEditorManager lets you explicitly register a Java class as a property editor for a given data type that uses the registerEditor() method. Alternatively, if a property editor for a given explicit type is not registered, the PropertyEditorManager will use design patterns to implicitly look for a corresponding property editor.

For instance, the following snippet of code uses the static method findEditor() from the PropertyEditorManager class to retrieve a PropertyEditor for the specified Beans component:

```
try
{
    Class target = Class.forName("myBean");
    PropertyEditor editor = PropertyEditorManager.findEditor(target);
    // Use PropertyEditor
}
catch(ClassNotFoundException e)
{
    System.err.println(
        "ClassNotFoundException: "+
        e.getMessage());
}
```

Class PropertyEditorSupport

The PropertyEditorSupport class implements the PropertyEditor interface, allowing you to extend PropertyEditor and use it to edit a property in your own bean without having to implement all the methods in the PropertyEditor interface. However, unlike the adapter classes you learned about for event handling in Chapter 6, this class does contain default functionality for each of its methods.

The following shows an example of using the PropertyEditorSupport class to avoid overriding all methods of the PropertyEditor interface. The editor allows editing of the property integer X in the following three ways:

- Using the pair of setValue() and getValue() methods to specify an integer argument.

- Using the pair of setAsText() and getAsText() methods to specify a string argument.

- Using a graphical interface approach in which the paintValue() method draws the current value in the specified Rectangle object. (Also, the isPaintable() method must return true in this case.)

Method getJavaInitializationString( ) returns the current property as a String object suitable for initialization of a Java object in the program's text:

```
class MyEditor extends PropertyEditorSupport
{
    private Integer X = new Integer(0);

    public void setValue(Object value)
    {
        if (value instanceof Integer)
            X = (Integer)value;
    }

    public Object getValue()
    {
        return (Object)X;
    }

    public void setAsText(String text)
        throws IllegalArgumentException
    {
        try
        {
            int newX = Integer.parseInt(text);
            X = new Integer(newX);
        }
        catch(NumberFormatException e)
        {
            throw new IllegalArgumentException(
                "Illegal value for X");
        }
    }

    public String getAsText()
    {
        return X.toString();
    }

    public String getJavaInitializationString()
    {
        return X.toString();
    }

    public boolean isPaintable()
    {
        return true;
    }
```

```
public void paintValue(Graphics g,
    Rectangle rc)
{
    g.drawString(X.toString(), rc.x,
        rc.y+rc.height-2);
}
}
```

Properties

Properties in the Java Beans API give you the ability to specify an attribute for a Beans component. This is a vital part of the Beans architecture and facilitates a key part of the functionality contained in a Beans component.

You can see a good example of a "property" looking at the Abstract Window Toolkit (AWT) component `java.awt.Button`. In it, two methods— `getLabel()` and `setLabel()`—let you read or specify the label for a particular button object. Since `Button` is technically a Beans component, `Button` follows the structure of a typical Beans component's property, in which you have a property and several methods that can be used to retrieve or set (if appropriate) the values for that property.

Note: The Java Beans architecture is not limited to specifying simple Java-data-type properties (`int`, `boolean`, `String`, and so on). You can also define property types to specify objects in the Java Class Library or objects of your own design (e.g., `java.awt.Color` and `COM.joshipublishing.stuff.MyClass`).

All properties are accessed via methods (which belong to the Beans component). However, there are a wide variety of ways to both access these methods and, in turn, access the properties for the bean. Scripting environments (e.g., JavaScript), other components, and component editors that utilize property sheets all can have access to a given bean's properties.

The Java Beans API also provides support for what are known as bound and constrained properties. However, these properties are rarely used in most basic bean implementations so they will only be mentioned here:

In brief, a *bounded property* is one that provides change notification to its container or another Beans component. This is done through event handling using the `java.beans.PropertyChangeListener` listener interface that gets passed a `java.beans.PropertyChangeEvent` object if the source (i.e., the bound property) property's value is changed. The Java Beans API also facilitates the `java.beans.PropertyChangeSupport` class used to keep track of all the `PropertyChangeListeners` and fire the `PropertyChangeEvent` events accordingly.

Constrained properties facilitate a transaction-like functionality wherein a property for a Beans component (and/or some other assigned object(s)) needs to validate the updated value or reject it and revert to the original value. Basically, you use the `java.beans.VetoChangeListener` to report whether the bound property has been updated and the `java.beans.VetoableChangeSupport` to keep track of instances of `VetoChangeListener` and fire `PropertyChangeEvent` events accordingly. In the event that a proposed change gets rejected, a `java.beans.PropertyVetoException` gets thrown and a `PropertyChangeEvent` event with the original value should be fired to update any listeners that may already have changed to the new value.

Note: Any set*XXX*( ) for a constrained property must throw or catch `PropertyVetoException`.

Example: A Simple Bean

This example shows a Beans component that can be used to graphically select numerical values from the given range. It works in a similar fashion to that of a scrollbar but has a different (and easily changeable) look and feel. Effectively, it is similar to the Windows control used to select sound level, screen size, and so on. This Beans component has only one property, called `value` (in this chapter, it's sometimes simply called "the Beans property"). This bean also acts as its own customizer (to notify its listeners about any changes in that property).

BeanScale

Create a text file entitled `BeanScale.java` and enter the following text (or you can copy it from this book's Companion CD-ROM):

```java
import java.lang.*;
import java.beans.*;
import java.awt.*;
import java.awt.event.*;

// Scale bean's control
class BeanScale extends Canvas implements Customizer {
    private int m_nValue=0;    // Current value
    private int m_nMinVal=0;   // Minimum value
    private int m_nMaxVal=0;   // Maximum value
    private int m_nTmpVal=0;   // Tempor. value
```

```java
    // Dragging flag
    private boolean m_bDragging=false;

    private PropertyChangeSupport m_ChSupp;

    // Constructor
    public BeanScale() {
        m_ChSupp = new  PropertyChangeSupport(this);
        addMouseListener(new MyMouseAdapter());
        addMouseMotionListener(new MyMouseMotionAdapter());
    }

    // Converts control's value to pixels
    private int ValToPixels(int nVal) {
        double dLen = getSize().width-10;
        if (m_nMaxVal > m_nMinVal)
        {
            int n = (int)(dLen*(nVal-m_nMinVal)/ (m_nMaxVal-m_nMinVal));
            return Math.min(Math.max(n, 0), (int)dLen) + 5;
        }
        else
            return 0;
    }

    // Converts pixels to control's value
    private int PixelsToVal(int nPix) {
        double dLen = getSize().width-10;
        if (dLen > 1)
        {
            int n = (int)((nPix-5)*(m_nMaxVal - m_nMinVal)/dLen)+m_nMinVal;
            return Math.min(Math.max(n, m_nMinVal), m_nMaxVal);
        }
        else
            return 0;
    }

    // Set value
    public void setValue(int nValue) {
        // Fire Property Change
        m_ChSupp.firePropertyChange("value", new Integer(m_nValue), new
Integer(nValue));

        m_nValue  = nValue;
        m_nMinVal = Math.min(m_nMinVal, m_nValue);
        m_nMaxVal = Math.max(m_nMaxVal, m_nValue);
        m_nTmpVal = m_nValue;
    }
```

```java
// Get value
public int getValue()   {
    return m_nValue;
}

// Set min. value
public void setMinVal(int nMinVal) {
    m_nMinVal = nMinVal;
    m_nValue  = Math.max(m_nMinVal, m_nValue);
    m_nMaxVal = Math.max(m_nMaxVal, m_nMinVal);
}
// Get min. value
public int getMinVal()   {
    return m_nMinVal;
}

// Set max. value
public void setMaxVal(int nMaxVal) {
    m_nMaxVal = nMaxVal;
    m_nValue  = Math.min(m_nMaxVal, m_nValue);
    m_nMinVal = Math.min(m_nMaxVal, m_nMinVal);
}
// Get max. value
public int getMaxVal()   {
    return m_nMaxVal;
}

// Draw current image
public void paint(Graphics g) {
    int nLen = getSize().width-10;

    // Draw scale's body
    g.setColor(Color.black);
    g.fillRect(5, 5, nLen+1, 4);
    g.setColor(Color.lightGray);
    g.fillRect(6, 6, nLen+1, 4);
    g.setColor(Color.gray);
    g.fillRect(6, 6, nLen, 3);

    // Draw grid
    g.setColor(Color.black);
    for (int k=0; k<5; k++)
    {
        int x = k*nLen/4 + 5;
        g.drawLine(x, 0, x, 4);
    }
```

```java
    // Draw cursor
    drawCursor(g);
}

// Draw cursor
protected void drawCursor(Graphics g)    {
    int x[] = new int[3];
    int y[] = new int[3];

    x[0] = ValToPixels(m_nTmpVal);
    y[0] = 11;
    x[1] = x[0] + 4;
    y[1] = y[0] + 7;
    x[2] = x[0] - 4;
    y[2] = y[0] + 7;

    if (m_bDragging)
        g.setColor(Color.red);
    else
        g.setColor(Color.blue);
    g.fillPolygon(x, y, 3);
    g.setColor(Color.black);
    g.drawPolygon(x, y, 3);
}

//  Erase cursor at current location
protected void eraseCursor(Graphics g)  {
    int x = ValToPixels(m_nTmpVal);
    int y = 11;
    g.clearRect(x-5, 11, 10, 8);
}



// MouseAdapter subclass
class MyMouseAdapter extends MouseAdapter {
    public void mousePressed(MouseEvent e)        {
        int x = ValToPixels(m_nValue);
        int y = 14;
        // Close enough to cursor
        if (Math.abs(e.getX()-x)<5 && Math.abs(e.getY()-y)<5) {
            m_bDragging = true;
            m_nTmpVal = m_nValue;
            drawCursor(getGraphics());
        }
    }
```

```java
        public void mouseReleased(MouseEvent e)      {
            if (m_bDragging) {
                m_bDragging = false;
                drawCursor(getGraphics());
                setValue(m_nTmpVal);
            }
        }

        public void mouseClicked(MouseEvent e)      {
            Rectangle lineRect = new Rectangle(5, 2, getSize().width-10,
10);
            if (!m_bDragging && lineRect.contains(e.getX(), e.getY())) {
                Graphics g = getGraphics();
                eraseCursor(g);

                int nStep = (m_nMaxVal-m_nMinVal)/10;
                m_nTmpVal = m_nValue;
                if (e.getX() > ValToPixels(m_nValue)+2)
                    m_nTmpVal += nStep;
                if (e.getX() < ValToPixels(m_nValue)-2)
                    m_nTmpVal -= nStep;
                m_nTmpVal = Math.min(Math.max(m_nTmpVal, m_nMinVal),
m_nMaxVal);

                drawCursor(g);
                setValue(m_nTmpVal);
            }
        }
    }

    // Inner MouseMotionAdapter subclass
    class MyMouseMotionAdapter extends MouseMotionAdapter {

        public void mouseDragged(MouseEvent e) {
            if (m_bDragging) {
                Graphics g = getGraphics();
                eraseCursor(g);
                m_nTmpVal = PixelsToVal(e.getX());
                drawCursor(g);
            }
        }
    }


    // PropertyChangeListener support
    public void addPropertyChangeListener(PropertyChangeListener Listener)
{
```

```
            m_ChSupp.addPropertyChangeListener(Listener);
    }

    public void removePropertyChangeListener(PropertyChangeListener
Listener) {
            m_ChSupp.removePropertyChangeListener(Listener);
    }

    public void setObject(Object bean) {}

}
```

Let's analyze the preceding code:

```
import java.lang.*;
import java.beans.*;
import java.awt.*;
import java.awt.event.*;
```

```
// Scale bean's control
class BeanScale extends Canvas implements Customizer {
    private int m_nValue=0;    // Current value
    private int m_nMinVal=0;   // Minimum value
    private int m_nMaxVal=0;   // Maximum value
    private int m_nTmpVal=0;   // Tempor. value
    // Dragging flag
    private boolean m_bDragging=false;

    private PropertyChangeSupport m_ChSupp;
```

Class BeanScale extends java.awt.Canvas to be able to paint itself (see the paint() method in the following code). It also implements the Customizer interface to utilize the Java Beans notification mechanism.

This class holds six private variables:

- **int m_nValue.** The current value of the Beans property.

- **int m_nMinVal.** The minimum value of the Beans property.

- **int m_nMaxVal=0.** The maximum value of the Beans property.

- **int m_nTmpVal=0.** The temporary value of the Beans property.

- **boolean m_bDragging.** The flag that indicates whether the user is currently dragging the bean's cursor.

- **PropertyChangeSupport m_ChSupp.** A reference to PropertyChangeSupport that takes care of listeners to the property value changes of this Beans component.

```
// Constructor
public BeanScale() {
    m_ChSupp = new  PropertyChangeSupport(this);
    addMouseListener(new MyMouseAdapter());
    addMouseMotionListener(new MyMouseMotionAdapter());
}
```

The public constructor provided for this bean creates a new instance of PropertyChangeSupport and registers respective instances of MyMouseListener and MyMouseMotionListener (two inner classes that will be analyzed shortly), to listen for certain mouse events.

```
// Converts control's value to pixels
private int ValToPixels(int nVal) {
    double dLen = getSize().width-10;
    if (m_nMaxVal > m_nMinVal)
    {
        int n = (int)(dLen*(nVal-m_nMinVal)/
            (m_nMaxVal-m_nMinVal));
        return Math.min(Math.max(n, 0),
            (int)dLen) + 5;
    }
    else
        return 0;
}
```

This method (for internal purposes only) is used to convert the bean's integer value into screen-pixel coordinates. It verifies that the bean is scaled correctly (i.e., maximum value is greater than minimum value) and calculates the distance in pixels from the left side of control based on the specified parameter nVal.

```
// Converts pixels to control's value
private int PixelsToVal(int nPix) {
    double dLen = getSize().width-10;
    if (dLen > 1)
    {
        int n = (int)((nPix-5)*(m_nMaxVal - m_nMinVal)/dLen)+m_nMinVal;
        return Math.min(Math.max(n, m_nMinVal), m_nMaxVal);
    }
    else
        return 0;
}
```

This method (also used for internal purposes only) does the exact opposite of the preceding method. In this case, it converts a specified screen-pixel coordinate into an integral value that can be used by the bean. It does this by verifying that the bean is resized correctly (i.e., length is greater than 1) and calculates the bean's current integral value based on the specified parameter nPix.

```
// Set value
public void setValue(int nValue) {
    // Fire Property Change
    m_ChSupp.firePropertyChange("value", new Integer(m_nValue), new
Integer(nValue));

    m_nValue  = nValue;
    m_nMinVal = Math.min(m_nMinVal, m_nValue);
    m_nMaxVal = Math.max(m_nMaxVal, m_nValue);
    m_nTmpVal = m_nValue;
}
```

This method is used to set a new property value for the bean. The method notifies listeners of this bean by invoking the PropertyChangeSupport.firePropertyChange() method with the property name (in this case "value") and two instances of java.lang.Integer for the old and new values. Then it sets the value and adjusts the minimum and maximum values if necessary.

TIP

Alternatively, you can use a constrained implementation for this property to prevent the value from being changed outside a certain range. In this case, since the user can't move the cursor outside the bean's range, it is not necessary.

```
// Get value
public int getValue()
{
    return m_nValue;
}
```

This method retrieves the current value for the bean's property. As you learned in the first half of this chapter, it is a necessary counterpart for the set*XXX*() method of some property in all Beans components.

```
// Set min. value
public void setMinVal(int nMinVal) {
    m_nMinVal = nMinVal;
    m_nValue  = Math.max(m_nMinVal, m_nValue);
    m_nMaxVal = Math.max(m_nMaxVal, m_nMinVal);
}

// Get min. value
public int getMinVal()  {
    return m_nMinVal;
}
```

Method setMinVal() sets a new minimum value for this bean and adjusts current and maximum values, if necessary. Method getMinVal() simply returns the current minimum value for this bean.

```java
// Set max. value
public void setMaxVal(int nMaxVal) {
    m_nMaxVal = nMaxVal;
    m_nValue  = Math.min(m_nMaxVal, m_nValue);
    m_nMinVal = Math.min(m_nMaxVal, m_nMinVal);
}

// Get max. value
public int getMaxVal()  {
    return m_nMaxVal;
}
```

Method setMaxVal() sets a new maximum value for this bean and adjusts current and minimum values, if necessary. Method getMaxVal() simply retrieves the current maximum value.

```java
// Draw current image
public void paint(Graphics g) {
    int nLen = getSize().width-10;

    // Draw scale's body
    g.setColor(Color.black);
    g.fillRect(5, 5, nLen+1, 4);
    g.setColor(Color.lightGray);
    g.fillRect(6, 6, nLen+1, 4);
    g.setColor(Color.gray);
    g.fillRect(6, 6, nLen, 3);
```

The paint() method can be implemented in all subclasses of java.awt.Component to specify how the component should draw itself. This bean first draws a quasi-3D scale's body by black and gray colors.

```java
    // Draw grid
    g.setColor(Color.black);
    for (int k=0; k<5; k++)
    {
        int x = k*nLen/4 + 5;
        g.drawLine(x, 0, x, 4);
    }

    // Draw cursor
    drawCursor(g);
}
```

The rest of the paint( ) method draws five equidistant lines to mark the cursor's position and draws a cursor by invoking the drawCursor( ) method.

```
// Draw cursor
protected void drawCursor(Graphics g)    {
     int x[] = new int[3];
     int y[] = new int[3];

     x[0] = ValToPixels(m_nTmpVal);
     y[0] = 11;
     x[1] = x[0] + 4;
     y[1] = y[0] + 7;
     x[2] = x[0] - 4;
     y[2] = y[0] + 7;
```

This method (drawCursor( )) draws a triangular cursor based on the specified Graphics reference. The method starts by creating two arrays of triangle coordinates. The X-coordinate of the first vertex is calculated using the ValToPixels( ) method for the current bean's value. The Y-coordinate is set to 11 (slightly below the scale's body). The other two vertices are placed in bottom-left and bottom-right directions from the first one.

```
     if (m_bDragging)
         g.setColor(Color.red);
     else
         g.setColor(Color.blue);
     g.fillPolygon(x, y, 3);
     g.setColor(Color.black);
     g.drawPolygon(x, y, 3);
}
```

Finally, the method fills the cursor's triangle with the color red if it is in a dragging state, or blue if it's in a nondragging state. The method also draws a thin triangular border around the cursor.

```
// Erase cursor at current location
protected void eraseCursor(Graphics g)  {
     int x = ValToPixels(m_nTmpVal);
     int y = 11;
     g.clearRect(x-5, 11, 10, 8);
}
```

As a counterpart to drawing the cursor, we need a way to erase it when it is moved. This method calculates the cursor's position in screen coordinates (using the ValToPixels( ) method) and erases the cursor using the Graphics.clearRect( ) method.

```
// MouseAdapter subclass
class MyMouseAdapter extends MouseAdapter {
    public void mousePressed(MouseEvent e)        {
        int x = ValToPixels(m_nValue);
        int y = 14;
        // Close enough to cursor
        if (Math.abs(e.getX()-x)<5 && Math.abs(e.getY()-y)<5) {
            m_bDragging = true;
            m_nTmpVal = m_nValue;
            drawCursor(getGraphics());
        }
    }
}
```

This inner class is used to implement the mousePressed(), mouseReleased(), and mouseClicked() methods (see Chapter 6 for details). The mousePressed() method will be invoked when the user presses a mouse button inside the Beans component's area. When this happens, the method verifies whether the mouse's cursor is located close enough to the cursor. If so, the method raises dragging flag m_bDragging, sets the temporary value m_nTmpVal to m_nValue, and redraws the cursor (with the red dragging color).

```
public void mouseReleased(MouseEvent e)        {
    if (m_bDragging) {
        m_bDragging = false;
        drawCursor(getGraphics());
        setValue(m_nTmpVal);
    }
}
```

The mouseReleased() method will be invoked when the user releases a mouse button that has been previously pressed inside the bean's area. When this happens, the method verifies whether the dragging flag was raised. If so, it drops the dragging flag (i.e., sets it to false), redraws the cursor, and sets temporary value m_nTmpVal to the bean's new value, using the setValue() method (which, as you know from the earlier discussion, will result in the notification of the bean's listeners). Note that the temporary value is actually calculated in the mouseDragged() method (discussed a little later in this analysis).

```
public void mouseClicked(MouseEvent e)        {
    Rectangle lineRect = new Rectangle(5, 2, getSize().width-10, 10);
    if (!m_bDragging && lineRect.contains(e.getX(), e.getY())) {
        Graphics g = getGraphics();
        eraseCursor(g);
```

The mouseClicked() method will be invoked when the user presses and releases a mouse button inside the bean's body area. When this happens, the method constructs a Rectangle object that covers the actual body area of the bean (and not just the borders). If the m_bDragging flag is false and the mouse is clicked inside the body area, this method creates an instance of Graphics to erase the cursor and draw it at the new location.

```
int nStep = (m_nMaxVal-m_nMinVal)/10;
m_nTmpVal = m_nValue;
if (e.getX() > ValToPixels(m_nValue)+2)
    m_nTmpVal += nStep;
if (e.getX() < ValToPixels(m_nValue)-2)
    m_nTmpVal -= nStep;
m_nTmpVal = Math.min(Math.max(m_nTmpVal, m_nMinVal),
m_nMaxVal);
```

Before we can draw the cursor at the new position (based on the user's click), we need to calculate the new value of the bean. The previous code shows the calculations based on a step value of one-tenth the bean's range. If the mouse was clicked on the side left of the bean's old cursor position, the bean's value will be decreased a step; otherwise, the value will increase a step. Finally the preceding code verifies that a new value lies in the bean's range and adjusts it, if necessary.

```
        drawCursor(g);
        setValue(m_nTmpVal);
    }
  }
}
```

This part of the mouseClicked() method redraws the cursor at the new position and sets a new property value using the setValue() method (resulting in the notification of the bean's listeners).

```
// Inner MouseMotionAdapter subclass
class MyMouseMotionAdapter extends MouseMotionAdapter {

    public void mouseDragged(MouseEvent e) {
        if (m_bDragging) {
            Graphics g = getGraphics();
            eraseCursor(g);
            m_nTmpVal = PixelsToVal(e.getX());
            drawCursor(g);
        }
    }
}
```

This inner class is used to implement the mouseDragged() method (see Chapter 6 for details). The mouseDragged() method will be invoked when the user drags the mouse inside the bean's area. When this happens, the method verifies that the dragging flag (m_bDragging) has been set to true. And if so, it erases the bean's cursor at the old position (using the eraseCursor( ) method), calculates the bean's new value corresponding to the current mouse position (using the PixelsToVal( ) method), and redraws the cursor at the new position (using the drawCursor( ) method).

Note: This method does not actually set a new value to the bean's property but only uses a temporary variable. Hence, the bean property remains unaffected (and the listeners will not be notified) until the user actually releases the mouse button.

```
// PropertyChangeListener support
public void addPropertyChangeListener(PropertyChangeListener Listener)
{
     m_ChSupp.addPropertyChangeListener(Listener);
}

public void removePropertyChangeListener(PropertyChangeListener
Listener) {
     m_ChSupp.removePropertyChangeListener(Listener);
}
```

These two methods are implemented from the Customizer interface. They add and remove instances of PropertyChangeListener to and from this bean by invoking the addPropertyChangeListener( ) and removePropertyChangeListener( ) methods on the PropertyChangeSupport instance m_ChSupp (that object will notify all registered listeners in the setValue( ) method).

```
public void setObject(Object bean) {}
```

This method is implemented from the Customizer interface but is not used by this class.

Save and compile the program.

BeanTest

The following applet is designed to show the BeanScale class in action. Create a text file named BeanTest and enter the following code text (or you can copy it from this book's Companion CD-ROM):

> **TIP**
>
> *Alternatively, if you have installed the BDK, you can test* BeanScale *in the Beanbox (a demonstration of which is beyond the scope of this book).*

```
import java.lang.*;
import java.awt.*;
```

```java
import java.awt.event.*;
import java.applet.*;
import java.beans.*;

import BeanScale;

public class BeansTest extends Applet
{
    TextField m_ShowVal;

    // Applet initialization
    public void init()
    {
        add(new Label(
            "Select value (0 - 100):"));

        m_ShowVal = new TextField(8);
        m_ShowVal.setEditable(false);
        add(m_ShowVal);

        // Create bean's control
        BeanScale scale = new BeanScale();
        scale.addPropertyChangeListener(new
            PropertyAdapter());
        scale.setSize(200, 20);
        scale.setValue(50);
        scale.setMinVal(0);
        scale.setMaxVal(100);
        add(scale);
    }


    // Adapter to take property changes
    class PropertyAdapter implements
        PropertyChangeListener
    {
        public void propertyChange(
            PropertyChangeEvent Evt)
        {
            Integer n = (Integer)Evt.
                getNewValue();
            m_ShowVal.setText(n.toString());
        }
    }
```

```
public static void main(String args[])
{
    Frame frame = new Frame(
        "Java Beans Applet");
    frame.setSize(300, 100);

    BeansTest appl = new BeansTest();
    frame.add("Center", appl);
    appl.init();
    appl.start();

    frame.addWindowListener(appl. new
        WndAdapter());
    frame.setVisible(true);
}


// Window Adapter
class WndAdapter extends WindowAdapter
{
    public void windowClosing(WindowEvent e)
    {
        e.getWindow().dispose();
        System.exit(0);
    }
}

}
```

Since most of this should be review for you, we will concentrate our analysis on the Java Beans–related code:

```
// Create bean's control
BeanScale scale = new BeanScale();
scale.addPropertyChangeListener(new PropertyAdapter());
scale.setSize(200, 20);
scale.setValue(50);
scale.setMinVal(0);
scale.setMaxVal(100);
add(scale);
```

This part of the applet's init() method creates a new instance of the BeanScale class. Then it adds a new instance of the inner class PropertyAdapter as a property change listener for this bean. The BeanScale component then is resized through a setSize() method call (this method is inherited from the java.awt.Component class).

Note: None of the methods in the BeanScale class relies on the component's size. Instead, they all retrieve the current size of the component on an as-needed basis. This allows for consistency in all resized instances of this Beans component.

The rest of the preceding code sets the bean's initial value as well as its minimum and maximum ranges, using the setValue( ), setMinVal( ), and setMaxVal( ) methods, respectively. Note that, since at this point the property change listener (PropertyAdapter) had been added, it will receive notification and, in turn display the initial value in the text field m_ShowVal of this applet. Finally, the code adds the Beans component to the applet's panel using the add( ) method.

```
// Adapter to take property changes
class PropertyAdapter implements
    PropertyChangeListener
{
    public void propertyChange(
        PropertyChangeEvent Evt)
    {
        Integer n = (Integer)Evt.
            getNewValue();
        m_ShowVal.setText(n.toString());
    }
}
```

Now look at the inner class PropertyAdapter. This adapter implements only one method, propertyChange( ), which will be invoked when the bean's property is changed. This method extracts the new value from the PropertyChangeEvent instance that is passed to the method and displays this value in the m_ShowVal text field.

Save BeanTest.java in the same directory in which you saved BeanScale.java. Then, compile and run BeanTest. Notice that the value in the text box changes as soon as you drag the bean's cursor or click the mouse over the bean's body (see Figure 10-2).

Figure 10-2: BeanScale example.

Moving On

In this chapter, you had an introduction to the component object model as well as Java Beans. You also learned about the Java Beans architecture and API. Finally, you had a chance to create a working Beans component and test it in a Java applet.

In the next chapter, you will get an introduction to one of Java's new GUI toolkits—the Java Foundation Classes (JFC). As you will see, some of the JFC is based on the AWT and Java Beans, and the material for these parts will be review for you. However, other parts of the JFC come from other GUI toolkits (i.e., Netscape's Internet Foundation Classes), as well as some completely new additions to which you will be introduced.

## PART III

Introducing the JFC

Introduction to the JFC

The Java Foundation Classes (JFC) represent an extension from the Abstract Window Toolkit (AWT), which you learned about earlier in this book. The JFC is also a conglomeration of Netscape's Internet Foundation Classes (IFC) technologies and some completely new functionality. In short, the JFC is a graphical user interface (GUI) toolkit specifically designed to create professional Java front ends.

In this chapter, we are going to take a preliminary look at the JFC and how it relates to the AWT and Netscape's IFC. We will also learn about the disadvantages of the AWT and the IFC, and how the JFC resolves these issues. Finally, we will cover the key features that make up the JFC. By the end of this chapter, you should have a good understanding of the JFC as well as a good understanding of where the JFC fits into the JavaSoft game plan.

Note: The JFC is still in a prerelease state at the time of this writing; some of features of the JFC may have been changed and/or enhanced by the time you read this or when it is officially released.

Defining JFC

The JFC is an application programming interface (API) that provides a suite of services as well as components to facilitate the development of professional front ends in any and all of your Java solutions. A single vendor (e.g., JavaSoft) is not developing the JFC; rather, it is a joint development project between

IBM, Netscape, and JavaSoft. With support for this development effort coming directly from JavaSoft, along with the backing of other major vendors, the JFC (when released) should quickly gain acceptance as the premier GUI development toolkit for any and all Java solutions.

Microsoft's Application Foundation Classes (AFC) vs. the JFC

Microsoft has developed a product comparable to the JFC, called Microsoft's AFC. The JFC is definitely in direct competition with the AFC, and as a result, Microsoft has remained conspicuously absent in JFC goings-on. Nonetheless, the JFC has JavaSoft's backing as well as an installed base of AWT and IFC users, giving it the JFC market share even before its release. For more information on the AFC, please go to http://www.microsoft.com/java.

Since the JFC is not proprietary to one vendor, it is receiving input from a number of organizations (for example, Apple Computer, which has stated it intends to support the JFC on the Macintosh), as well as from the general public, to better address the needs of Java GUI developers. Both the AWT and the IFC are being used as the foundations for the JFC. So, if you have any experience in either of these GUI toolkits (if you read Chapters 5 and 6, you should be more than a little familiar with the AWT), you will find the JFC familiar territory. At this point, let's take a closer look at both the AWT and IFC to explore the key advantages and disadvantages these toolkits brought to Java, and why they are being included in the JFC.

Looking Back at the AWT

In Chapter 5, you were introduced to the AWT, its components and services. As you may have noticed, when compared to GUI toolkits from other platforms outside Java, the AWT contained only a handful of components and an uncompleted list of services. For example, the java.awt.TextArea component does not have any sort of word-wrapping functionality; therefore, if a string of text goes beyond the borders of this component, it will not be "wrapped" to the next line (a common built-in feature in other environments). Also, services such as undo/redo currently are unavailable in the AWT.

Note: Knowing that the AWT is an integral part of the JFC, you can distinguish between them. The AWT 1.1 (included in Java 1.1) is sometimes referred to as the JFC. This is because so many of the features in the AWT 1.1 are transparently present in the JFC. However, for purposes of clarity, when we refer to the JFC in this book, we are referring to the one that contains IFC features and (at the time of this writing) is still under development.

By design, the AWT was focused on front-end solutions used for the development of Java applets that are executed inside a browser and not necessarily designed for a commercial-grade stand-alone application with a complete and more traditional user interface (UI). Although this proved to be a perfect fit for the initial release of Java (while the Java application market was just budding), with the advent of applications and more sophisticated applets, the AWT is beginning to outlive its usefulness. That is why it is being superseded by the more feature-rich and robust JFC.

The Advantages of the AWT

When the AWT was released, it brought two distinct strengths to GUI development. It was introduced as the first completely portable GUI toolkit (at both the source and the binary level), and it could assume its native environment's *look and feel*. These two strengths were the focal points of functionality for the AWT and helped make Java much of what it is today.

Defining Look & Feel

Look and feel is used to describe all of the major and minor designs, layouts, colors, and overall appearance of a given platform (or component). From one perspective, all GUI toolkits are very similar; for example, the Windows, Macintosh, and Motif environments all have the GUI component button. However, the overall look and feel for the button (for example, its framing, colors, location, and so forth) can vary greatly from one platform to the next.

We have already discussed platform independence in Java. However, it is important to clarify that a Java program's ability to assume the native look and feel of its hosting environment gave Java the leverage necessary to develop really cool applets. It also proved to be one of the most powerful aspects of the AWT. However, the AWT's implementation of this native look and feel, as well as its overall lack of functionality/flexibility, has proven a challenge for developing professional GUI-intensive Java programs, about which we will learn more in the next section.

The Disadvantages of the AWT

Though the AWT was hugely successful at first, its actual implementation was not designed in a very flexible or extendable way. This was not a flaw on JavaSoft's part. Rather, it was the result of ensuring that the AWT met the time deadlines for the initial release of Java.

The AWT utilizes what is known as the *peer model* for its implementation of giving components their native look and feel. In this model, when a component is instantiated, there is a call to create another instance of that same component in the native environment (that is, the component's peer). Obviously, depending on the environment, the looks of the native peer will differ. By creating a Java component and a native counterpart, Java can facilitate platform independence. Effectively, the source and binary code for the AWT components you create in Java are layered on top of a native implementation. Unfortunately, using a peer model is akin to cheating, because such an implementation is not truly platform independent all the way through; rather, it simply adds what could be termed "layers of abstraction" to an otherwise platform-dependent foundation.

TIP

In Java, peer-based components are termed heavyweight. *The term was chosen to describe the extra baggage the native peer brings to a given AWT component. Fortunately, as you will learn later in this chapter, the components presented in the JFC are* lightweight *(that is, they do not have the extra baggage of a native peer), thus freeing them from the inflexibility and restrictions of the peer model.*

Back when the AWT was first introduced, it appeared to free developers from a single platform. However, with the advent of professional-level Java applications, the peer model has begun to expose its overall inflexibility and limitations. Specifically, using the peer model does not allow customization of the look and feel of a given AWT component (at least not easily). You are stuck with the look and feel of whatever environment you happen to be running. Furthermore, the peculiarities, bugs, and/or platform-dependent restrictions present in a native GUI environment will crop up in this peer model to the actual AWT components (even though they are written in Java).

> **TIP**
>
> *If you want to customize the look and feel for a given AWT component, the typical solution would either be to extend the* java.awt.Canvas *class (for components), overriding its* paint() *method to draw the component of your choice, or to extend the* java.awt.Panel *class (for containers), doing likewise with its* paint() *method. At best, this is a workaround and a long way from perfect, because these custom components must still be rendered in a nontransparent native peer window, resulting in an inability to layer them.*

As you will learn a little later in the chapter, the JFC has resolved these issues that plagued the AWT by not using the peer model. Right now, however, let's take a look at Netscape's IFC to learn a little more about what it is and why it is being added to the JFC.

Note: Programs written in the AWT should be compatible with and easily portable to the JFC.

Looking Back at the IFC

Not long after Java's initial release, Netscape recognized limitations in the AWT. As a result, they started their IFC project. The IFC is a set of APIs designed to effectively sit on top of the AWT both to provide smoother implementations for some of the existing AWT features and components, and to add some new features or components that the AWT did not currently support.

For example, the IFC added a completely new component—ColorChooser (among several others)—which can be used as a dialog to let a user visually choose a color. An excellent instance of the IFC improving on the AWT is the additional layer of abstraction to the java.awt.GridBagLayout layout manager, which enables the developer to use this layout without being forced to overcomplicate the user interface. Aside from adding new components and enhancing the existing features of the AWT, the IFC added completely new functionality (most notably drag and drop), which otherwise was unavailable to a typical AWT user.

> **TIP**
>
> *A detailed introduction and overview of the IFC is beyond the scope of this book. For more information, including a more complete listing of the technical aspects of the IFC, take a look at the IFC section in Ventana's* Official Netscape ONE Developer's Guide, *2nd Edition [ISBN: 1-56604-710-2].*

In the end, the IFC proved to be a key third-party ingredient in many Java development solutions. However, its third-party status put it at a disadvantage and proved to be a major roadblock in its acceptance in the mainstream. The IFC had to be installed and added as "extra baggage" to Java. Thus, despite the improvements the IFC made to the AWT, it was definitely a compromise.

Note: The primary exception to the "extra baggage" rule is that most Netscape products (for example, Navigator) have added the IFC as a standard part of their run-time environment for Java.

As you will learn in the following sections, the JFC is proving to be a win/win situation for the IFC, because all of the key features of the IFC are included in the JFC; and, unlike the IFC, the JFC will be an integral part of the Java platform. Let's take a closer look at the overall features that make up the JFC.

Note: Programs written in the IFC will be able to execute on any Java platform (whether or not the JFC is present). However, such programs are not directly portable to use the JFC alone without porting the code to the JFC and recompiling. Nonetheless, JavaSoft states that the migration tools will be available to assist in the porting of IFC solutions directly to the JFC.

Key Features of the JFC

Now that you have learned a little bit about the JFC's origins, let's turn our attention to the direction in which the JFC is heading. One of the JFC's powerful features is its framework's design—flexible, extendible, and an integral part of the Java platform. Let's take a look at the features of the JFC.

Accessibility for the Physically Challenged

One of the completely new features of the JFC is the Accessibility API. This API is designed to convert standard user interfaces created in the JFC to other formats that can be accessed by physically challenged individuals. Specifically, there will be a *screen reader*, which converts a given UI to some speech-synthesized equivalent; a *Braille terminal*, which (in a similar fashion to the screen reader) converts a given UI into Braille; and a *screen magnifier*, which enlarges the screen for this UI to as much as 16 times its original size.

Note: Microsoft's AFC has a similar API known as the Active Accessibility API, but this API works only with AFC solutions and is proprietary to Microsoft's Java virtual machine.

Beans Compliance

The Java Beans architecture you learned about in the last chapter is a key ingredient in the overall infrastructure of the JFC. Furthermore, all JFC components are actually Beans components and use the Java Beans component-object model. This improves their ability to be used (and reused), extended, and incorporated into visual development solutions. For more information on the advantages of Java Beans, please refer to Chapter 10.

Clipboard/Data Transfer

Cut, copy, and paste operations (services currently available in the AWT), as well as the framework for general data transfer will be available in the JFC. The JFC (like the AWT) will be able to support normal clipboard operations in Java-program-to-Java-program as well as Java-program-to-native-program solutions. For more information on this, please refer to Chapter 6.

Desktop Color Integration

This service also is available currently and is being copied over from the AWT. It allows you to customize your UI to follow the color scheme (as closely as possible) that's being used on the native environment. For a demonstration, please refer to Chapter 6.

Delegation Event Handling

As you learned in Chapter 6, event handling in Java is part of a delegation process. In summary, an object (designed to respond to a certain event type) is assigned to listen to some event source, and when an event object of the corresponding type (or types) is created, it then is delegated to the object assigned and designed to handle it. This type of event handling is much more effective for an object-oriented language like Java than are large conditional statements—usually switch statements—which are more error prone. For more information on delegation-event handling, along with a number of runnable examples, please refer to Chapter 6.

Drag & Drop

This feature has been carried over from the IFC. The IFC has defined the foundation for having a given object in Java be both draggable and droppable in a Java-to-Java solution. The JFC has borrowed and extended this functionality so that it provides a foundation to very easily add drag and drop capabilities in Java-to-Java as well as Java-to-native solutions. The general structure for data transfer was touched upon in the clipboard section of Chapter 6.

Graphics/Image Enhancements

Various enhanced graphics and image handling functionality are key features added from the AWT. Key enhancements include better graphics handling and image generation on the fly. A detailed discussion of these enhancements is beyond the scope of this book, but a closely related topic is the 2D API, which is a new addition to Java and a key feature in the JFC.

Printing Functionality

As you learned in Chapter 6, printing is an important part of the AWT. This same printing functionality is also available in the JFC.

Lightweight Framework

As mentioned earlier in the chapter, all JFC components are lightweight. This improves the performance, extendability, and appearance of all JFC components. The lightweight component concept was pioneered in the IFC and has been incorporated as the framework for the JFC. With this lightweight framework, it is very easy to incorporate third-party Beans components or custom components of your own design in the JFC. The next chapter gives a little more detail regarding this framework and the actual components present in the JFC.

Mouseless Operation

If you happen to be familiar with the AWT 1.0 (which was included in the JDK 1.0), you know that UIs created with this version were not keyboard traversable (that is, the only way to interact with the UI was through the mouse). The IFC first introduced the concept of using the keyboard to interact with a Java

UI. Then, as you learned in Chapter 6, the AWT 1.1 has included this type of functionality as well. The JFC also will inherit the mouseless functionality with a few enhancements.

Pluggable Look & Feel

Not too long ago, the look and feel between platforms (for example, Windows, Macintosh, Motif, etc.) were quite segregated. However, since the commercialization of the Net, the lines have been blurred, and the native look and feel functionality used in the AWT is proving to be restrictive for certain solutions. Today, with the advent of thin clients (that is, NC computers) and the emergence of universal look and feel, programs need to be flexible in their look and feel. The JFC uses a pluggable look and feel, meaning that a given JFC-generated UI can easily assume (and even switch to) any available look and feel. You will have a chance to learn more about how this is done in the next chapter.

Swing Set Components

The term *swing set* is used to describe all of the components that make up the JFC. The components making up the swing set are, by default, lightweight Beans components. At this time, the number of components still is not known, but when completed, the JFC will contain components from the AWT and the IFC, as well as several completely new ones. The next chapter's main focus will be to introduce you to the swing set and how it works and to demonstrate some of its functionality.

Undo/Redo Support

One of the new features to be added to the JFC (unavailable in both the AWT and the IFC) is undo/redo support. This API lets users backtrack and move forward again (if they so desire) to various actions they performed in the UI.

Note: This is particularly useful for solutions that call for users to write and edit large amounts of text in your UI.

2D API

A new API known as the 2D API will be included in the JFC. This API will extend from the java.awt and java.awt.image classes, providing a rich set of features for the creation, portation, and manipulation (even during the rendering process) of various graphics. One of the key features of the 2D API is that it will treat all graphics in the same way, regardless of their type (drawing, text, image, etc.).

Moving On

In this chapter, you had a chance to learn about the AWT and IFC and how they are being integrated into the JFC. You also learned about key services and features in the JFC, including where they came from, as well as many references for more information.

In the next chapter, we are going to focus on the swing set to learn about the various JFC components available (or currently in development). Some of this may be review from Chapter 5, while other parts will be uncharted territory.

The Swing Set

When the last chapter introduced the Java Foundation Classes (JFC), one of the key features mentioned was the Swing set. The Swing set is the term used to denote the suite of components that will be present in the JFC. As you learned with the Abstract Window Toolkit (AWT), the actual components for a graphical user interface (GUI) toolkit make up at least half of its functionality. The same holds true for the JFC.

This chapter is going to introduce you to Swing components. It will also go into a little more depth about how they are different (and better) than traditional AWT components. You will also have a chance to learn about a number of the classes that make up the Swing set and to create a few examples. Finally, you will have a look at other features/functionality that will be available as the Swing set (and the JFC) comes nearer to completion.

Note: At the time of this writing, the Swing set is still in a prereleased state; some of the features discussed here may be changed or added by the time the JFC is officially released.

Swing Architecture

The Swing architecture is based on two key technologies: Java Beans and pluggable look and feel. Since we already thoroughly discussed Beans architecture in Chapter 10, we will not discuss it here. At this point, it is important just to note that all Swing components are Java Beans compliant. However, the following section will take a closer look at the pluggable look and feel architecture and how it is being implemented in the Swing set.

Pluggable Look & Feel Architecture

As mentioned in the last chapter, pluggable look and feel represents a more flexible alternative than the rigid native look and feel used in the AWT. With the pluggable alternative, you can choose the look and feel that you want your front end to utilize.

Note: Choosing a look and feel is performed at the program's run time and can be changed dynamically (without even needing to reinitialize the program itself).

Swing's pluggable look and feel architecture also allows for different users of the same program to potentially choose a different look and feel. Hence, one program can be executed dynamically (at the same time) in more than one look and feel. For example, one program could be executed in three locations, the first using a Windows-based look and feel, the second using a Solaris-based look and feel, and the third using the Accessibility application programming interface (API)—discussed in the prior chapter—to convert the look and feel to a Braille terminal.

What Kinds of Look and Feel Are Available?

Included with Swing (and therefore the JFC) are two kinds of look and feel. The first (named Basic) facilitates the standard 32-bit Windows look and feel. The second (named Rose) shows the standard look and feel used by Netscape. However, once the JFC is released, there will be a number of other kinds of look and feel available for the other major platforms. And it is very feasible for you (the developer) to create your own custom look and feel as well.

Model View Controller

How is all this functionality technically possible? Simply stated, Swing uses a *Model View Controller* (MVC) design. Based on Swing's implementation of this design, the overall functionality of a given component is segregated into three distinct parts:

- **Model.** The part representing the internal state for a given component.
- **View.** The visual appearance (i.e., the look and feel).
- **Controller.** Acts as the bridge between the View and the Model. Effectively, the controller makes sure that user input from the View is correspondingly updated in the Model.

Based on the needs of Swing, a completely segregated view and controller are not necessary. Swing has implemented an MVC in which there is segregation only between the model (M) and the view controller (VC). The VC part is known as the *delegate* for a given Swing component. This is a good name, as it effectively acts as a delegate between the user and the actual data for the given Swing component.

Note: All MVC parts are interchangeable, and more than one delegate can be present for a given Swing component. This is how the versatility described at the beginning of this section is technically possible.

Swing Component Architecture

So far, this discussion has remained fairly theoretical. At this point, though, we are going to look at the necessary classes that actually make up a Swing component. Doing so should help clarify and make sense out of some of the previous theory. In this case, we will take a look at Swing component Button, in which there are five distinct classes (or interfaces):

- **Interface ButtonModel and Class JButtonModel.** This interface defines the non-look-and-feel-related state for the Swing component. Implementations of this interface use a name convention based on the standard prefix of J and suffix of Model; hence, the one Swing class implementing this interface is called JButtonModel.

- **Interface ButtonUI and Class BasicButtonUI.** This interface defines the look-and-feel-specific state for the Swing component. This interface must extend ComponentUI in some way. The default implementation of this interface is based on the 32-bit Windows look and feel. Note the UI prefix and the name Basic.

- **Class JButton.** This is the actual component. This class must extend JComponent (which extends java.awt.Container) either directly or indirectly.

Note: All Swing components have been prefixed with the letter J to differentiate them from normal AWT components.

Looking at the previous discussions of MVC and the Swing components, implementations of ButtonModel represent the controller, implementations of ButtonUI represent the view, and the class JButton represents the model.

Note: The JButton class is the only class with which you need be concerned if you are interested simply in using a given Swing component.

However, as mentioned earlier, a more common alternative implementation is to have the view and controller combined into one object. For example, take a look at the ToolBar component:

- **Interface ToolBarUI and BasicToolBarUI.** This interface defines the entire state (both the look and feel and internal state) for the Swing component.

- **Class JToolBar.** This is the actual Swing component.

Here, implementations of the ToolBarUI interface (i.e., BasicToolBarUI) act as both the view and controller for this Swing component.

UI Factories

In Swing, a given pluggable look and feel is managed by the abstract UIFactory class. This class is responsible for handling the given look and feel for all the components for a look and feel theme. This factory contains a "default" look and feel for itself. It also contains the functionality necessary to customize, override, and/or update the look and feel for a specific component (or components) belonging to a given factory.

A given UI factory is a concrete subclass of UIFactory and uses the naming convention of its name followed by the word Factory. So, for example, on the default look and feel facilitated by the Swing called Basic, the UI factory is correspondingly BasicFactory. Using this class, you can specify attributes (such as the background color) that will be used by all components in this factory. The factory class's other key roles are to initialize resources (e.g., images), to return new instances of the UI object for a given Swing component (on demand), and to install new UI objects if there is a change from the default factory.

Note on the Multiplexing UI Factory

Swing is also defining a multiplexing factory called MultiFactory that allows you to mix and match UI factories for various components. This is useful for situations in which you wish to have more than one view for a given component (or set of components). The multiplexing UI factory also lets you define more than one controller, leaving the view the same. For example, the multiplexing factory comes in handy in situations in which you are using the Accessibility API in which a UI is being interpreted to Braille, audio, and visual format.

Basically, this factory lets you mix and match UIs from the default UI factory as well as a list of auxiliary factories. The multiplexing factory accomplishes its task by acting as a sort of intermediary between a given component (requesting a UI) and the current default factory. Effectively, calls are sent to the multiplexing factory (as opposed to the default factory), thereby allowing you to use the default factory's UI for this component and/or one from an auxiliary factory.

Auxiliary factories are specified in the AuxiliaryProperties property of the uimanager.properties file. You also can override the default multiplexing factory by specifying the MultiplexingFactory in the uimanager.properties file as well. However, for most implementations, the multiplexing factory that comes with Swing will be more than sufficient.

The UIManager is responsible for determining whether multiplexing should be used by seeing if the AuxiliaryProperties property exists and has specified at least one valid auxiliary factory. Otherwise, the current default factory will be used directly.

However, unless you intend to create your own look and feel, the key class that you will work with in typical solutions is UIManager. This class manages a list of installed (e.g., available) UI factories with one that is marked specifically as the default. This class also contains a number of utility methods that relate to its management of the UI factory list. Table 12-1 lists and explains the methods available in the UIManager class.

Method	Explanation
addUIChangeListener(Window)	Adds the specified Window to be notified in the event that the default UI look and feel should change.
deinstallUIFactory(String)	Removes the specified UI factory from the persistent list of available UI factories managed by this UIManager. Note that you need to specify the full path (e.g., com.java.sun.MyFactory) or a ClassNotFoundException is thrown.
getAuxiliaryFactories()	Used in multiplexing to return an array of UIFactory objects specifying the available auxiliary factories or null if multiplexing is not defined.
getDefaultFactory()	Returns a UIFactory object that specifies the current default UI factory specified for this UIManager.
getInstalledUIFactoryList()	Returns an Enumeration of the class names for all of the factories currently installed in this UIManager.
getUI(String, String, JComponent)	Returns a ComponentUI implementation for the specified Swing component from the default factory. Note that the first parameter specifies the component name, the second specifies an alternate class if the default factory cannot provide a UI for this component by using the multiplexing factory (if available), and the third specifies a reference to the actual Swing component whose UI is being requested.
getUIFactory(String)	Returns a UIFactory reference for the specified UI factory.
installUIFactory(String)	Installs the specified UI factory and adds it to this UIManager's list. When specifying the UI factory, note that you need to put the full path (e.g., com.java.sun.MyFactory) as needed.
removeUIChangeListener(Window)	Removes the specified Window from the list to be notified in the event that the default UI look and feel should change.

Method	Explanation
setInstalledUIFactoryList(String[])	Installs the specified list of UI factories and adds it to this UIManager's list. When specifying the UI factory, note that you need to put the full path (e.g., com.java.sun.MyFactory) as needed.
setUIFactory(UIFactory, Container), setUIFactory(String, Container), setUIFactory(UIFactory, Container, boolean)	Sets the default UI factory to be used by this container, resetting the UI for components in the specified Container. If you use a String to specify the UI factory, you need to put the full path (e.g., com.java.sun.MyFactory) as needed. Also, you can specify a boolean to save the default UI factory property.

Table 12-1: Static methods in the UIManager class.

The Swing API

At this point, we are going to put on our programming hats to take a closer look at the key components and/or services that come with Swing. Unfortunately, not all of the components or services have been fully provided for with this early release, so some key components and/or services may have been skipped over. However, at the time of this writing, here are the Swing packages available:

- **com.java.sun.swing**. The package containing all the Swing components and their interfaces.

- **com.sun.java.swing.accessibility**. The Accessibility API.

- **com.sun.java.swing.basic**. The package used for the Basic UI factory, which has a Windows 95 look and feel and is the default factory for Swing.

- **com.sun.java.swing.border**. The package containing the border-based Swing components.

- **com.sun.java.swing.event**. The package containing event-handling classes for some new event types to handle the events for the new Swing components.

- **com.sun.java.multi**. The package used for the multiplexing UI factory.

- **com.sun.java.rose**. The package used for the Rose UI factory, which represents the factory that has a Netscape look and feel.

- `com.sun.java.swing.table`. The package used for the `JTable` Swing component.

- `com.sun.java.swing.text`. The package used for texts.

- `com.sun.java.swing.undo`. The package used for the undo/redo Swing service.

Installing the Prerelease of the JFC

If you intend to try the examples in this chapter, you will need to download a prerelease of the JFC from the following site: http://www.javasoft.com.

Once downloaded, unzip the files into a directory (let's say `c:\jfc`). Then you will need to update your `CLASSPATH` environment variable to specify the locations of `swing.jar` and `rose.jar`. An example of a typical `CLASSPATH` might look like the following:

`set CLASSPATH=c:\java\lib\classes.zip;c:\JFC\swing.jar;c:\java\JFC\rose.jar;`

Note that the prerelease of the JFC works only with the Java Development Kit (JDK) 1.1.X.

Once this is installed, you can import the various classes and/or subpackages from what is called the `java.swing` package by using an import statement. For example:

`import com.sun.java.swing.*;`

Note that when Java 1.2 is released, it will contain Swing as part of the core Java platform in the `java.swing` package.

Starting with the basic Swing components (most of which were carried over from the AWT), let's take a closer look.

Basic Swing Components

In this section, we are going to cover the basic Swing components. None of these components should be new to you, because they have been copied (most with only a few minor changes) from the AWT. Figure 12-1 diagrams the class hierarchy for the basic components discussed in the following subsections.

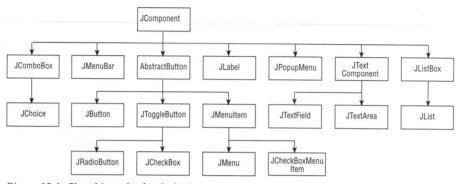

Figure 12-1: Class hierarchy for the basic components.

Note: A number of AWT components have been ported over to the JFC; so far, however, they have not undergone any significant changes/improvements and are not being discussed. Since JFC is still under development, these unmentioned components may end up undergoing changes.

Button

Probably the most simple GUI component is the button. The Swing button component, `swing.JButton`, is practically a copy from the `java.awt.Button` AWT component you learned about in Chapter 5. The one addition that is worth mentioning is the support for both text and icon labels in a given `JButton` object.

Icons

One of the new features to the Swing set is the ability to have icons appear in a label that is used by any Swing component that contains a label, including the label Swing component (which you will learn about a little later on). This is facilitated by the addition of the `Icon` interface and its implementation `ImageIcon`. The `ImageIcon` class lets you create a cached icon version of any image. You can construct an `ImageIcon` by specifying a path and filename (as a string), a Uniform Resource Locator (URL), or a normal `java.awt.Image` reference.

The following example demonstrates two `JButton` instances that belong to two different panels. The first panel (i.e., the westward one) uses the `Rose` UI factory, while the second panel (i.e., the eastward one) uses the `Basic` UI factory (this source code is available on this book's Companion CD-ROM).

```
import java.awt.*;
import java.awt.event.*;
import com.sun.java.swing.*;

public class SwingButtonTest extends JFrame implements ActionListener {
JButton myButton1;
JButton myButton2;

    public SwingButtonTest() {

        JBufferedPane basicPanel = new JBufferedPane();
        //Set the UI manager for basicPanel
        try {

            UIManager.setUIFactory("com.sun.java.swing.basic.BasicFactory",
basicPanel);
        } catch (Exception e) {}

        //Create the first button
        myButton1 = new JButton("Basic");
        myButton1.addActionListener(this);
        basicPanel.add(myButton1);

        //Add the panel to the frame
        add(basicPanel, "East");

        JBufferedPane rosePanel = new JBufferedPane();
        //Set the UI panel for basicPanel
        try {

            UIManager.setUIFactory("com.sun.java.swing.rose.RoseFactory",
rosePanel);
        } catch (Exception e) {}

        //Create the second button
        myButton2 = new JButton("Rose");
        myButton2.addActionListener(this);
        rosePanel.add(myButton2);

        //Add the panel to the frame
        add(rosePanel, "West");

        addWindowListener(new WndAdapter());
        setSize(300, 200);
        setVisible(true);
    }
```

```
        // Event-handling for the buttons
        public void actionPerformed(ActionEvent event) {
            if (event.getSource() == myButton1)
                System.out.println("Basic was clicked.");
            else if (event.getSource() == myButton2)
                System.out.println("Rose was clicked.");
        }

        // Event-handling for the Frame
        class WndAdapter extends WindowAdapter {

            public void windowClosing(WindowEvent event) {
                event.getWindow().dispose();
                System.exit(0);
            }
        }

        public static void main(String args[]) {
            new SwingButtonTest();

        }


    }
```

Notice that the preceding code uses a number of Swing containers in exactly the same way that you learned to use AWT containers. Also, notice that JButton uses the same action-based event-handling mechanism as the AWT button. Except for several J's being added, nothing should be new to you. The setUIFactory( ) method call is used to specify which UI factory we want the specified container (in this case, a JBuffered instance, which is the equivalent of a Panel in the AWT) to use. Figure 12-2 shows the previous code in action.

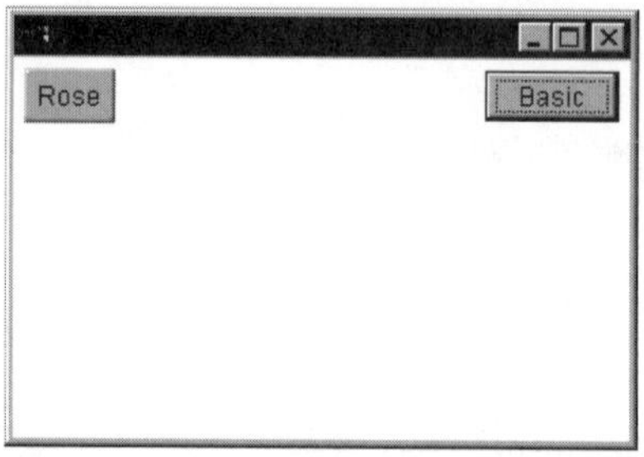

Figure 12-2: SwingButtonTest in action.

Look at the two buttons closely. Notice that the fonts and corners are different. Also, click both of the buttons and notice that the Rose button does not display a dotted rectangle around its label when it has focus. Throughout the rest of this chapter, you will have a chance to gain exposure to the pluggable look and feel concept by comparing Rose and Basic with identical components. We may not point out all the visual details (as we did here), but be sure to note them as you go along.

Note on DebugGraphics

With the advent of pluggable look and feel, the JFC has provided capabilities for developers to debug their UIs as they are being made. This is facilitated through the DebugGraphics class, which is a subclass of Graphics. Through this class, you can see graphics (in red) as they are being drawn and get detailed internal information on how the drawing is taking place.

To use the DebugGraphics class, you use the methods getDebugGraphicsOption() and setDebugGraphicsOption(), which are present in any JComponent subclass (i.e., any Swing component). The debugOptions property has three states:

- DebugGraphics.LOG_OPTION. Used to display a textual log.

- DebugGraphics.FLASH_OPTION. Used to cause the drawing to repeatedly flash, allowing you to see how it is being drawn.

- DebugGraphics.BUFFERED_OPTION. Used to see the off screen view operations being performed in the buffer.

By default, all Swing components' debugOptions property is set to DebugGraphics.NONE_OPTION.

For a simple demonstration, add the following line of code to the constructor for the SwingButtonTest class (shown previously):

```
myButton1.setDebugGraphicsOptions(DebugGraphics.LOG_OPTION);
```

Run the example and pay close attention to the command box from which you executed, and you will see a detailed log (displayed in the console) of the construction of the UI for this Java program. You can also try to specify other debug options in the modified SwingButtonTest program.

RadioButton

Radio buttons may look like a new addition to Swing. However, they are merely the result of a name change from the CheckboxGroup that you learned about in the AWT chapter. Instead of Checkbox instances that belong to a CheckboxGroup instance, you have JRadioButton, which belongs to a ButtonGroup instance.

Note: Unlike the Checkbox class, if you use JRadioButton by itself (i.e., it does not belong to any group), it is still a JRadioButton that simply belongs to an empty group.

The following example demonstrates two JRadioButton instances that belong to the same ButtonGroup. Notice that in this example we use an icon for each JRadioButton (both the icons and source code are available on the Companion CD-ROM):

```java
import java.awt.*;
import java.awt.event.*;
import com.sun.java.swing.*;

public class SwingRadioButtonTest extends JFrame implements ItemListener {
JRadioButton myRadioButton1;
JRadioButton myRadioButton2;

    public SwingRadioButtonTest() {

        super("Where do you want to go today?");
        setLayout(new BorderLayout());

        //Construct the icons
        ImageIcon myEarthImage = new ImageIcon("images/earth.gif");
        ImageIcon myMarsImage = new ImageIcon("images/mars.gif");

        //Create the Radio button group
        ButtonGroup myRadioGroup = new ButtonGroup();

        //Create the first radio button
        myRadioButton1 = new JRadioButton("Earth", myEarthImage);
        myRadioButton1.addItemListener(this);

        myRadioGroup.add(myRadioButton1);
        add(myRadioButton1, "West");

        //Create the second radio button
        myRadioButton2 = new JRadioButton("Mars", myMarsImage);
        myRadioButton2.addItemListener(this);

        myRadioGroup.add(myRadioButton2);
        add(myRadioButton2, "East");

        addWindowListener(new WndAdapter());
        setSize(300, 100);
        setVisible(true);
    }
```

```
// Event-handling for the radio buttons
public void itemStateChanged(ItemEvent event) {
    if (event.getItemSelectable() == myRadioButton1)
        System.out.println("Earth is checked. Mars is unchecked.");
    else if (event.getItemSelectable() == myRadioButton2)
        System.out.println("Mars is checked. Earth is unchecked.");
}

// Event-handling for the Frame
class WndAdapter extends WindowAdapter {

    public void windowClosing(WindowEvent event) {
        event.getWindow().dispose();
        System.exit(0);
    }
}

public static void main(String args[]) {
    new SwingRadioButtonTest();

}

}
```

Nothing in the preceding code should be new to you, except JRadioButton does not use a constructor parameter to specify the ButtonGroup to which it should belong (as the Checkbox class did); instead, you use an add() method from the ButtonGroup class. Figure 12-3 shows the preceding in action.

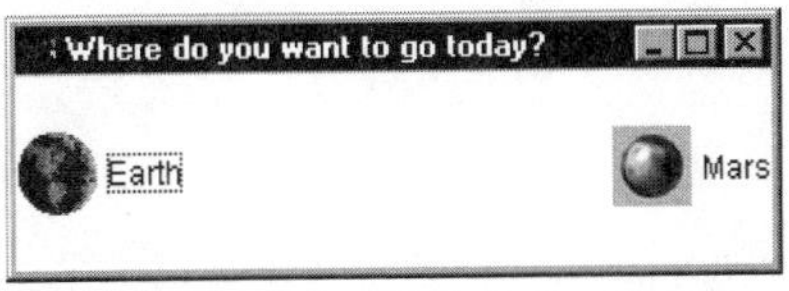

Figure 12-3: SwingRadioButtonTest in action.

Notice in Figure 12-3 how the icon goes into a depressed state when you choose a radio button.

Checkbox
In Swing, the JCheckBox class represents nothing more than a checkbox. Unlike the Checkbox class from the AWT, JCheckBox does not provide for checkbox groups.

Note: The API for checkbox groups is provided for in JCheckBox, but it is deprecated. It is highly recommended that you use the JRadioButton class discussed in the last section.

The following example demonstrates two CheckBox instances using the Rose and Basic look and feel respectively. Notice that in this example we use an icon for each JRadioButton (both the icons and source code are available on this book's Companion CD-ROM):

```java
import java.awt.*;
import java.awt.event.*;
import com.sun.java.swing.*;

public class SwingCheckboxTest extends JFrame implements ItemListener {
JCheckBox myCheckbox1;
JCheckBox myCheckbox2;

    public SwingCheckboxTest() {

        JBufferedPane basicPanel = new JBufferedPane();
        //Set the UI manager for basicPanel
        try {

            UIManager.setUIFactory("com.sun.java.swing.basic.BasicFactory",
basicPanel);
        } catch (Exception e) {}

        //Create the first button
        myCheckbox1 = new JCheckBox("Basic");
        myCheckbox1.addItemListener(this);
        basicPanel.add(myCheckbox1);

        //Add the panel to the frame
        add(basicPanel, "East");

        JBufferedPane rosePanel = new JBufferedPane();
        //Set the UI panel for basicPanel
        try {

            UIManager.setUIFactory("com.sun.java.swing.rose.RoseFactory",
rosePanel);
        } catch (Exception e) {}

        //Create the second button
        myCheckbox2 = new JCheckBox("Rose");
        myCheckbox2.addItemListener(this);
        rosePanel.add(myCheckbox2);
```

```
        //Add the panel to the frame
        add(rosePanel, "West");

        addWindowListener(new WndAdapter());
        setSize(300, 100);
        setVisible(true);
    }

    // Event-handling for the buttons
    public void itemStateChanged(ItemEvent event) {
        if (event.getItemSelectable() == myCheckbox1)
            System.out.println("Basic is " + myCheckbox1.isSelected() + ".");
        else if (event.getItemSelectable() == myCheckbox2)
            System.out.println("Rose is " + myCheckbox2.isSelected() + ".");
    }

    // Event-handling for the Frame
    class WndAdapter extends WindowAdapter {

        public void windowClosing(WindowEvent event) {
            event.getWindow().dispose();
            System.exit(0);
        }
    }

    public static void main(String args[]) {
        new SwingCheckboxTest();

    }


}
```

In the preceding code, notice that the isSelected() call—in the itemStateChanged() method above—is inherited from the AbstractButton class (JCheckBox's supersuperclass). Figure 12-4 shows the preceding in action.

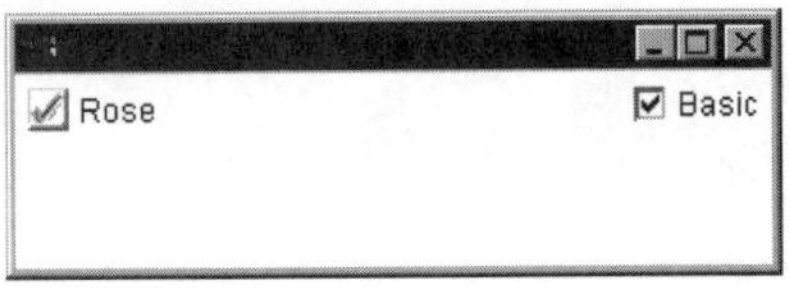

Figure 12-4: SwingCheckboxTest in action.

Combo Box

The combo box is something that you are already familiar with from the AWT, except that in the AWT it was referred to as a choice. The Swing component JComboBox is used for drop-down list implementations in the JFC. There are several methods used to add, edit, and remove objects from a given JComboBox instance. Table 12-2 details these methods.

Method	Explanation
addPossibleValue(Object)	Adds the specified Object to this JComboBox.
getCurrentValue()	Returns an Object containing the current value.
getCurrentValueIndex()	Returns an integer representing the current value (or −1 otherwise).
insertPossibleValue(Object, int)	Inserts the specified Object at the specified index.
removePossibleValue(Object)	Removes the specified Object from this JComboBox.
removePossibleValueAt(Object, int)	Removes the item from the specified index.
removeAllPossibleValues()	Clears this JComboBox.
setCurrentValue(int), setCurrentValue(Object)	Sets the current value.

Table 12-2: Useful methods for adding, editing, and removing items in JComboBox.

Note: For backward compatibility, the Swing set also has included a JChoice component (which is a subclass of JComboBox). However, it is highly recommended that you use JComboBox whenever possible.

The following example demonstrates a JComboBox instance using the Rose look and feel (the source code for this is available on the Companion CD-ROM):

```java
import java.awt.*;
import java.awt.event.*;
import com.sun.java.swing.*;

public class SwingComboBoxTest extends JFrame implements ItemListener {
JComboBox myComboBox;

    public SwingComboBoxTest() {

        setLayout(new FlowLayout());

        //Set the UI panel for basicPanel
        try {

            UIManager.setUIFactory("com.sun.java.swing.rose.RoseFactory", this);
        } catch (Exception e) {}
```

```
        //Create the combo box
        myComboBox = new JComboBox();
        myComboBox.addPossibleValue("1998");
        myComboBox.addPossibleValue("1997");
        myComboBox.addPossibleValue("1996");

        myComboBox.addItemListener(this);
        add(myComboBox);

        addWindowListener(new WndAdapter());
        setSize(200, 100);
        setVisible(true);
    }

    public void itemStateChanged(ItemEvent event) {
        if (event.getItemSelectable() == myComboBox);

System.out.println(((JComboBox)event.getItemSelectable()).getCurrentValue());
}

    // Event-handling for the Frame
    class WndAdapter extends WindowAdapter {

        public void windowClosing(WindowEvent event) {
            event.getWindow().dispose();
            System.exit(0);
        }
    }

    public static void main(String args[]) {
        new SwingComboBoxTest();

    }


}
```

Figure 12-5 shows the preceding code in action.

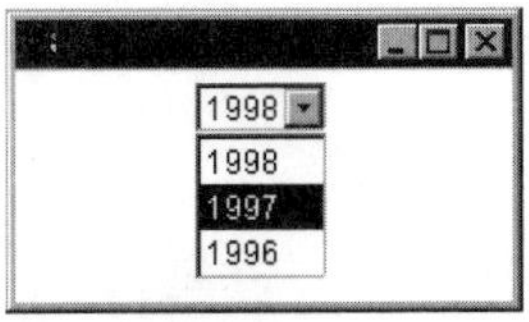

Figure 12-5: SwingComboBoxTest in action.

Label

The JLabel Swing component is like the Label AWT component, except it has the added functionality to display an icon by itself or in conjunction with a single line of text. Along these lines, JLabel also has the added functionality to allow you to specify the relative positioning and alignment of the text and icon in a given JLabel instance as well as the overall positioning and alignment for the label.

Note: JLabel is used as the label for other Swing components, including JButton, JCheckBox, JRadioButton, and JMenuItem (which will be discussed shortly).

The following example demonstrates a JLabel instance using the Rose look and feel, which contains both text and an icon (the source code and icon image are available on the Companion CD-ROM):

```java
import java.awt.*;
import java.awt.event.*;
import com.sun.java.swing.*;

public class SwingLabelTest extends JFrame {
JLabel myLabel;

    public SwingLabelTest() {

        //Create the label with text, an icon, and center alignment
        myLabel = new JLabel("Check this out!", new ImageIcon("images/
check.gif"), 0);

        //Set the icon/text gap to 10 pixels
        myLabel.setIconTextGap(10);

        add(myLabel);

        addWindowListener(new WndAdapter());
        setSize(300, 100);
        setVisible(true);
    }

    // Event-handling for the Frame
    class WndAdapter extends WindowAdapter {

        public void windowClosing(WindowEvent event) {
            event.getWindow().dispose();
            System.exit(0);
        }
    }
```

```
public static void main(String args[]) {
    new SwingLabelTest();
}

}
```

Figure 12-6 shows the preceding code in action.

Figure 12-6: SwingLabelTest in action.

List Box

Swing's list box is a portation from the java.awt.List component you learned about, except it has been renamed JListBox. The JListBox Swing component differs from the AWT component List in that you can declare an array of Objects and pass this array to the constructor of JListBox, so that each item in the array will be an element in the list box.

Just like the combo box described earlier, one of the key advantages to JListBox is that you can add objects to be elements of the list box rather than just simple text strings. Note that if you do use strings in a JListBox, they are encapsulated in a JLabel subclass. Also, just like the combo box, you are notified of changes in the selection (or selections in the case of list boxes) through an ItemEvent instance.

Note: For backward compatibility, the Swing set has also included a JList component (which is a subclass of JListBox). However, it is highly recommend that you use JListBox whenever possible.

The following example demonstrates a JListBox instance using the Rose look and feel, which contains an array of three ImageIcon objects (the actual images and source code are available on the Companion CD-ROM):

```
import java.awt.*;
import java.awt.event.*;
import com.sun.java.swing.*;
```

```java
public class SwingListBoxTest extends JFrame {
JListBox myListBox;

    public SwingListBoxTest() {

        setLayout(new FlowLayout());

        ImageIcon[] images = { new ImageIcon("images/new1.gif"), new
ImageIcon("images/new2.gif"), new ImageIcon("images/new3.gif") };

        //Set the UI panel for basicPanel
        try {

            UIManager.setUIFactory("com.sun.java.swing.rose.RoseFactory",
this);
        } catch (Exception e) {}

        //Create the List box
        myListBox = new JListBox(images);
        add(myListBox);

        addWindowListener(new WndAdapter());
        setSize(200, 100);
        setVisible(true);
    }

    // Event-handling for the Frame
    class WndAdapter extends WindowAdapter {

        public void windowClosing(WindowEvent event) {
            event.getWindow().dispose();
            System.exit(0);
        }
    }

    public static void main(String args[]) {
        new SwingListBoxTest();

    }

}
```

Figure 12-7 shows the preceding code in action.

Figure 12-7: SwingListBoxTest in action.

Menus

At the time of this writing, Swing menus are still under serious development. For the most part, though, the menus you learned about in the AWT will still hold here (with the exception of a few changes and enhancements). Probably the single biggest change to menus in Swing is that everything is now under JComponent (which is an eventual subclass of java.awt.Component). Previously, we had a java.awt.MenuComponent class (which directly extends java.lang.Object) for the menus-related components as well as the standard java.awt.Component class (which directly extends java.lang.Object). So, things are now greatly simplified, and the overall object-oriented design (OOD) is improved for menus in Java. At this point, let's take a quick look at each of the Swing menu components:

- **JMenuBar**. This class directly extends JComponent and will be enhanced to support a help menu as well as a menu of more than one row. JMenuBar event types are of the java.awt.ComponentEvent and/or java.awt.ContainerEvent type.

- **JMenu**. This class directly extends JMenuItem. The event handling for JMenu will be updated with the new event type swing.event.MenuEvent. Correspondingly, you will register swing.event.MenuListeners to handle MenuEvents originating from a given JMenu.

- **JMenuItem**. This class directly extends the swing.AbstractButton class. JMenuItems (just like their predecessors, AWT MenuItem components) will be an ActionEvent source and be able to have shortcuts associated with them. One key enhancement worth noting is that JMenuItem will include a status bar help mechanism.

- **JCheckBoxMenuItem**. This class directly extends JMenuItem and is comparable to the AWT CheckboxMenuItem component.

Note: Support for radio buttons using the JRadioButton Swing component in a menu will be provided for by Swing.

- **JPopupMenu**. This class directly extends JComponent and is comparable to the AWT PopupMenu component. One indirect enhancement that will be added to all Swing components (via a method addition to the JComponent class) is the ability to associate a given popup menu to a container by registering the menu as a InputEvent listener to some container. When this event occurs, the popup menu will automatically post/unpost itself.

Scrollbar

The JScrollBar Swing component is almost a duplicate of the AWT Scrollbar component you learned about. JScrollBar is a Swing component. So, internally it has standard Swing features (e.g., uses an MVC data model, is Java Beans compliant, etc.). Externally, the only real change has been to the two methods, getUnitIncrement() and getBlockIncrement(), which have been updated (and the older versions deprecated) to take an extra parameter to specify direction, so subclasses of JScrollBar can better manage its edges.

Note: Since JScrollBar and Scrollbar are closely related, no example is being provided. If you wish, you can update the Scrollbar example in Chapter 6 to JScrollBar.

Text Component, TextField & TextArea

JTextComponent has been redesigned to provide support for more than just simple text, like its AWT TextComponent counterpart. At the time of this writing, things are still under development, but so far JTextComponent will facilitate support for international strings and for graphics. Also, support will be added to accommodate Standard Generalized Markup Language (SGML). So, for example, you could define a JTextComponent subclass to support the HyperText Markup Language (HTML) tag <CODE>. Finally, JTextComponent's corresponding event type TextEvent and listener TextListener have been replaced by DocumentEvent and DocumentListener, respectively.

Note: Standard Generalized Markup Language is a generic markup language used to format text for better appearance and overall information design. HTML is an example of a markup language built on top of SGML.

The JTextField and JTextArea Swing components almost duplicate AWT TextField and TextArea, save the getPreferredSize() and getMinimumSize() methods, which have had their visibility reduced, and the addition of the two methods getColumnWidth() and getRowHeight().

Miscellaneous Swing Components

So far, you have been introduced to Swing components, which have roots stemming from the already-familiar AWT components. At this point, we are going to introduce some of the miscellaneous Swing components, which may have roots with the AWT, the IFC, or may be completely new. Figure 12-8 diagrams the class hierarchy for the components discussed in this section.

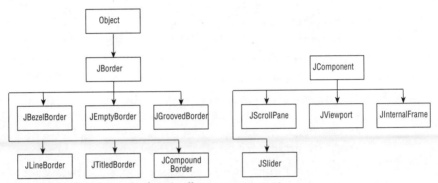

Figure 12-8: Class hierarchy for miscellaneous components.

> **Note:** One new miscellaneous addition to the JFC is the increased customizability of cursors. The Swing toolkit facilitates the method `createCustomCursor()`, which lets you specify an image, hot spot, and name for the cursor you wish to create. Thus, in Swing, you no longer are limited to the standard cursors (or the standard colors) that were available in the AWT.

Borders

The Swing set allows you to put a custom border around a given Swing component. The functionality for borders is provided by the `swing.border` package. The interface `Border`, which defines two methods—`paintBorder(Graphics g, int x, int y, int width, int height)` and `getBorderInsets()`—is in this package. Any class needing to be a border must implement this interface. Fortunately, for most solutions, you do not need to concern yourself about creating `Border` implementations, because Swing already has facilitated seven (also located in the `swing.border` package):

■ **BezelBorder**. This draws a bezel border (either raised or lowered, based on your preference) around a given Jcomponent, with several color specifications for each part of the bezel.

■ **EmptyBorder**. This is used to specify a border with no visual presence (similar to that of java.awt.Insets). In its constructor, you specify the four coordinates (x, y, width, and height) for the dimensions of the border.

■ **GroovedBorder**. This draws a grooved border. You can use a default constructor, which uses black and white for the highlight and shadow, or use its other constructor and specify your own color for the highlight and shadow.

■ **LineBorder**. This draws a simple line around a given JComponent based on a specified color and pixel thickness.

■ **TitledBorder**. This is an interesting border, as it takes (in its constructor) the target JComponent, another Border reference, and some text. Effectively, this border draws the specified border and transposes a title using the specified text into the target JComponent.

■ **CompoundBorder**. This is the most complicated because it allows you to nest borders to varying levels.

To actually use a border, all you need to do is to use the setBorder() method on the target JComponent specifying the Border object you wish to use.

TIP

Alternatively, you can use borders through the JBorderedPane Swing component from the swing package. JBorderedPane is a container that takes a Border reference, which it uses as its own border.

The following example demonstrates the various Border implementations by creating arbitrary borders around five JButton instances (this source code is available on the Companion CD-ROM):

```
import java.awt.*;
import java.awt.event.*;
import com.sun.java.swing.*;
import com.sun.java.swing.border.*;
```

```
public class SwingBorderTest extends JFrame {
JButton myButton1;
JButton myButton2;
JButton myButton3;
JButton myButton4;
JButton myButton5;

    public SwingBorderTest() {

        setLayout(new FlowLayout());

        //Create the buttons and set the borders
        myButton1 = new JButton("Lined");
        myButton1.setBorder(new LineBorder(Color.green, 3));
        add(myButton1);

        myButton2 = new JButton("Grooved");
        myButton2.setBorder(new GroovedBorder(Color.green, Color.blue));
        add(myButton2);

        myButton3 = new JButton("Empty");
        myButton3.setBorder(new EmptyBorder(10, 10, 10, 10));
        add(myButton3);


        myButton4 = new JButton("Bezel");
        myButton4.setBorder(new BezelBorder(BezelBorder.RAISED, Color.black,
Color.gray, Color.white, Color.pink));
        add(myButton4);

        myButton5 = new JButton("Titled");
        myButton5.setBorder(new TitledBorder(myButton5, new
LineBorder(Color.white, 5), "Border Title"));
        add(myButton5);

        addWindowListener(new WndAdapter());
        setSize(200, 150);
        setVisible(true);
    }
```

```
// Event-handling for the Frame
class WndAdapter extends WindowAdapter {

    public void windowClosing(WindowEvent event) {
        event.getWindow().dispose();
        System.exit(0);
    }
}

public static void main(String args[]) {
    new SwingBorderTest();

}


}
```

Figure 12-9 shows the preceding code in action.

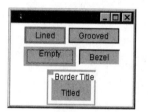

Figure 12-9: SwingBorderTest in action.

JViewport

The JViewport Swing component allows you to fit a given component inside a view. You can then specify a view port (which is usually smaller than the view) to show a cropped version of the normal component. While you can use the JViewport class directly, it is not uncommon to subclass it with your own custom functionality.

The following example demonstrates the use of two JViewport instances to crop a very large JButton instance and a JLabel instance, which contains a very large image. Before looking at the example, take a look at the full icon image to be set in the JLabel instance in Figure 12-10.

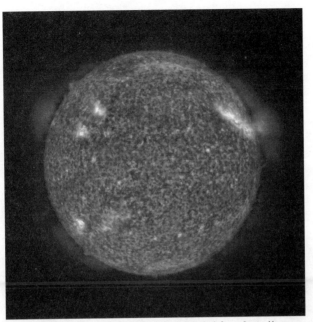

Figure 12-10: Image of the Sun (downloaded from http://www.nasa.gov).

The following shows the source code of the example (both the source code and the image are available on the Companion CD-ROM):

```
import java.awt.*;
import java.awt.event.*;
import com.sun.java.swing.*;

public class SwingViewPortTest extends JFrame {
JButton testButton;
JLabel testLabel;

    public SwingViewPortTest() {

        setLayout(null);

        //Create the button
        testButton = new JButton("Big Button");
        testButton.setBounds(10, 25, 400, 400);
```

```
        //Create the buttons viewport
        JViewport view = new JViewport();
        view.setSize(200, 100);
        view.setView(testButton);
        view.setLocation(10, 25);
        add(view);

        //Create the label
        testLabel = new JLabel(new ImageIcon("images/Sun.gif"));
        testLabel.setBounds(10, 25, 600, 600);

        //Create the label viewport
        JViewport view2 = new JViewport();
        view2.setSize(200, 200);
        view2.setView(testLabel);
        view2.setLocation(10, 230);
        add(view2);

        addWindowListener(new WndAdapter());
        setSize(500, 500);
        setVisible(true);

    }

    // Event-handling for the Frame
    class WndAdapter extends WindowAdapter {

        public void windowClosing(WindowEvent event) {
            event.getWindow().dispose();
            System.exit(0);
        }
    }

    public static void main(String args[]) {
        new SwingViewPortTest();

    }

}
```

Figure 12-11 shows the preceding code in action.

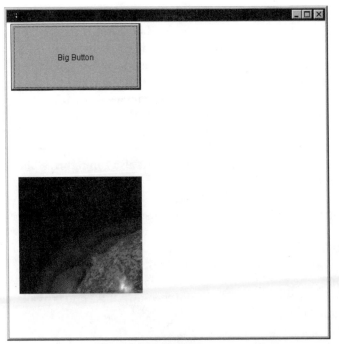

Figure 12-11: SwingViewPortTest in action.

First notice that, using viewports, both of these components are able to exist on the same frame. Otherwise, testButton's view size of 400 x 400 and testLabel's 600 x 600 would most definitely overlap and/or go off the frame. Second, notice that testButton was able to adapt to the viewport size and correctly display itself without being cropped. This is possible because the JViewport class uses a layout manager named (obviously enough) JViewportLayout. The JViewportLayout layout by default resizes the specified component view to be collinear with the viewport for this JViewport. On the other hand, testLabel's icon image was not so lucky: As testLabel was resized, its large icon was cropped.

·   What if we wanted to add scrolling functionality to testLabel as a way to work around this cropping? JViewport does provide the methods getViewSize() and getExtentSize(), which you could use to retrieve the size of the view, the cropped viewport, and the difference between the two to implement non-pixel-based (i.e., a logical-based) scrolling format. However, as you will learn in the next section, using JScrollPane provides a very easy way to add scrolling behavior.

JScrollPane

The JScrollPane Swing component should be familiar to you, because it comes from the AWT ScrollPane component. Aside from the standard ScrollPane features you learned about, JScrollPane has the added granularity to set your scrolling policy for the vertical and horizontal scrollbars separately. Also, functionality has been added to allow subclasses of ScrollPane to add their own scrollbars, as well as horizontal and vertical column heads (using the setRowHeading() and setColumnHeading() methods, respectively). The getUnitIncrement() and getBlockIncrement() methods have been modified so they no longer simply return a constant but also can return some computed value, which is useful for adding scrolling to part of a view as well as better managing items of variable heights (to be scrolled).

Note: Just like JViewport, JScrollPane also has a layout manager called JScrollPaneLayout whose job is to manage the laying out of the viewport, the scrollbars (if needed or specified), and column and row heads (if available), as well as any specified corners (if available).

The following example uses JScrollPane by using the testLabel instance (which contains the satellite image of the Sun) (this code is available on the Companion CD-ROM):

```java
import java.awt.*;
import java.awt.event.*;
import com.sun.java.swing.*;

public class SwingScrollPaneTest extends JFrame {
JLabel testLabel;

    public SwingScrollPaneTest() {

        //Set the UI
        try {

            UIManager.setUIFactory("com.sun.java.swing.rose.RoseFactory", this);
        } catch (Exception e) {}

        //Create the label
        testLabel = new JLabel(new ImageIcon("images/Sun.gif"));

        //Create the scrolling pane
        JScrollPane scroll = new JScrollPane();

        //Set the viewport to testLabel
        scroll.getViewport().add(testLabel);
        add(scroll);
```

```
            addWindowListener(new WndAdapter());
            setSize(300, 200);
            setVisible(true);

        }

        // Event-handling for the Frame
        class WndAdapter extends WindowAdapter {

            public void windowClosing(WindowEvent event) {
                event.getWindow().dispose();
                System.exit(0);
            }
        }

        public static void main(String args[]) {
            new SwingScrollPaneTest();

        }

}
```

Figure 12-12 shows the preceding code in action.

Figure 12-12: SwingScrollPaneTest in action.

Internal Frame

The JJFrame Swing component is comparable to the AWT Frame component. However, Swing has also added a new component called JInternalFrame. This Swing component allows you to create a frame that can exist only inside another frame, which is useful for Multiple Document Interface (MDI) solutions. To use JInternalFrame, you create an instance as you would a typical component. From there, you can add components as well as specify a layout just as if it were a normal frame. Finally, you need to add your JInternalFrame instance to the Swing component JLayeredPanel or else it will be trapped in the parent's layout and other restrictions.

The following shows an example of a simple JInternalFrame (the source code is on the Companion CD-ROM):

```java
import java.awt.*;
import java.awt.event.*;
import com.sun.java.swing.*;

public class SwingInternalFrameTest extends JFrame {

JInternalFrame myInternalFrame;
JLayeredPane lp;

    public SwingInternalFrameTest() {

        //Create the internal frame
        myInternalFrame = new JInternalFrame("Internal Frame", true, false,
true, true);
        myInternalFrame.setBounds(10, 25, 200, 100);
        myInternalFrame.add(new JLabel("This is an internal frame."));

        //Create the layered pane
        lp = new JLayeredPane();
        lp.add(myInternalFrame);
        add(lp);

        addWindowListener(new WndAdapter());
        setSize(300, 200);
        setVisible(true);

    }

    // Event-handling for the Frame
    class WndAdapter extends WindowAdapter {

        public void windowClosing(WindowEvent event) {
            event.getWindow().dispose();
            System.exit(0);
        }
    }

        public static void main(String args[]) {
        new SwingInternalFrameTest();

    }
}
```

Figure 12-13 shows the preceding code in action.

Figure 12-13: SwingInternalFrameTest in action.

Slider

JSlider is a new Swing component that is similar to the BeansScale slider you created in the chapter on Java Beans. Using JSlider is very similar to the functionality of a scrollbar, which you learned about earlier in this chapter. JSlider's event type and listener are swing.event.ChangeEvent and swing.event.ChangeListener. Change events occur whenever the state of the source component changes.

The following shows an example of a simple JSlider (the source code is on the Companion CD-ROM):

```java
import java.awt.*;
import java.awt.event.*;
import com.sun.java.swing.*;
import com.sun.java.swing.event.*;

public class SwingSliderTest extends JFrame implements ChangeListener {
JSlider mySlider;


    public SwingSliderTest() {

        //Create the slider
        mySlider = new JSlider(SwingConstants.HORIZONTAL, 4, 1, 10);

        //Set the ticks for this slider
        mySlider.setPaintTicks(true);
        mySlider.setMajorTickSpacing(1);

        mySlider.addChangeListener(this);
        add(mySlider);
```

```
        addWindowListener(new WndAdapter());
        setSize(200, 100);
        setVisible(true);
    }

    public void stateChanged(ChangeEvent event) {
        System.out.println(((JSlider)event.getSource()).getValue());
    }

    // Event-handling for the Frame
    class WndAdapter extends WindowAdapter {

        public void windowClosing(WindowEvent event) {
            event.getWindow().dispose();
            System.exit(0);
        }
    }

    public static void main(String args[]) {
        new SwingSliderTest();

    }


}
```

At the time of this writing, the JSlider component is still under development, so no figure is provided here.

Advanced Swing Components

In this section, we are going to take a look at the more sophisticated Swing components. Figure 12-14 shows a diagram of the class hierarchy for these components.

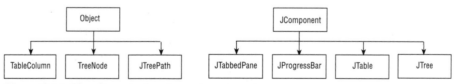

Figure 12-14: Class hierarchy for advanced components.

Progress Bar

A component like JProgressBar is common to all professional GUI platforms. It effectively displays a "read-only" slider that gives a visual representation to the progress of some given time-consuming task. The JProgressBar Swing component can use a ChangeEvent to notify you of the state (i.e., the value) of the component changes. The key methods you use to update a JProgressBar instance are setValue() and getValue().

The following example demonstrates a JProgressBar instance using the Rose look and feel. The example puts a counter on a thread so that it will slowly increment from 0 to 100 with the JProgressBar displaying its progress (the source code is on the Companion CD-ROM):

```java
import java.awt.*;
import java.awt.event.*;
import com.sun.java.swing.*;

public class SwingProgressBarTest extends JFrame implements Runnable {
JProgressBar myProBar;

    public SwingProgressBarTest() {
        setLayout(new FlowLayout());
        //Set the UI to rose
        try {

            UIManager.setUIFactory("com.sun.java.swing.rose.RoseFactory",
this);
        } catch (Exception e) {}

        //Create the  progress bar
        myProBar = new JProgressBar();
        myProBar.setOrientation(JProgressBar.HORIZONTAL);
        myProBar.setMinimum(0);
        myProBar.setMaximum(100);

        add(myProBar);

        addWindowListener(new WndAdapter());
        setSize(200, 100);
        setVisible(true);
    }
```

```java
//Used by the thread
public void run() {
    while(true) {
        //Sleep for a little while
        try {
            Thread.currentThread().sleep(200);
        } catch (Exception e) {
            System.err.println("Error trying to sleep: " + e);
        }

        //Update myProBar
        if (myProBar.getValue() >= 100) {
            System.out.println("Done!");
            break;
        } else {
            myProBar.setValue(myProBar.getValue()+1);
            System.out.println(myProBar.getValue() + "%");
        }
    }
}

// Event-handling for the Frame
class WndAdapter extends WindowAdapter {

    public void windowClosing(WindowEvent event) {
        event.getWindow().dispose();
        System.exit(0);
    }
}

public static void main(String args[]) {
    SwingProgressBarTest testBar = new SwingProgressBarTest();
    Thread t = new Thread(testBar);
    t.start();
}


}
```

Be sure to pay close attention to the command box from which you executed this program, as it displays each new value for the counter every time
it is incremented. Figure 12-15 shows the previous code in action.

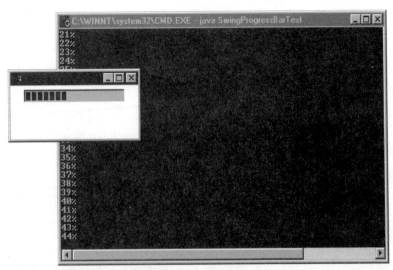

Figure 12-15: SwingProgressBarTest in action.

Tabbed Pane

Tabbed windows are a common feature in modern GUIs, in that you have a window containing several panes, each of which has a tab. Depending on which tab you choose, a particular pane will be brought to the front (covering all the others). Figure 12-16 shows an example of a window in NT that contains a set of tabbed panes.

Figure 12-16: A Windows NT tabbed-pane example.

Implementing such functionality was possible in the AWT. However, it involved using several instances of Panel and the CardLayout manager (in which you would have a bottom panel using the CardLayout layout and a top panel with some Button objects to traverse between the cards in the layout for the bottom panel). In the end, you would have something that only resembles a real tabbed pane at best.

The introduction of Swing presents a better alternative: the JTabbedPane Swing component. This Swing component lets you add components as its pane and use tabbing labels with all the bells and whistles of a typical JLabel. After constructing a JTabbedPane instance, you use the addTab() method to add tabs. When you're done, you merely add this JTabbedPane instance to your parent window.

Note: JTabbedPane precipitates ChangeEvents, so if you wish to be notified for these events, you will need to register a ChangeListener object.

The following example demonstrates a JTabbedPane instance by adding three panes that hold three panels. The first buffered pane contains a button, the second an image, and the third a label (the source code and images are available on the Companion CD-ROM):

```java
import java.awt.*;
import java.awt.event.*;
import com.sun.java.swing.*;

public class SwingTabbedPaneTest extends JFrame {
JTabbedPane myTabbedPane;

    public SwingTabbedPaneTest() {

        myTabbedPane = new JTabbedPane();

        //The first tab
        JBufferedPane panel1 = new JBufferedPane(new FlowLayout());
        panel1.setBackground(Color.lightGray);
        panel1.add(new JButton("OK"));

        //Add the panel to the tabbed pane
        myTabbedPane.addTab("First", null, panel1, "Click Here");
        myTabbedPane.setSelectedIndex(0);

        //The second tab
        JBufferedPane panel2 = new JBufferedPane();
        panel2.add(new JLabel(new ImageIcon("images/Sun.gif")));
```

```
                //Add the panel to the tabbed pane
                myTabbedPane.addTab("Second", new ImageIcon("images/new1.gif"),
                panel2);


                //The third tab
                JBufferedPane panel3 = new JBufferedPane();
                panel3.setBackground(Color.lightGray);
                panel3.add(new JLabel("Welcome!"));

                //Add the panel to the tabbed pane
                myTabbedPane.addTab("Third", null, panel3);


                //Add the tabbed pane to the frame
                add(myTabbedPane);

                addWindowListener(new WndAdapter());
                setSize(300, 200);
                setVisible(true);
        }


        // Event-handling for the Frame
        class WndAdapter extends WindowAdapter {

            public void windowClosing(WindowEvent event) {
                event.getWindow().dispose();
                System.exit(0);
            }
        }

        public static void main(String args[]) {
            new SwingTabbedPaneTest();

        }


}
```

Figure 12-17 shows the preceding code in action.

Figure 12-17: SwingTabbedPaneTest in action.

Note: As you move your mouse over the First tab, a tip of Click Here will appear. This tab-based tip was specified as the fourth parameter in the addTab( ) method for that tab in the previous code.

Table
The Swing set has included a whole package (swing.table) of classes used for the JTable Swing component. This component lets you create a two-dimensional array of objects. Usually the data are added as a multidimensional array of objects. For each column, you can specify an object (such as a Swing component) that will be used to render the data for the cells in that column. This is accomplished by using the TableColumn.setCellRenderer( ) method, passing it a TableCellRenderer instance. You also can specify an object used as the editor for a given column using the corresponding TableColumn.setCellEditor( ) method, passing it a TableCellEditor instance.

For example, if you have a column of boolean values, you can set a JCheckBox reference as the object to use for rendering, thus embedding in each cell a JCheckBox instance containing the corresponding boolean setting from the specified array of data. JTable is very useful for creating spreadsheet-based solutions that let you perform grid-based displaying of data and allowing for in-place editing. At the time of this writing, it is still under development, so an example has not been provided here.

Tree
Another Swing component similar to JTable is JTree. This component is used to visually display data to the user in the form of a hierarchy of nodes (represented as a JTreeNode instance). A given tree node can contain other tree nodes (a.k.a. subtree nodes), allowing you to create a complete tree of directories and entries through which a user can navigate to choose the hierarchy. There is also a JTreePath class used to represent a path as specified by an array of objects.

Event handling for trees is based around some new special change event types including TreeExpansionEvent (and its corresponding TreeExpansionListener), TreeModelEvent (and its corresponding TreeModelEvent), and TreeSelectionEvent (and its corresponding TreeSelectionEvent), all of which are members of the swing.event package. The first, TreeExpansionEvent, is used for notification if some branch in the tree is expanded. The second, TreeModelEvent, is used for notification if the state of the tree has changed in some way (e.g., some nodes were added/removed). The third and final, TreeSelectionEvent, is used for notification if some entry has been selected by the user.

Note: The JTree Swing component provides an excellent way to visually display directories and/or any files contained therein for a user to navigate through.

The following example demonstrates JTree by generating an arbitrary hierarchy of TreeNode instances. Event handling also has been put in place for notification of selections made in the tree (the source code is also available on the Companion CD-ROM):

```
import java.awt.*;
import java.awt.event.*;
import com.sun.java.swing.*;
import com.sun.java.swing.event.*;

public class SwingTreeTest extends JFrame implements TreeSelectionListener {
JTree myTree;

    public SwingTreeTest() {

        //Create the stuff node.
        TreeNode myStuffNode = new TreeNode("Stuff");

            //Create the a node.
            TreeNode myANode = new TreeNode("A");
            myStuffNode.add(myANode);

                //Create the fruit node.
                TreeNode myFruitNode = new TreeNode("Fruit");
                myANode.add(myFruitNode);

                    //Add entries to fruit.
                    myFruitNode.add(new TreeNode("Apples"));
                    myFruitNode.add(new TreeNode("Apricots"));
                    myFruitNode.add(new TreeNode("Artichoke"));
```

```
            //Create the b node.
            TreeNode myBNode = new TreeNode("B");
            myStuffNode.add(myBNode);

                //Add entries to b.
                myBNode.add(new TreeNode("Baseball"));
                myBNode.add(new TreeNode("Basketball"));


        //Create the tree.
        myTree = new JTree(myStuffNode);
        myTree.addTreeSelectionListener(this);
        add(myTree);

        addWindowListener(new WndAdapter());
        setSize(300, 200);
        setVisible(true);
    }

    // Event-handling for the tree.
    public void valueChanged(TreeSelectionEvent event) {
            System.out.println(event.getPath() + " is selected.");
    }

    // Event-handling for the Frame.
    class WndAdapter extends WindowAdapter {

        public void windowClosing(WindowEvent event) {
            event.getWindow().dispose();
            System.exit(0);
        }
    }

    public static void main(String args[]) {
        new SwingTreeTest();

    }


}
```

Figure 12-18 shows the preceding code in action.

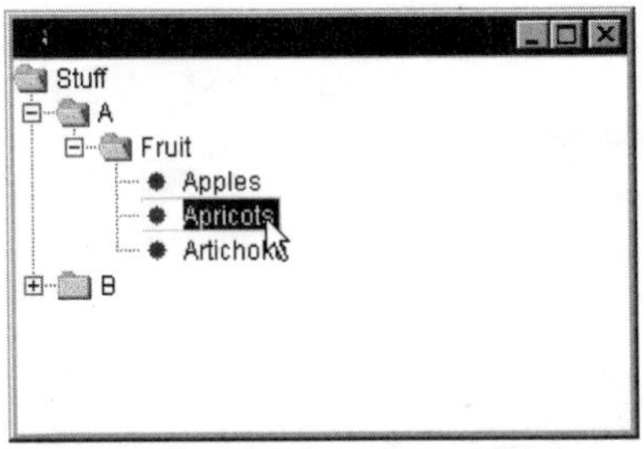

Figure 12-18: SwingTreeTest in action.

Moving On

In this chapter, we've had a chance to get a first look at some of the things going on with Swing. We also got to look at several examples. At this point, things are still under development, and a number of Swing components as well as services (e.g., drag and drop) are still in the works. More Swing components, services, and features will definitely be present before Swing is officially released. Nonetheless, through these last two chapters, you have had a good opportunity to learn about the JFC and get your feet wet with a few examples.

PART IV

Appendices

About the Companion CD-ROM

The Companion CD-ROM included with your copy of the *Official Netscape Java 1.1 Programming Book* contains useful source code for many of the exercises described in the book.

To Navigate the CD-ROM

To find out more about the CD-ROM and its contents, please open the README.HTM file in your favorite browser. You will see a small menu offering several links.

Software on the CD-ROM

To review the directory and file listings, please refer to DIR.TXT.

All of the source code on the CD-ROM is uncompiled. To obtain a freely available Java 1.1.x compiler, visit http://www.javasoft.com.

Note: In order to use the source code in the ch12 subdirectory, you must download and install the Swing pre-release packages. Also, any Swing-related Java programs specifically require a Java 1.1.2 (or higher) compiler.

The image Sun.gif was downloaded from NASA at http://www.nasa.gov/ and all the other images were downloaded from "Andy's Art Attack" at http://www.andyart.com.

Technical Support

Technical support is available for installation-related problems only. The technical support office is open from 8:00 A.M. to 6:00 P.M. Monday through Friday and can be reached via the following methods:

- Phone: (919) 544-9404 extension 81
- Faxback Answer System: (919) 544-9404 extension 85
- E-mail: help@vmedia.com
- FAX: (919) 544-9472
- World Wide Web: **http://www.vmedia.com/support**
- America Online: keyword *Ventana*

Limits of Liability & Disclaimer of Warranty

The authors and publisher of this book have used their best efforts in preparing the CD-ROM and the programs contained in it. These efforts include the development, research, and testing of the theories and programs to determine their effectiveness. The authors and publisher make no warranty of any kind expressed or implied, with regard to these programs or the documentation contained in this book.

The authors and publisher shall not be liable in the event of incidental or consequential damages in connection with, or arising out of, the furnishing, performance, or use of the programs, associated instructions, and/or claims of productivity gains.

Index